Edward King

The Golden Spike

Fantasie in Prose

Edward King

The Golden Spike
Fantasie in Prose

ISBN/EAN: 9783743349049

Manufactured in Europe, USA, Canada, Australia, Japa

Cover: Foto ©Thomas Meinert / pixelio.de

Manufactured and distributed by brebook publishing software (www.brebook.com)

Edward King

The Golden Spike

THE GOLDEN SPIKE

Fantasie in Prose

BY

EDWARD KING

AUTHOR OF "THE GENTLE SAVAGE," ETC.

BOSTON
TICKNOR AND COMPANY
1886

TO

W. W. CLAPP,

OF THE

Boston Journal.

CONTENTS.

THE GOLDEN SPIKE

THE GOLDEN SPIKE.

CHAPTER I.

MORNING IN CRAVEN STREET.

"CRAVEN STREET is not exactly the spot that I should choose to die in, Mistress Cragg," said Colonel Amory J. Hodges to his landlady, as she came to inspect the serving of his morning meal. "If one were lingering on, for instance, with a mortal malady, ma'am, Craven street might, — well, it might hasten the sad event. But I believe I am in comfortable health in spite of my old wounds, and I propose to weather the gloom of Craven street until the first of December. I have written to my dear wife that we will take our Christmas dinner under a live-oak tree, in the open air, if you please, Mistress Cragg, at the very point where the new canal is to be begun. Of course I look forward to that time with much pleasure, so much that the smoke and mist of London in August do not affect me. So you need not apologize for them. Did the earl call yesterday?"

There was a perceptible tremor, a faint sign of discouragement, in the voice of Colonel Amory J. Hodges as he asked this question; and the landlady hesitated a minute before she answered: —

"No, sir, the herl 'as not been. You came in so very late, sir, or we should ha' told you last night."

"I wonder, now," said Colonel Hodges, musingly, and addressing himself to one of the long windows of the drawing-room rather than to Mrs. Cragg, — "I wonder, now, if the earl received those oysters?"

"Is everythink quite right, sir?" timidly inquired the landlady, inspecting the back of Col. Hodges' head as if she expected the answer to arise therefrom; and, receiving an affirmative oral response, she murmured, "Thank kyou," in the humble manner traditional with her class, and disappeared.

"Mistress" Cragg, as the Floridian colonel called her, was by no means in the habit of calling upon each of her lodgers to inquire how he enjoyed his breakfast; but she cherished her "first floor," this tall, ceremonious American, as the immediate apple of her eye. It was now some fifteen months since he first appeared at her door, encumbered with two enormous valises, out of which in process of time he had evolved a gentlemanly wardrobe and a formidable mass of printed matter. The serving-maid had said to her, on the morning after the colonel's arrival, "Please, missus, it's another of them foreign gentlemen come to float a company;" and on hearing this, she had comfortably smoothed her cap-strings, and inwardly congratulated herself on having a good customer. She had seen dozens of these people in her day, and liked them well; for they had a cheerful way of spending money, regardless of the condition of their prospects, which made her prosperous. Sometimes a critical turn in their fortunes brought her a small loss; but she accepted it in the true commercial spirit, and did not allow it to prejudice her against the class.

For Colonel Hodges she had a respect not unmingled with reverence. It had been prompted by two things: the old-school gallantry with which the colonel invariably treated her, and the fact that he was the first of her speculative lodgers who had ever possessed sufficient influence to bring to his own lodgings, as visitors, certain members of the "upper classes." From the day that she had seen a live marquis holding conversation with the colonel in his rooms she had begun her series of morning visits. By a few minutes of talk with the American she fancied that she caught some of the reflected glory of his aristocratic visitors. Besides, the colonel was nice in his tastes. He spurned the simple eggs and bacon, the coffee, and stale bread which other lodgers considered good enough, and commenced his morning meal with a brace of oranges, after which he disposed of a small and succulent steak, flanked with mealy potatoes and a delicate bunch of celery. His coffee was ground to his order, and caused the cook many a pang. From time to time he received a mysterious barrel, covered with odd labels; and from this transatlantic receptacle he would bring forth wild ducks, oysters, and toothsome hams, which he always sent to the kitchen, with the modest request that the landlady would accept them for herself, only now and then serving him a bit to remind him of the "home flavor."

One day, when Colonel Hodges was absent from town, Mrs. Cragg, passing through her front hall, saw a footman handing a card to the servant. When the tiny bit of pasteboard was laid upon the receiver she read on it the name of "The Earl of Offast." This was one of the colonel's new acquaintances, and it would be difficult precisely to calculate the pitch of august dignity to which this raised him in Mrs. Cragg's mind.

It was of this noble earl that Colonel Hodges was thinking as he sat alone on the morning when he had indulged in his little homily on the characteristics of Craven street. The colonel was sad, and it was not the leaden dulness of the morning which had affected his usually buoyant spirits. For the first time since his arrival in London he began to feel discouraged. He had come to the mighty metropolis feeling like a successful invader who had but to dictate his own terms. "The Ocala Canal and Land Company," which he had intended to found and place upon the London market in six weeks, had hung like a millstone about his patient neck for one year and three months, and the colonel was compelled to admit that it was growing heavy. But as in the days of the Civil War, when he had fought through the glades of Southern Georgia with his handful of ragged men against the clever and disciplined troops of the Union, so now he was unwilling to admit that his situation was desperate. "No," he said, musingly, as he finished his coffee and took up the "Times," "it will all come right, — although this is the last chance. The earl is *sure* (the colonel pronounced it *sho*) to go into the thing, and that will consummate the success. And I really must be at home by Christmas-time."

He had said the same thing about Christmas to himself on the preceding year, and he remembered it now, smiling bitterly, as he reviewed the many obstacles and deceptions which he had encountered. The memory of his troubles told upon his nerves, and he arose and paced to and fro, in and out among the tables and rusty *étagères* with which the long and somewhat shabby drawing-room was encumbered. The colonel was a tall man, "six feet two in his stockings," and he had once been singularly handsome. But now he was like one of those symmetrical, yet torn and buffeted trees that one sometimes sees on an Alpine height. He was slightly lame, and stooped a little forward, as if it hurt him to carry his head erect. The fact is that he had been shot almost to pieces during the war. "It was a miracle, I reckon, that I ever grew together again," he used to say to his personal friends. Colonel Hodges was a gentleman, in the true American sense, and he accepted the fortunes of war like a gentleman. He refused to have anything to do with the squabbles of reconstruction, and went up to Washington, where he earned a modest living by the practice of his profession — the law — and by occasionally promoting the interests of a Southern railroad. Every year, at Christmas, he went home to his family at Ocala; each year they besought him to stay and "carry on" the little plantation, which was all he had saved after the war out of the wreck of his investments; and each year he made the same answer — that he must get "on the track of some scheme with which to make a fortune."

It was while on one of his home visits that he conceived the idea of "The Ocala Canal and Land Company." By means of a new water-way he proposed to connect the great St. John's river with a vast tract of country composed of alternate swamps and uplands, now only to be reached through tortuous and shallow streams, some of which were navigable but a few months in the year. A powerful company, formed in London, should buy up the lands and construct the canal, and should then proceed to make an enormous fortune out of the reclaimed land, the founding of a second company for the planting and working of endless orange groves, etc. The colonel had an imagination as warm as a Floridian sunset, and he let it run riot while he was editing his prospectus. He wrote with true Southern eloquence of the vast industries which might be developed at trifling cost so soon as the canal had opened a way to the sea; of the sugar and indigo and other costly produce for which there was an unlimited demand in London, and of the fabulous dividends which the stock would pay. He went to London with his pockets filled with letters of introduction to aristocratic gentlemen who did not disdain to examine into proposed investments. Besides, he found that a certain bullet-mark which had been left upon his face by a Union rifle proved a good passport to many genteel circles, where sympathy with the Confederacy had been strong enough when the struggle was in progress. He was given a dinner and reception by a member of Parliament who liked to dabble in American schemes. He was invited to country-houses and to town entertainments. He even had an audience of the Rothschilds, and received a letter from a noble duke, giving several reasons why his grace could not just then lend his patronage to the Ocala matter. After three months of endeavor he secured some attention from a Hebrew gentleman, who sent the prospectus to his solicitor, which personage kept the papers six months and then made an appointment a fortnight off to discuss the matter. The discussion brought about a new delay, which lasted until the close of the "London season." Then the colonel had to hunt up his people at Brighton, in Paris, in Scotland. They were always considerate and polite, always on the point of engaging heart and soul in the enterprise, if it were not for some sudden drawback which none of them had foreseen.

So the poor man was tossed about between hopes and fears until the end of his first year in London, when a most unpleasant thing occurred. A strong company was formed for the cutting of a ship canal directly across the peninsula of Florida, and the London market smiled on the new organization. This seemed to overshadow and in some mysterious manner to annihilate the colonel's smaller enterprise. People said, when Colonel Hodges' "Ocala Canal and Land Company" was brought to their notice, "The canal business is overdone in Florida. If you had gone into *the* Canal Company, now"— And thus it is that in London every year hundreds of small schemes are ruined by the sudden apparition of larger and more powerful ones of similar character.

At this juncture Colonel Hodges happened to make

the acquaintance of the Earl of Offast. The earl had always been renowned as an enthusiastic sportsman; and he took a fancy to the American, because of some of his picturesque descriptions of Floridian sport. The colonel had a fund of dry humor, too, and his memory was well stored with grotesque stories which he was fond of telling. The earl found these stories vastly amusing. He began to laugh when the colonel began a tale, and laughed uninterruptedly to the close. Sometimes he understood, and sometimes he did not; but he never failed to laugh heartily. "It was the accent," he said, "and the — the repose of the fellow — don't you know," that were so mirth-provoking. Colonel Hodges found, at the end of a month, that he had seen a great deal of the earl; that he had invited him to Ocala to shoot birds, turtles, and alligators; that he had dined frequently with the earl at his club; but that he had never lisped a syllable to the earl about his cherished canal project. One day, when he felt a touch of despair, he thought reticence as to his personal affairs was no longer a virtue; so he said: —

"I regret that I must decline your lordship's invitation for Scotland, for the affairs of my canal are pressing. I had forgotten to tell you that I am interested in a Florida canal company — not *the* big one — but a most interesting" —

"Of course you are," said the earl; "no bright American comes to London nowadays without a plan for a company in his pocket. And what is your particular project like?"

The colonel talked, and the earl listened for two hours. At the end of that time Colonel Hodges fancied that he had made a hit. He regained his elasticity of temper; he had visions of fat fields stretching away in every direction from Ocala; of shining avenues of water reflecting the phenomenal colors of the Southern sunsets; of agreeable dividends fluttering down in neatly written checks upon the office tables. If the earl would but take up the thing fortune was at hand. With the Earl of Offast at the head of the board of directors all could be accomplished in a week. He said so, frankly.

"Hum!" said the earl; "you say the shooting is good, and the climate not too bad. And there would be a great rise in the value of the lands. I'll think it over. Look here! You write me a letter, a month from this time, to remind me of the affair, and if I can see my way clear I'll go into it. For the next thirty days I can do nothing. Write me, with all the details."

Colonel Hodges felt that this was his last chance. Here was the season once more drawing to a close, and people would soon be scattered anew. The Floridian had drawn too heavily upon his slight resources, and was beginning to be worried about money. He passed an anxious month. Toward the middle of it he ventured to send to the earl's address a barrel of the small Florida oysters to which he had previously invited the aristocratic gentleman's attention at a breakfast given at the Star and Garter, and which had, on that occasion, given complete satisfaction. Then, at the appointed time, he launched forth his letter to the earl, who had come down from Scotland after a series of brilliant successes in grouse-shooting. By return of post he received this note: —

My dear Colonel: — I will drop in a day or two hence, and we can then decide our little matter.

Yours heartily,

Offast.

This looked well; but days passed, and the earl came not. And now, as Colonel Hodges paced his room, the suspense seemed almost intolerable. He could *not* wait longer; he must write again — or call — or — Ten o'clock sounded melodiously from "Big Ben" in the clock tower of Westminster Palace. The colonel sat down, wrote two letters, tore them up, took a furtive chew of tobacco — a license which he allowed himself only when excessively nervous — laid out two copies of his prospectus where they would be handy, and — sighed like a furnace.

A little before eleven the bell rang at Mrs. Cragg's door, and a minute afterward there was a knock at the entrance to Colonel Hodges' apartment. "Come in!" cried the colonel, hoping it was the servant with the earl's card. When he looked around a faint flush arose about the bullet-mark on his face; for he saw, advancing to greet him, the Earl of Offast, accompanied by a young and charming lady.

"I beg your lordship's pardon," he stammered; "but I had no idea" —

"Don't mention it, my dear colonel, I beg of you," said the earl. "It's all our — er — fault, I assure you. The servant said you were in, and always received — er — visitors in the morning; so I ran up — er — American fashion — don't you know."

Colonel Hodges had by this time placed his right hand in the breast of his elegant blue-cloth coat, and assumed a dignified attitude beside one of the tables on which his prospectuses were piled.

"And — you see we were looking at some old books — most interesting — on angling — near by — so we felt — er — we must profit by the occasion to see you. So I said to Lady Helena — (my cousin, Lady Helena Roderick — Colonel Hodges) — er — 'Lady Helena,' I said, 'you are always talking about American investments. Now — er — I shall take you up to the colonel's drawing-room and present you. I hope you will excuse the lack of ceremony, because, I tell you — er — frankly that we don't mind it the least bit in the world.'"

"Very courteous to honor my poor den with a visit," stammered the colonel. "Madam, will you kindly take a seat?" The earl strolled to a table laden with pamphlets, and picked up the prospectus of the Ocala project. Lady Helena looked amused, and Colonel Hodges perceived the delicate smile hovering like a tiny vagrant sunbeam about her lips. The thought flashed through his mind that she might have found his sudden assumption of dignity amusing; so he hastily took his hand from his breast, dropped the Websterian pose, and became himself again. Meantime the young lady had seated herself on an old-fashioned sofa near a window, after thanking the colonel for his invitation, and was gazing about her with that unruffled serenity and seeming indifference peculiar to her country and her class. The small smile had died away, and her eyes, which for a moment the colonel had thought mischievously merry, were tender and a little sad.

Lady Helena had not been laughing in her sleeve at Colonel Hodges, but at her cousin, the earl, as she watched his endeavors to assume the brisk and unceremonious ways which he was pleased to attribute to Americans. The earl had never been in America, but it was a favorite remark of his that "he knew how to take Americans." He was determined that they should not outdo him in *brusquerie*, and that they should never be troubled by the superiority which he felt certain was inseparable from his rank. In addition to this he was naturally a trifle bluff; he felt more at home on a Scotch moor than in the House of Lords. But he was not awkward, and there were circles in which he was thought to be brilliant. He was tall, slender, forty, fair in type; his features were regular and pleasing, although there were cruel lines about the mouth which indicated an unbending will, and had possibly been deepened by his unbounded passion for slaughtering the lower orders of the animal creation. He was bald, with the exception of a long wisp of chestnut hair, which had been spared in some miraculous manner, and which he brought over his forehead exactly as he would have done had the other locks not been absent. He wore his beard closely clipped, in foreign style. When he was not equipped for sporting, his garments were in excellent taste; but when he sallied forth to hunt or fish he wore such variegated raiment that he seemed like a walking rainbow. His brother sportsmen said that he dressed so in order to inspire terror among the animals.

The conversation became animated, and the colonel was too clever a diplomat to bring it at once to the subject of the canal. He was very ceremonious in his politeness to Lady Helena, and brought out for her inspection a large album of photographs of Western scenery, in which she seemed especially interested. Presently the earl came to the topic of American investments. The colonel felt a twinge of nervous excitement in his old wounds. *Now* was his chance.

"I don't mind telling you that most of my investments are made in the States nowadays," said the earl. "It's the country — er — of the future — don't you know. I'm not one of those who believe that the Irish will get the upper hands of you. I should think some of our best fortunes were being invested in America and in Egypt just now. Egypt's a nice country; beautiful cotton. Ever been in Egypt? No? I should fancy Egypt must be something like Florida."

The earl had seated himself on the sofa beside Lady Helena, and the tall colonel stood looking down at them, as he said: —

"I hope your lordship has not lost your interest in my Florida Canal Company?"

"Well, no, not exactly that," answered the earl. "I've been thinkin' (he was in the habit of suppressing the g's at the end of present participles, as if he considered them an affectation) a good bit about your canal. But you see the other — the *big* one — rather puts it in the shade, and so I'm afraid to go in for it. Very sorry — er — and I wish you had a better thing."

Colonel Hodges swallowed his chagrin, and tried to smile. But the bullet-mark in his face seemed to hurt him. "I confess," he said, "that I am disappointed. And it is getting so late in the season."

"Quite so," interrupted the earl. "I am disappointed myself. But the truth is that my friends in the other canal scheme would not like my coöperation in yours; and then — I had forgotten to tell you that Lady Helena and I had made some investments in the West, or the North-west, I am told they call it, and these are turning out so well that we fancy we should like to visit the countries where they are" —

"And perhaps invest some more. Ah! the West is a terrible competitor," said the colonel.

"The North-west is quite the thing, is it not?" said Lady Helena; "I am sure every one tells us so. If you only had a canal in the North-west, now, Colonel Hodges! But perhaps they do not need one there?" She leaned forward, clasping one small gloved hand over the other, and looking up into the southerner's face gravely and sweetly. He admired her with all his might, and still he had a lurking suspicion that she was laughing at him.

"I fear, madam," he said, "that my interests cannot be moved from their present location; but if I can offer any advice about investments in general, even in the North-west, I shall be most happy" —

"Well, you see," remarked the earl, "we have

received a very cordial invitation — Lady Offast and myself — to join an excursion party going to the North-west, at the close of the month. Extraordinary affair — invitations by hundreds — real American fashion — er. We should like to know — er — if you think it would be select enough to warrant our going. You see — er — Lady Offast is rather particular, not about the Americans — but the English, don't you know — that she might meet on the excursion. I think the party starts from Minnesota" —

"Minnesota! what a pretty name!" said Lady Helena. "It *must* be a pretty place. It is in Missouri, is it not?"

"Nonsense, cousin," said the earl, laughing. "You must not air your ignorance of the geography of the region in which you have invested. Minnesota is in Montana, isn't it, colonel?"

"It is in that neighborhood, sah, in that neighborhood," answered the Floridian. "Before I advise your lordship as to the excursion, may I ask if the invitation to it is similar to this?" He drew from the breast-pocket of his coat a large and handsome card and handed it to the earl.

"Precisely similar," was the answer, in which there was the vaguest hint of coldness — not because the earl was sorry the colonel had been invited, but because of a certain indefinable indisposition suddenly to be placed on the same footing with him. The colonel, in whose ingenious brain a new plan had blossomed with startling rapidity, was too acute not to perceive this ; but he carefully concealed his impression, and talked with much eloquence about the wonders of the Yellowstone, the great fields of Dakota, the Montana mines, and the rich lands on the Pacific slope, engaging the earl to go on the excursion and to take his "good lady" with him. When the colonel said "good lady" the earl's solitary scalp-lock seemed inclined to rise in amazement. The result of the colonel's conversational powers, however, was an invitation to lunch for the morrow — not at the club, as heretofore, but at the earl's own house. "If we decide to go you must tell us all about the sporting, you know ; what to buy, and all that sort of thing," said the earl, as he went downstairs. "Half-past two, without ceremony, American fashion."

"Cousin," said Lady Helena, as they returned to the carriage, "will you kindly stop at Stanford's and buy me a map of the States? I should really like to know where my investments are, and I *know* I was right about Minnesota."

"Stop a bit," said the earl, halting, and taking the invitation card for the excursion from his pocket. "This document reads: 'The Earl of Offast and the ladies of his family.' If Lady Offast will go, Lady Helena, you shall go with us and perfect your notions of Western geography."

CHAPTER II.

THE GATE OF THE MISTS.

Lady Helena did not content herself with the purchase of one map; she bought a dozen, and as many guide-books, and accepted the invitation of her cousin to accompany him on the excursion. This unexpected inclination of Lady Helena's for the wilds of the American North-west settled the wavering mind of the countess; that "good lady," as Colonel Hodges called her, forthwith announced that she had been for years dying of curiosity to see America; and the two ladies were soon so busy with their preparations for the journey that the earl saw little or nothing of them until the day before the party was to depart for Liverpool, to take ship. All that he could learn was that they had much enjoyed two shopping excursions to Paris, as well as innumerable visits to London shops; and that they were equipped for travel around the world, as they had a vague suspicion that the earl might decide to "keep on" when he reached San Francisco. Colonel Hodges had been to the house at lunch several times, and the countess had been pleased to say that he seemed "very polite and — useful." She admired the bullet-mark in his face, and liked to say rather more about the shattered fortunes of the Southern aristocracy than he cared to hear. The countess was, as she never wearied of telling him, entirely Southern in her sympathies; but Lady Helena confessed to having always had an idea that the North was in the right. Colonel Hodges was a born gallant, and he managed to commit himself to the opinion of neither lady, while he flattered them both. It was understood, now, that the colonel was to sail on the same steamer with the earl's party, and that, if certain pressing business in New York did not interfere, he would avail himself of his invitation to the transcontinental excursion, and go with them through the North-west.

"I will help you to find Minnesota," he said to Lady Helena, with a quizzical smile.

The truth is that the colonel was glad to get some relief from the monotony of his existence in London. The thought of his hundred fruitless journeys to Lombard street, of his profitless so-journs in antechambers in Abchurch lane, clouded his brow. He was weary of meeting the same despairing faces in the same nooks and corners of London's financial centre. He shuddered as he remembered that he might in time become like the seedy and loud-voiced speculators who frequented the smoking-rooms of the Grand Hotel and the Langham, men who were forever talking of dazzling successes contingent on the use of capital which they never obtained. "I must neglect no opportunity," he said to himself. "If I have not persuaded the earl to insure the success of my Canal and Land Company before we have finished our jaunt to the Pacific coast, I'll sell my hopes for a song, and be satisfied to live in a third-rate boarding-house in Washington for the remainder of my days." The prospect of revisiting his native shores seemed to fortify his courage. He told Mrs. Cragg that he was going for a little run across America with the Earl of Offast; after which he intended to go South to see his beloved wife and to persuade her to return to London with him. "We must give up the Christmas dinner under the live-oak tree, Mistress Cragg, for this year at least," he said majestically; "our interests here are too vast to allow me long to remain away from London;" and "Mistress" Cragg had such unbounded respect for him that she could have fallen on her knees and worshipped him before he left Craven street.

It was a misty morning in mid-August when the Earl of Offast and the two ladies arrived in Liverpool. In fact, it was an unearthly hour in the morning; for the earl, with his mania for doing things in American fashion, had insisted that the countess and Lady Helena should accede to his desire to leave London by the midnight train from Euston station, and to travel to Liverpool in a "sleeping-car." He was so firm that the countess was just a bit frightened, and entreated him not to "begin the journey by lugging them into all sorts of low and horrible places;" at which he laughed; whereupon she waxed tearful and became silent. She went through the door of the Pullman car with the air of a saint going to the stake, and immediately besought her maid to hand her the "salts," declaring that the "atmosphere of the atrocious vehicle was detestable." Lady Helena was anxious to like the car, but could not help calling it "an absurd little drawing-room on wheels." But the earl was so busy watching his servants, as they in their turn watched the railway employés who were stowing the small mountain of luggage in the van, that he could pay no attention to the complaints of his fair companions until after the train had started. When he came in he found his wife standing bolt upright in a corner, holding Lady Helena tightly by the hand, and looking as if she had thunderbolts of speech in store for him.

"This is really too dreadful!" she said. "It is so repulsively public! Pray look at that gentleman in the farther corner. He is actually having his bed made up in some shocking fashion or other by that creature in uniform. I hope he does not expect" — and here she stopped short, and made a mute appeal to Lady Helena for sympathy.

"Good heavens!" said the earl, "has Jenks gone quite mad?" The maid started at hearing her name, and looked guilty. "Did I not tell her when we came in that a 'drawing-room' was specially reserved for you?"

Jenks blushed violently, and in a rapid and unpunctuated speech asseverated that she had seen nothing in the carriage which bore the remotest resemblance to a "drorin' room." Upon this the earl showed some temper, and escorted the ladies to a snug and handsomely decorated section of the car, where they were able to ensconce themselves behind doors which shut out the odious public, and where most comfortable beds awaited them.

"There," he said to the wife of his bosom, "is not that a fascinating boudoir? You can, I am sure, sleep as soundly there as in your little blue room at our country-house in Branley." Then he went away to the forward car, in which there was a smoking compartment, knowing that he should find the colonel there enjoying an excellent Havana. The ladies, left alone, "cuddled" together upon one of the beds without taking off their cloaks or hats, and prepared to be miserable, while the wretched Jenks took up a position of observation on the couch opposite them. In half an hour Jenks perceived that the criticisms on the Pullman car and its detestable democracy had ceased, and that both ladies slept. So she covered them with shawls and blankets, and, returning wearily to the friendly berth, soon followed them to the land of dreams.

. . . .

When Lady Helena awoke her first impulse was to be angry. She had willingly adhered to all that the countess had said against the odious American "car;" and yet she had been rocked to sleep in it. Now the train was at a stand-still. Through the closely drawn curtains came no ray of light. Could it be possible that the journey to Liverpool was over? And was that limp mass of rugs and waterproofs, faintly agitated by an almost noiseless breathing, was *that* Jenks? It must be so; yet Lady Helena was a trifle confused. "I am not half awake," she whispered to herself; "and I believe I should like to go back to my dream, although it was most strange."

It was, indeed, a strange dream. She had been transported by some unseen and resistless energy through great spaces, among the constellations, high into the inner heavens, and there she had seen winged creatures strewing stars downward from huge sieves, scattering the shining orbs beneath them as a careless child might scatter pearls from a casket. One star would not go down, but fluttered up, and up, and up; and, perceiving this, one of the sowers said, scornfully, "Let it go; it is not of the first magnitude!" While she fixed her gaze upon this vagrant star she awoke, but the voice kept resounding in her ears. It had a familiar tone, and she strove with all her might to remember where she had heard it before. There was no noise outside; the lamp suspended from the car-roof gave but a feeble gleam; the countess was peacefully sleeping, regardless of the ravages made by the pressure of the pillow against her new travelling-hat, fresh from Madame Virot's. Lady Helena opened and closed her daintily gloved hands, to make sure that she herself was not asleep. Suddenly she started, for she heard that voice once more. But this time it was not talking of stars; it was saying: —

"Very well; have the small bags put in the cloak-room, and bring me the ticket for them. I will walk up."

No, she could not remember where she had heard it; but she knew that it stirred her heart pleasurably and awakened there a vague and indefinable regret.

Finding that the countess and the maid were not at all disposed to awaken, she gave herself up to revery, and she sat with her shapely head bent slightly forward, her hands clasped together and her lips parted, in the attitude of listening, as when she had started from her dream. The owner of the mysterious voice had departed, but he had left behind him a lasting impression. The shadows danced upon the girl's face and seemed to linger lovingly on her pretty brow and chin. Lady Helena was not beautiful; but she had something better than beauty — a permanent and never-to-be-forgotten charm, difficult to analyze or resist. Yet she was commonly called cold, and sometimes hard-hearted, by persons of her own rank. Inferiors contented themselves with affirming that she was "haughty." Her dark brown hair was combed smoothly back from her forehead and caught in a simple knot at her neck. Had she been willing to torture it into grotesque forms, as some women would have done, the effect of her face would have been more picturesque, but it would also have been less charming. She had been brought up to abhor affectation or artifice; and the severe simplicity which characterized her during her first two seasons in London was, now and then, cited as a reproach against her.

Lady Offast had, at one time, manifested a tendency toward the æsthetic school. But Lady Helena had been so keen and effective in her ridicule of the disciples of the superlatively intense and the indescribably utter that the passion for ugly China and lank lilies never secured a footing in the earl's household. The earl and his wife were sincerely fond of their clever and amiable cousin, who was herself the daughter of an earl, and who, as Lord Boughton, one of her enthusiastic admirers, was fond of saying, "would be the most popular woman in London if she were not so unworldly." She was quite unconscious of the resentment aroused in many masculine and feminine minds by her indifference to the vanities and the small pleasures of conventional society; but even had she realized the bitterness of the criticism which she excited, she would not have heeded it. Lady Helena had inherited strength of will and independence from her father, the robust old earl, and originality and fineness of motive from her mother. The one grief of her life had been the loss of these parents, both in the same year. She possessed a handsome fortune, bequeathed to her by an uncle, who had coined his liver into silver and gold in India; and many a young nobleman looked at her with more than usual attention when she began to appear in the society for which she cared so little, and of which she might be so conspicuous an ornament. One or two dowagers who had attempted to give Lady Helena advice, and had been skilfully snubbed for their pains, said that unless the girl minded her ways she would never find a husband. These malicious critics, with the cunning of their kind, never mentioned the fact that Lady Helena, notwithstanding her seeming coldness, had, before she was four and twenty, had more offers than usually fall to the lot of one woman. Yet there she was, fast nearing the dangerous ground of twenty-five, and unmarried. It was a burning shame, said the dowagers, that such a fine fortune as Lady Helena's should be allowed to run to waste. The headstrong girl was frittering it away, they were told, in all sorts of disreputable American investments. What would her father say if he were alive, on learning that his daughter permitted good English money to leave the country? Once or twice some busybodies ventured to question the earl about Lady Helena's *penchant* for transatlantic financial ventures; but their reception was so extremely frosty that they concluded they had made a mistake, and withdrew just in time to save their necks; for the earl was rapidly making up his mind to throw them out of the window.

Lady Helena had ideas of her own on politics, and was much more liberal in sentiment than she fancied herself to be. The word "radical" had an unpleasant sound in her ears; it invariably suggested something vaguely disreputable, and she would have doubtless been much mystified had she discovered that on many social questions she was more in sympathy with the outcast radicals than with the eminent conservative statesmen whom she knew. The Earl of Offast once told her that one of his brother peers, after having sat next to her at dinner in the earl's house, reported that she was a "veritable little radical, her ideas tempered only by good-breeding and education."

The countess, who was a pretty and lazy creature, excessively fond of comfort and luxury, but decidedly emphatic in her notions as to the rights and privileges of the aristocracy, had at first objected to having Lady Helena visit America, lest a sojourn in that land of unbridled democracy should make the charming cousin an out and out revolutionist. But the earl laughed at these fears, and insisted on the necessity for their cousin of a personal inspection of her investments. "Besides," he added, in a tone which completely broke down the lingering opposition manifested by Lady Offast, "our opportunities for investing our available cash will be much better than they are at present, if we are thought in any way to influence such a capitalist as Lady Helena in the disposal of her means. I can look after the girl and see that she does nothing rash, while at the same time we can do ourselves a good turn."

Riches had never brought any happiness to Lady Helena. She would have been exactly as happy with a few hundreds of pounds annually as she was with a great many thousands. Perhaps she would have had longings for costly works of art beyond her reach if she had been poor; but she now had plenty of wishes that no money could gratify. If she invested in many things it was in obedience to the advice of her relatives and intimate friends, rather than from any desire for large results or from any prudent instincts. The earl was often her adviser, and strove to be a faithful one. She usually agreed with his suggestions, and he hesitated at making any unless he believed them as well calculated to promote her welfare as those that she might receive from others. His plan was very simple. A duke, who was an excellent friend of his, employed an agent, — a sound-hearted, clear-headed man, — to travel up and down the world and make investments for him. The earl attentively watched the movements of the agent, and, when that acute personage had found something remarkably good for the duke, took measures to be "let in" to the scheme. In this manner the earl had been led first to invest, in Spain, in certain mines supposed to possess fabulous-wealth; next, in Egypt, in the broad and inexhaustible lands which are in the near future to supply Great Britain with its wheat; and, finally, in the North-west of the United States. The agent came back from America, after two or three careful visits of inspection, convinced that the ducal resources might with safety be lavished there. The earl soon "got the tip," as he called it in his sporting jargon; and the thousands which Lady Helena and he himself were able to spare out of their annual incomes went to America in the wake of the duke's treasure. "The agent would not dare to put us into a bad thing, my dear," said the earl to his wife; "for, if we were to shake the duke's confidence in him, his mission would be at an end."

Just as Lady Helena was falling asleep again there was a knock at the door, and the earl's voice was heard inquiring if the fair travellers were aware that they had been in Liverpool for two hours; that eight o'clock was near at hand; and that, whenever they chose, they could emerge from their seclusion, and go to the apartments engaged for them at the hotel. Then there was much discomfiture on the part of Jenks, who was awakened by the countess, that lady appearing not to have had her temper refreshed by her slumbers.

By and by they left the car and walked through the huge station, which had not yet thoroughly awakened to its day of haste and bustle, out into the streets.

"The journey is like a dream," said the countess, sleepily; "I know we left London at midnight, but

I know nothing else, except that this is a land of dreams. How unreal everything seems, seen through the veil of these mists!"

There was a kind of glamour in the warm and omnipresent mists which had crept in from the sea on this August morning, and had transformed Liverpool into a weird and enchanted place. Houses peeped out of the blankness for an instant and then disappeared again, as if they were alarmed at the presence of these new-comers. A boy driving a butcher's cart, seen a little way off, looked like a giant mounted on an elephant. An old woman, clad in a filthy black gown, a torn shawl, and a tattered straw hat, reeled out from an alley, taking her uncertain course through the door of a public-house, over whose gaudy entrance lamps were burning. Lady Helena thought of a poor animal disappearing in the maw of some dreadful dragon with fiery eyes, as she saw this. St. George's Hall loomed up majestically, a black mass, appearing to the countess, according to her own statement, "as large as a peak of the Himalayas," which, by the way, she had never seen. The equestrian figures of Her Gracious Majesty and the Prince Consort appeared as if flying through the air, for the fantastic mist had shrouded their pedestals, while allowing the figures themselves to remain visible. Over all the avenues leading down to the river the curtain hung, now wavering lightly to and fro in obedience to some vagrant breeze, and disclosing acres of smoke-blackened walls, mysterious recesses filled with squalid hovels, vast squares lined with noble public buildings, court-yards in which screaming women and drunken men were fighting, or corners on which hucksters were peddling cheap food from their tiny carts. There were moments when the veil was drawn so tightly over all things that the earl and the ladies could not see a dozen paces before them. "Heaven knows what would have become of us had we taken a cab," sighed the countess. "We might have been driven into the Mersey and drowned!"

They were to be at the Prince's landing-stage at four that afternoon, to take their steamer, and the countess, after breakfast, retired to her cosey room in the North-western Hotel, asserting that she must make up for lost sleep, or she could not face the terrors of the ocean with equanimity. Lady Helena and the earl, feeling adventurous, went for a walk by the water-side. "In a few hours we shall sail through the gate of the mists, yonder," said the earl, pointing down stream, "and shape our course for the Western sunshine. What a depressing spectacle!" He pointed to the broad river, along which the mists and fogs lay in solid banks. Birkenhead was concealed under the pall; now and then there came through the distance a dismal groan from a straggling ferry-boat, or a dignified warning bellow from a great steamship, striving to get through the misty gate of which the earl had spoken. The sun was dimly visible, a ball of red in the east; he seemed half inclined to go back, as if disgusted with the scene which he had arisen to witness. Voices came seemingly out of the depths of the waters; tugs and steamers, carrying hundreds of emigrants and costly merchandise, puffed by unseen; and a song, sung by invisible boatmen, the regular dip of whose oars could be heard close at hand, was so ghostly that it made Lady Helena shudder.

In the course of their walk they came upon Colonel Hodges, who immediately threw away a fine Havana cigar, which he had just lighted, and assumed an air of deep contemplation as he perceived Lady Helena.

"I am waiting," he said, when they came up and stirred him from his feigned revery, "for my good friend, Captain Jobson. He is one of the salt of the earth, sah," addressing himself to the earl. "I reckon you must have heard of him."

"I compute not," said the earl, determined to be as mathematical as the colonel.

"Not salt of the earth, but salt of the sea, you should say, Colonel Hodges," said Lady Helena. "I have had the pleasure of meeting Captain Jobson. It was — in the country — last season. 'Sir,' I said, 'by your conversation I judge that you have seen much of the ocean.' 'Madam,' he replied, with the most *beautiful* American inflection, — 'Madam, I was master of the finest ship in the world for twenty years. She was built of mahogany, and she sailed out of the port of New York.'" Here Lady Helena laughed merrily, but checked her gayety instantly, saying: —

"And there comes the captain now, bearing down this way with his wonted impetuosity."

CHAPTER III.

CAPTAIN JOBSON.

"I HAVE just learned something," said Colonel Hodges, turning around to gaze at the approaching mariner, "which quite surprises me."

"Nothing unpleasant, I hope," remarked the earl. "I think surprises are usually — er — disagreeable. For my part I begin to feel as that Schopenhauer fellow said he felt when his door-bell rang. I say, 'What bad news is this?'"

"It's a feeling we all have after we are thirty-five," sighed the colonel. He had certainly had it a good many times in the last six months. "We are all more or less frightened as we begin to go down the hill of life, and each one tries to conceal his alarm as best he can. Some succeed better than others at this game of concealment, and so pass for jolly and contented mortals. Excuse my didactic vein. I was about to say that I was surprised to find among our fellow-passengers on the 'Athabaska' no less than six people who are invited to join the excursion to the North-west. And among them is this old and good friend, Captain Jobson."

"Really. How strange!" said Lady Helena, glancing at her cousin. She knew well enough of what he was thinking. The earl's face wore a look of vague apprehension. Lady Helena fancied she could hear him saying, "Now here, by my lack of caution, I have got myself into a mess! Just fancy —er—six more persons—all of whom will find out that we are going for the excursion—er—and who will come about scraping acquaintance and—er—offering their nasty civilities. Bah! I wish I were well out of it." And the girl read her cousin's mind very correctly. If it had not been undignified he would have taken to his heels when the captain came up. That passion for exclusiveness, that insatiable desire to have something that others cannot possess, which is such a shining characteristic of the British aristocrat's mind, ruled the earl's thought for a moment. But he was master of himself, and had mustered all his grave and somewhat frosty politeness by the time Captain Jobson had arrived, had greeted Colonel Hodges in a rapid allocution which was as picturesque as varied, and had recognized Lady Helena and paid her a sugared compliment with a grace which the earl envied.

"You are the gentleman of the mahogany ship," said the young lady. "Did you expect that I could ever forget you? And that story about Chinese pirates, which you never finished?" —

"And you are the lady with the dazzling eyes!" said the gallant captain. "Do you think that I could ever forget *that?* You don't mind an old man's compliments? Very good of you to remember my poor story. It had one merit, that it was true. All my stories *are* true. Some uncharitable persons think the contrary, because I tell them marvels. But, bless their souls! I've *seen* marvels. Where were we? — on the river — the Tamoon river. Ah! now it all comes back!" The captain's voice rose a little. He had been holding Lady Helena's hand, but now he released it, and, making a formal bow, full of the grace of that "old school" which was so much better than the new, he concentrated all his energy upon his story, as if it had been interrupted but a few minutes instead of a few months.

"The Tamoon river, yes! I remember it as if it were yesterday. I had told you — yes — about Fernandino Bernardez — my worthy employer."

"You had," said Lady Helena, laughing again. "You said that he was a mixture" —

"Of Portuguese, Chinese, and the Evil One.

Quite right. In those days Canton was a rough place. Funny people there. Funniest of all was Fernandino Bernardez. My ship — my mahogany craft — was on the berth in Canton for some months, and not liking to be idle I took charge of a steamer belonging to my long-name friend. My duty was to tow junks and to chase pirates. Now I tell *you* that I didn't sleep *more'n* half of the twenty-four hours every day. The junk-towing was genuine fun, because the Chinese are such cowards. The very name of pirate is enough to take all their strength away. It was my first expedition after pirates that I started to tell you about — I really hope I am not keeping that gentleman waiting."

Lady Helena glanced around for the earl. He had retreated to some distance from the captain and his audience, and was gazing steadfastly into the mists, as if he were determined to frown them down and frighten them out of his range of vision.

"It is my cousin, the Earl of Offast," she said, mischievously. "Will you let me call him? He is so fond of American tales."

"The Earl of Offast, great sportsman; certainly; knew his father very well; we are to be fellow-travellers in the North-west; most happy;" said the captain, with a pleased twinkle in his sharp eyes, but without the slightest manifestation of trepidation at the presence of a member of the nobility.

"The earl is a particular friend of mine," said Colonel Hodges, in a low voice, as Lady Helena stepped back to call her cousin.

"Ah, ha! Enough said; I never want mysteries explained. I shall do my best to be agreeable."

He did so well that in five minutes the earl, who had fancied that he should dislike him, was heartily pleased with him and that he was to be of the excursion party, and was laughing aloud as the captain steered dexterously through the sinuous stretches of his story.

"My first expedition after pirates was in 1849, eighty-five miles south of Macao, on the Tamoon, near Lafien, a place never visited by an outside barbarian before," said the captain. "I was after a craft belonging to a Macao merchant; he said it had been taken by pirates. So we got our guns loaded and everything ready for work, and we ran up on the north side of the Island of St. John, the place where Saint Francis Xavier was first buried — don't you remember? Now, this island was a regular nest of pirates, and I knew we should find some of those gentlemen not far up-stream. Sure enough, twenty miles from the mouth of the Tamoon what did I see but the passage stopped by a row of long piles driven into the river bed! Here was fun. Just beyond these swinging and swaying piles was the craft that we were in search of. I ran in close to the piles, made a rope to a number of them at a time, backed astern and drew them out. Then you should have seen the pirates pop over the sides of the craft, taking to the water in all directions! With good shooting we picked off eighteen out of twenty-five swimmers, and then we lowered a boat and caught three more. Do you know the reason why I started to tell you the story?"

"No, I'm *sure* I can't imagine," answered Lady Helena. "But tell me, Captain Jobson, do you mean to say that you and your men shot and killed those pirates?"

"Most decidedly, and kept up the game for six weeks after that, until"—

"How delightful! Isn't it quite romantic?" cried Lady Helena, appealing to her cousin, who replied that it was, and that he must get Captain Jobson to tell him what muskets they used in those days, and whether there were any other kinds of sport on the Tamoon.

"Until," continued Captain Jobson, "I happened to see my tripartite friend with the Portuguese name in close colloquy with one of the worst pirates of Canton. This set me to thinking. Here was my employer, who sent me out to kill pirates, conversing in the most confidential manner with one of their chieftains. I studied that matter out, and found" —

"Oh, let us hope that he was a pirate, too!" cried Lady Helena, clapping her hands.

"And found that he played a double game. Up to that time it had worked beautifully. He kept a fleet of piratical cruisers knocking about, with instructions to capture any unprotected junks they observed beating along the coast. The pirates were to murder and plunder the crews of the junks and turn the vessels afloat, after which my variegated employer would send me out to tow the derelicts in, and would claim handsome sums from the owners for the service. And, once in a while, the Portuguese gentleman had me attack his pirates, just to keep up the illusion! Cute feller, wasn't he? We towed junks to protect them from our pirates, so to speak, and we towed them after they had been attacked by our pirates! Well, having found the truth out, I thought I had had enough of that; so I discharged myself; and, as my own ship was still in berth, I went over to California, built a river steamer (light draught, to run up the Chinese rivers with) on the Pacific coast. I brought her across the Pacific Ocean without starting a timber; made eighteen thousand dollars in six months! Yes, —— ——, I met an old captain, this very morning, who was in Canton in 1849. 'Jobson,' says he, 'you're seventy-two, if you're a day, but you look younger'n you did a generation ago.' I tell him it is this English air."

Colonel Hodges coughed faintly, as if he could not subscribe with enthusiasm to this sentiment. They moved on together toward the landing-stage whence they were to depart that afternoon, the captain escorting Lady Helena as if he had known her for twenty years, and telling her how it was that he came to be numbered among those invited on the excursion. "You see, my friend Dalkyn — old Dalkyn, who was in the China trade in 1840 — immense concern — he was invited — and wrote me from Boston, 'I'll go if you will.' We were in San Francisco when there were only three houses there. Dalkyn knew I couldn't say no — and when my invitation came — of course I accepted, and my boy is packing my bag this minute at my little house over yonder on the hill. Dalkyn ought to remember me; I took him on my ship — the mahogany one — in the port of Canton, sailing for San Francisco, and he says to me, 'Captain Jobson, I'm a dead man. Nothing can cure me; I shall die on your hands, and just bury me at sea, without any nonsense.' — 'Friend Dalkyn,' said I, 'you shall not perish away under my care;' and I brought him into the Golden Gate a well man. He said I talked the life back into him, and I made him eat."

The stalwart policeman at the entrance to the landing-stage touched his hat as the party approached. The earl, at first, fancied that this salute was in recognition of his own position, but he speedily discovered that it was for Captain Jobson, who appeared to be on the best of terms with every one down by the water-side. The earl had studied the captain a bit while the aged mariner was telling his tale of exploits among pirates in China, and had decided that this was another American in whose presence he would unbend, and in whose peculiarities he should find perpetual delight. Captain Jobson was one of those wonderful men on whom Time leaves but few marks, as if loath to hasten them out of a generation to which they contribute so much enjoyment and activity. He was wont to refer to himself as having been "master for five and thirty years of the finest ship that ever took the water;"

yet he was not weather-beaten, neither did he have a rolling gait, nor was his conversation interlarded with nautical phrases. His long voyages had been full of adventure, and many a time he had taken his life in his hand; but one might have supposed him a prosperous city missionary rather than a retired ocean rover. His strong, well-balanced features framed in iron-gray whiskers; a certain coquettishness of attire which yet did not transgress the bounds of excellent taste; a smile which instantly restored confidence that might have been a trifle shaken by any extravagant incident which he had happened to relate, and a vivid and picturesque gesticulation, rare among Anglo-Saxons, joined to a fluent and pleasant delivery, — these were all combined in the minds of any new acquaintances in a favorable first impression, which there was never any occasion to change. Captain Jobson was more than seventy, and looked less than fifty, years of age. He lived in a small and comfortable house in a suburb of Liverpool, spending his days in renewing old friendships and making new ones on the docks — the wonderful docks of the Mersey — where the representatives of every civilization under the sun set their feet at least once or twice in their lives; and in the evening he wrote out, in a clear, round hand, in neatly ruled note-books, the story of his life, copied from "logs" innumerable. Each year he gave the dock porters a dinner at a temperance tavern; and every week he dined Tuesdays with a Catholic and Wednesdays with a Church of England clergyman. These reverend gentlemen alleged as the reason of their fondness for Jobson, that he brought them the air of the outside world, and seemed to put them into closer relations with humanity than by their own unaided efforts they managed to get. When he disappeared, as he occasionally did, on voyages to America, to France, or Spain, there was something lacking on the banks of the Mersey, and, although every one would have been puzzled to say exactly what it was, in point of fact it was Captain Jobson. Although he was American-born, the good mercantile folk of Liverpool never thought of the captain as of any especial country; he was a cosmopolite, a fine old craft, not carrying any particular flag, which had come in with the tide one day after circumnavigation infinite, and which had brought to anchor in the Mersey.

Thanks to the mysterious intervention of Captain Jobson, it was arranged that the earl and his party should go off to the "Athabaska" in a private tug half an hour before the departure of the regular one, which, as the earl observed, would "most probably be oppressively crowded." So grateful was the earl for the attention which he felt was due to his station, yet which he might perhaps have asked for in vain himself, that he expressed the earnest hope that Colonel Hodges and the captain would not fail to accompany him and his cousin on the private tug. "We shall feel quite anxious — er — to have you do so," he said to Captain Jobson, who, when alone with Colonel Hodges, a minute afterward, remarked: —

"That was pretty good, after I got the privilege, and asked him to share it! I wonder if I shall ever understand these fellows?"

Lady Helena was delighted with everything she saw, especially with the troops of wild-eyed emigrants, embarking in the mist of enormous masses of soiled mattresses, frowzy blankets, and clattering tin ware, for the land of the setting sun. She went down among the Norwegian babies, and the Italian children undergoing exportation to become organ-grinders, and the old Irish women with coarse shawls pulled over their unkempt hair, and with short black pipes between their teeth. The crones flattered her until she had no sixpences left, and when her back was turned spat on the ground and cursed her for a "Saxon." But she seemed to bring sunshine into the mist, and many a pallid mother, whose nerves were weary with the endless care of a clamorous brood of children impatiently awaiting the tedious embarkation, felt soothed and comforted by the kind words of the soft-voiced and brilliant-eyed young lady, who did not seem at all concerned if her garments happened to brush against theirs.

They wandered to and fro, merry and inquisitive, until the colonel said that it was noon, and that he must go to the Adelphi; and Lady Helena suddenly remembered with a pang that the countess was most likely pacing her apartment in the North-western Hotel, and grimly imagining that some dread adventure had befallen her husband and cousin, who had been foolhardy enough to venture forth in the mists. So she was about to suggest a speedy return, when the earl said: —

"Cousin, the captain says that by going a little out of our way home we can get a glimpse of the 'poor quarter' of Liverpool. I suppose that, as conscientious Britons, it is our duty to see all the horrors that exist in our beloved country. Have you courage? Shall we see one of the circles of the Inferno before we set sail?"

"I should be delighted to go with you," said

Lady Helena, whereupon the colonel discovered that his appointment, which was in reality with a dish of whitebait and a pint of champagne, could wait. And so they struck boldly into a labyrinth of ill-smelling streets, and left civilization behind.

As they went on, coming every moment upon some new horror, the earl said: —

"I really didn't know there was anything quite so bad as this in Liverpool! And we can't be — er — more than ten minutes' walk from St. George's Hall."

"This should all be swept away!" cried Lady Helena, whose eyes were dilated with surprise and disgust.

"A great many ancient uses and abuses will have to be swept away before this can be remedied," said Captain Jobson, turning to the enthusiastic young lady with a quaint smile on his firm lips. "Just look down this lane — it can't be called a street."

Lady Helena looked, drawing her breath hard. Her heart beat loudly, and she felt inclined to run away. She saw long rows of dirty and crazy houses on either side of an avenue choked with filth, and into which the sun — on the rare occasions when that luminary condescended to make his appearance in Liverpool — could never peep.

The habitations were horrible; they had a sinister look; the windows, grimy with dirt, were tightly closed. Nowhere was there a flower or a child singing, or a group of babies engaged in some pretty game. Children born in these slums could only be expected to yell, to claw each other fiercely, to fight as soon as they were old enough, and to engage in childish imitation of the vices of their elders. Rickety steps led down to damp cellars; and, through the narrow entrances to these noisome dens, the visitors could see young and old women with discolored faces, matted hair, and eyes which glared suspiciously, like those of wild beasts, at passers-by. In some of the cellars women were fighting; in others they were screaming and scolding drunken men, who had just staggered in from adjacent public-houses to sleep off the effects of their debauch in the kennels which they called homes; and in still others, old men and women, clad in rags, sat mute and desolate, looking as if they would find nothing so cheering as the approach of Death, who alone could relieve them from their woes.

"Well," said Colonel Hodges; "I thought I had already seen every variety of wild animal, but here is a new species."

"Let us go," said Lady Helena. "I am certain

that they are beginning to worry about us at the hotel, and I feel quite faint."

They left the mouth of the alley and turned into a long and broad street, which, according to Captain Jobson, was the "nearest way home." On the right was a foreign-looking public-house, with a quaint lettering upon a creaking sign. A narrow flight of wooden steps, protected on each side by a railing painted blue, led to a stout door with oaken panels. In front of this door, as if she had just closed it behind her, stood a Norwegian peasant girl, neatly dressed in a simple costume; and at the foot of the steps was a young man sketching. Near him was an old fellow in a fur cap, a long blue coat and knee-breeches, presumably the father of the Norwegian damsel.

"That fellow has found a picturesque subject," said the earl; "but it must have required a good bit of courage to come into such a hole as this in search of sketches."

The artist turned as he heard the party's footsteps. He frowned slightly, and seemed inclined to move away; but in a moment he fixed his attention anew on his work, and, motioning to the girl to stand a little to one side, he said: —

"I know you don't understand me; but it is my

duty to tell you that you look quite bewitching like that. Now, may Heaven preserve you in just that attitude until I have finished my sketch!"

Lady Helena was near enough to hear what the artist said. Her color came and went quickly. The voice of this man was the voice that she had heard in her dream — had heard before she had dreamed the dream — and had heard outside the Pullman car that very morning.

Now what was the magic of this voice?

She hoped to get a good look at the artist's face, thinking that possibly she might recognize him as some person whom she had met in drawing-room or at watering-place. But the face was bent over the work as Lady Helena and her party passed, and she could not even see whether the man were young or old.

CHAPTER IV.

AN ATLANTIC DAY.

About thirty hours after Lady Helena had threaded the inodorous mazes of the "poor quarter" in Liverpool she was reclining in a steamer chair on the upper deck of the "Athabaska," and was endeavoring, with a persistence of will rare enough on shipboard, to collect her scattered thoughts. It was Lady Helena's will which had brought her on deck, and which now kept her there, on the swaying and plunging planks which, to her feminine apprehension, seemed every minute more and more likely to be plunged beneath the green waters capped with white foam. Supported by the stout arms of Captain Jobson and by his kindly counsels, she had managed to reach this chair, which was securely lashed to an iron rod; and once well wrapped up, and with her dainty head laid upon a comfortable pillow, she whispered to herself, "This plunge of waters is terrifying to look at, and I feel as if it would certainly swallow me up; but I would rather be drowned than to stir from this chair now I am ensconced in it."

The "Athabaska" was a great monster with colossal engines and with such a ponderous upper deck that she was unduly weighted down. Many an old sailor shook his head after he had been to sea in this craft, and averred that he would "never again be caught on a steamer that shipped so much water on the lee side." Her power seemed almost resistless; in a rough day, when the riotous waves were inclined to trifle with the monotonous regularity of Her Majesty's mails, the mighty ship dashed along at her ordinary rate of speed, and the discomfited ocean retired, not exactly crestfallen, but at least browbeaten. Naturally such a swiftly moving steamer was also a most remarkable "roller;" and the countess had declared, after ten hours of consecutive rolling, from the moment they were out of sight of Queenstown, that she should feel the dreadful rocking in her brain for the next ten years. As for Jenks, she was utterly demoralized. The wretched Jenks had been happy all the way down Channel, and had frequently asseverated that if "that was all goin' to sea amounted to she was sure for *her* part that she would be willing to go every day of her life." She repudiated the odious insinuation of Captain Jobson "that there was always a gale blowing somewhere," and that it was not entirely improbable that one might be encountered before reaching New York. Then came her day of confusion. "O Lor'!" she cried, when the rocking, rolling, and pitching began, "this *is* the sea, and I *know* it will kill me." Over the sorrows of Jenks, as she crawled on hands and knees to and from the sofa on which her mistress reclined, the historian must draw a veil. When she was not crawling she was sitting on the floor, with her head propped against the berth, and wishing the world might come to an end.

The day was not cold, and the sky was filled with pretty and fleecy clouds, through which the sun occasionally cast a shy glance, as if anxious to see how the "Athabaska" would make her way this time in a particularly fresh gale. The horrors with which Lady Offast and her maid (and perhaps Colonel Hodges must be added) were appalled had no existence save in their imaginations, and would presently have been dissipated by the serene and vivifying influences of light and air. That a fresh gale had come up in the night there was not the smallest doubt, and the captain was likely that noon to inscribe upon his log, "Heavy sea; frequent squalls."

"Oh, what was that?" said Lady Helena, with a startled look. But there was no excitement in her voice.

"That, your ladyship, was the merest nothing," remarked the imperturbable captain, who had just returned from below, bearing in his firm grasp a plate on which a cup of bouillon was sliding to and fro, like the "Athabaska" on the waves. "That was only a couple of tons of salt water which the spirits of the deep wished to add to our cargo! B-r-r-! " And the captain stood, grim, angry, still griping his plate, and severely drenched by a second hasty arrival of "merest nothing." Lady Helena thought from the rushing and roaring that this time she was surely lost; but she felt no hurt, and, opening her eyes, and, observing the almost comical grimness of the old navigator, she could not help smiling as she said: —

"Captain, I fear you have allowed some of that sea-water to get into my bouillon."

"Even the cup is gone! Oh, no! there it is by the nettings." He walked "down the roof of the house," as Lady Helena expressed it, and recovered the vagrant article with ease. "I never had any such doings as this on my ship," he remarked. "We used to be content to take our water on the weather-side."

"What is the weather-side, captain?" said Lady Helena, faintly.

"The sea has made you giddy," said the old man, as gently as if she were his daughter. "I'll skip down and get some more bouillon. And some fruit. Nothing like fruit. One day when I was in the China Seas — coming up from — But never mind that now. I know all about fruit, and I'll tell you."

"I wonder if my cousin would be so gallant," thought Lady Helena, as she awaited with some impatience the captain's return. Her cousin was just at that moment in the smoking-room, enjoying the modest luxuries of a short pipe and a bottle of Bass. Seated at a dignified distance from the other inmates, he was intently studying them and meditating as to the expediency of knowing some of them. Impervious to sea-sickness, he rather enjoyed the rough weather; it added a certain hilarity, which he veiled under a placid exterior, to his spirits. He had assured himself that Lady Offast had the usual purgatorial period to go through, and that Lady Helena was well cared for; so he enjoyed his pipe, and his beer, and the storm, and the fact that he was an earl; or, as the clumsy English phrase has it, he "enjoyed himself."

Thanks to the captain, Lady Helena got a good breakfast, considering the exceptional situation, and only one sweep of water came across the deck while she was taking this meal.

"Do you never eat, captain?" she asked.

"Twice a day, madam," he said; "twice a day — noon and six o'clock — nothing between meals, and no appetizers. You see that I thrive on that system. In 1853 — no, it was in 1854 — I first adopted the French plan. But never mind that. It was in the Philippine Islands. But never mind that, either."

"I *do* mind, though, Captain Jobson," she said, very sweetly, "and I should like to hear all about the circumstance."

"Bless your heart, you wouldn't believe it! It is a marvel, and you, charitable as you are, would *not* give it credence. However, I left Macao — in" —

Lady Helena was destined never to know at what time Captain Jobson left Macao, nor what marvel he encountered in the Philippine Islands; for just then the "Athabaska" gave one of her treacherous lurches, and mountainous masses of water came pouring in upon the lower deck, while wind-blown clouds of spray and a few leaping jets came even to where Lady Helena was sitting. The ship trembled like a big monster in rage and pain, and it was some time before she righted — so long that many nervous passengers manifested more emotion than they would afterward have been willing to admit. The long row of chairs filled with invalids in various stages of recovery from sea-sickness was emptied of its occupants, who rolled, or sprang, or tumbled, down to the rail, upon which the demons of the deep seemed to be fixing their sinuous clutch, preparatory to whelming the unlucky travellers in the waves. Blankets flew along the deck, children screamed, women shrieked, and there was not the least uncertainty about the profanity indulged in by numbers of the men, for the noise of it rose above the roar of the ocean. Lady Helena alone was saved from this unceremonious hustling by the prompt action of the captain, who threw himself on his knees in front of her and, grasping the handles of her chair, held on, as he himself oddly expressed it, "like grim death to a dead Chinaman."

"If the rope had snapped," said Lady Helena, reaching up with her slender gloved hand to touch the cord which held the chair to the rod, "should we have been out *there* now?"

The captain arose, somewhat painfully, and wiping the spray from his face, looked at the sea. "Out *there?* No, indeed; not the smallest danger, for we are not diaphanous enough to be carried between those railings. Isn't that a glorious sight, now? Think of staying on land when you can see such sights on the ocean! Do you notice that bark yonder — Norwegian — (she should be, by the build of her), and how she rises and falls on the waves? Lovely! I beg pardon!"

A tall young gentleman had touched the captain's arm, recalling him from the height of enthusiasm at which he was contemplating the changeful wonders of the deep, and had said: —

"Will you allow me to ask your help, sir? I think this little girl has broken an arm."

Lady Helena looked up at the sky for a moment (the captain had told her it was the way to steady her head), then she turned her gaze full upon the speaker. His eyes met hers, and then she remembered where she had first heard this voice, which now came again to stir the blood at her heart as it had never been stirred by any other sound, nor by any sight whatsoever.

"Poor baby!" cried the captain, stooping with the stranger to raise and replace in the chair in which she had been sitting a pretty girl seven or eight years old, who had been thrown out by the lurch, and who now, white with pain and just coming out of a swoon, was beginning to call for her mother.

"Are you the doctor?" said the captain.

There was an affectation of half humorous indignation in the gentleman's answer.

"Now, come, sir, do I look like a steamship surgeon? If I do I will never pray more. Steady, little girl, we are only lifting you up to make you more comfortable, and then we will send for your mamma and for the doctor, if he can do any good."

But the small girl was thoroughly frightened, besides being exasperated by sharp pain, and she screamed and insisted that she would not arise until her mother came.

"She *must* be raised," said the captain. "Tell us where your mother is."

The small girl indicated without specifying names, that the mother was in her state-room, going through the same purgatorial experience as Lady Offast and the melancholy Jenks.

"Give me the child here in my arms," said Lady Helena, in the commanding voice which she used when she went visiting among her cousin's poor people in the country. When she found that neither the captain nor the stranger seemed inclined to obey her she frowned and then blushed violently.

Captain Jobson came to her rescue. "I am afraid your ladyship could not hold the little sufferer," he said; "she kicks stoutly."

"Which would indicate," remarked the "gentleman with the influential voice," as Lady Helena was beginning to designate him to herself, "that I was mistaken in my supposition of the broken arm."

"Not at all," said Lady Helena, coldly. "Please give me the child."

There was no other lady near; the alarmed passengers were thinking of nothing so much as a safe arrival at the gangway; so Captain Jobson yielded, and the two men took the screaming girl up and gently lowered her into Lady Helena's lap. This action brought both the gentlemen to their knees, where they remained a moment, and the four, thus grouped, made a pretty picture. The child, suddenly pacified, and finding that her pain had not been increased, clung to the lady and, ceasing to scream, began to sob violently.

"I'll stand guard while you run for the doctor," said the captain to the new acquaintance; and that passenger hastened away on his errand, with a sure foot, which showed that he had traversed oceans before. "Don't disturb the mother, yet," shrieked Captain Jobson after him.

"I'm not likely to do that, since I don't know her name," shouted back the voice.

"Yes," — Lady Helena was thinking, as she held the child tenderly — "that is the very man. And it was in Paris that I first saw him. In Paris the last time that Lady Offast and I were shopping there. I bought this very wrap I have on at this minute on that day. And where did we see him? It was in that odd house in the Rue Croix des Petits Champs, where we had to climb so many stairs to find Lady Offast's habit-maker. We rang at a door, and it opened so quickly that we were a little alarmed. There stood this — gentleman." Lady Helena hesitated as she thought out this word, and finally gave it a great emphasis in her mind, as if she were at last very much determined indeed that he *must* be a gentleman. "Of course, he is a painter, for as he stood there in the light which streamed out from a brilliant room lined with warm red papers, I remember that we caught a glimpse of tapestries and an easel. And then that royal voice, when he informed us of the mistake, which we had already perceived, and showed us that the habit-maker's abode was on the landing below! And now he is going to America; and has been our fellow-traveller from London, and we saw him yesterday sketching that Norwegian girl in Liverpool. Pshaw! We only saw his back. But what is seeing, when you know a voice so well as that? And just fancy his being on the 'Athabaska.'"

"How fast your heart beats!" said the child, muffling her sobs and looking up with tear-stained eyes at Lady Helena. "Are you frightened? Do you think we are going down?"

Lady Helena smiled and kissed the girl. "Perhaps you hear your own heart, my dear," she said. "I do not think there is anything the matter with mine." But in her secret soul she was not quite certain of that.

Captain Jobson began telling a "marvel," to beguile the time until the doctor came, but Lady Helena did not listen. She looked out over the water, taking a lazy pleasure, now that her faintness and nausea had vanished before a genuine excitement, in watching the perpetual fight of the watery legions, as they met upon the crests of ephemeral hills which were succeeded by vacillating plains, that in their turns became dreadful gulfs. She tried to imagine the lonely stretches of moving and shifting and moaning waters which lay beyond the horizon; she fancied them scourged for days by capricious winds, or lying chill and silent for weeks beneath leaden skies; or glittering like beaten silver under the morning light. She courageously wondered what she would, could, or should do in case the "Athabaska" should be wrecked, or driven for days out of her course encumbered with broken machinery. This stormy North Atlantic, with its fleets of icebergs, its embracing fogs, its mysterious storms, its dread legends of collision, had a strong fascination for her. Captain Jobson's face grew a trifle dull when he discovered that his fair companion was not vouchsafing him the least attention, and he was relieved when the doctor approached, accompanied by the gentleman with the "royal voice."

"But it does beat horribly fast!" said the small girl, returning with the irresponsible and unabashed persistence of childhood to her notion about Lady Helena's heart. "Are you quite sure that you are not frightened? Oh, now it says toc, toc, toc! as plain as plain can be! Can't you hear it, sir?" she said, raising her tear-stained eyes up to encounter and interrogate the weather-beaten visage of Captain Jobson.

"What a strange child!" said Lady Helena, in her iciest tone, and making an involuntary movement to deposit the little creature on the deck. Then she recovered herself with a start. It was vexatious; all the more so that these remarks with regard to her perturbation were made just exactly at the moment when the man with the voice stood beside her chair again.

It was a considerable task to get the child conveyed along the deck to the gangway, and thence, slung in a blanket carried by the doctor, the deck steward and Captain Jobson, down the stairs to the ladies' saloon, whither the anxious mother was summoned, to find that no bones were broken after all. The doctor said that, with the exception of some slight bruises, the girl was unhurt, and that she would soon be able to resume her place on deck, and laugh at the waves which on this day had given her such a fright. Captain Jobson had recommended Lady Helena to remain on deck, lest the excitement of attending to the child, and the bad air of the cabin, should, as he quaintly expressed it, "tickle Davy Jones;" and, to her astonishment, as well as somewhat to her dismay, she found herself alone on the deck, with the gentleman whose sudden apparition had caused her so many pleasant and — the truth must be owned — so many violent sensations. What would he do? Would he have the courage to recognize her and to speak so that she might give him a cold and haughty answer, and send him about his business; or would he walk away, with that assured tread, which she could not help admiring and envying?

This is what he did: He unstrapped a glass from his waist, adjusted it, took a long look through it at the Norwegian vessel, now some distance astern, and then, turning to her as if he had known her for a century, he remarked: —

"The child seems to have been pacified very quickly by your care. I think you must be fond of children."

Lady Helena had a gold-bowed glass, which she sometimes raised to her eyes with a gesture amply sufficient to frighten into silence and confusion the most pertinacious and audacious of London dandies; but a delicate instinct warned her that it would be useless on this occasion. She kept her hands folded in her lap and answered, as if she were addressing one of the sailors, and were communicating to him a most commonplace piece of information: —

"I love children, as I fancy all ladies love them. It would be most unnatural, I am sure, not to sympathize with them in their frights, and especially in their hurts. I hope this little one's injuries will not prove serious."

"Oh, at that age bones and hearts are soon mended!" was the answer. "There was a poor old creature, at least seventy years old, thrown down in the steerage early this morning when the heavy rolling began, and I fear she can never be put together properly again."

"Ah!" Lady Helena's voice betrayed a strong disposition to resent this familiar and forcible manner of stating the case of the "old creature;" but in a moment more all her other feelings were subordinated to pity, and she half rose to her feet, saying: —

"How dreadful! Just fancy! And in that odious steerage! Do you not think that I could be of some service to her?"

"I hardly think so; but it is exceedingly kind of you. Oddly enough, I have a sort of interest in the tragedy of this old woman's fatal fall, for I believe she will die. I was wandering about Liverpool on our sailing day, impatient to be on board ship, when I saw a picturesque family of Norwegians at the door of a foreign lodging-house. There they were, father, mother, and daughter, as primitive and as interesting — as — as — possible. The old woman ran in-doors when I approached, and so I entered into conversation with the father, who knew a few words of German. I begged permission to sketch the pretty daughter and her costume, and they were good enough to allow me that privilege" —

"Yes — I — we — saw you."

Lady Helena would have given all her investments, an instant afterward, to recall what she had said. For now this curiously indifferent and unceremonious young man turned boldly around and looked at her respectfully yet searchingly. Lady Helena could have cried with vexation. Here was a gentleman who did not seem at all afraid of her, but who had no trace of impudence in his demeanor. This was no languid swell who could say detestably rude things in a soft and polished way; it was a man who thought it perfectly natural and proper to converse with her without the formality of an introduction; who did not intrude nor seem to admit the possibility of an intrusion; who was, in short, so far as her experience went, thoroughly novel, and not without piquancy. She wondered what he would do next.

"I beg your pardon if I am mistaken," he said (here he was becoming apologetic just as she had made up her mind that he could not be so), "but I think we have met before. Was it not in Paris that I had the pleasure of giving you some information"—

"On a peculiarly damp and dark staircase in the Rue Croix des Petits Champs," said Lady Helena, completely recovering her equanimity.

"And at the door of my own *atelier*," he continued, with a smile. "I was quite sure that I had seen you again on this steamer yesterday morning"—and here he stopped short and bit his lips, for it became evident to him that he was perilously near the verge of something which might be interpreted as a confession, and possibly be cut short. As Lady Helena had imagined, his ease had been due to his unconsciousness. He was conscious enough, now, and the advantage was to be hers.

"If you are a painter," she said, with a determination to seem as natural and unconstrained as he at first had been, "perhaps you will be good enough to tell me the exact name for that delicious color—that one, away to the right—look quickly, or it will be gone!—on the very topmost wave."

"Before I try to do that," he said, "I must be

allowed to ask you if you are yourself familiar with painting? For to any one who has not a practical knowledge of the art, an explanation of colors and their values offers some — well — some radical difficulties."

"Indeed!" Lady Helena's color rose, and there would have been no trouble at all in defining *that*. "Then you may, if you please, treat me as if I were an absolute tiro. Ah! now it's gone — the beautiful tint — so it does not matter. I have always heard it said that painters were renowned for the assumption of mystery in everything relating to their art."

"I am sorry, madam," said the young man, "if I have offended you. I did not intend to assume anything whatever. It is so difficult to define a color" —

"Quite right — the gentleman is quite right," said the earl, who had come round the corner of the deck cabin near which Lady Helena was sitting, and had heard the last few words. "What *we* mean by such and such colors means — er — just nothing at all — er — to painters."

"Why, cousin, you steal upon one like a ghost," cried Lady Helena, not at all sorry that he had arrived; for she felt that she was tempted to say more than she felt was prudent. "I thought you were making the acquaintance of the gentlemen in the smoke-hole, smoke-room — what do you call it?"

"Yes — er — I spoke to one fellow; English — going to Montana; horses — he called them 'osses; I thought — er — he wouldn't do. Spoke to another — English, going to Virginia; eyed me carefully, and — er — began to talk lordship; thought he wouldn't do. Spoke to a third; English; he had evidently been drinking before breakfast; said he was tired of England; what had England done for him — er — and so on — and — er — wanted the House of Lords abolished — er; so I came on deck for a change of air."

The earl blew a huge cloud of smoke from his pipe, settled himself carefully in the chair next to Lady Helena, banged his lawn-tennis shoes cheerfully together, and, looking up at the young man, who was just moving away, said: —

"Don't let me interrupt your discussion about color. I only put my word in — er — American fashion — don't you know?"

"It was hardly a discussion, sir." The earl looked flattered at this "sir," the exact purport of which he misunderstood. "The lady asked me for a definition, which I was unable to give, and I am afraid she thought me over-precise in a matter of *technique*."

"Now, how was that?" queried the earl, blowing another cloud of smoke. "Won't you — er — sit down — it's dangerous standing — and tell us all about it?"

In a few minutes they were chatting merrily and earnestly by turns on this vexed question of the names, durations, and values of colors, and Lady Helena had quite forgotten that there was such a thing as imminent sea-sickness. It did not occur to her to mention to the earl that she had met this artistic young gentleman before; nor did the young gentleman himself manifest the least intention of mentioning it. The charm of the voice was for her greater than the charm of the "much-resounding sea," which was hourly getting mightier in its wrath.

The earl and his cousin presently discovered that their new acquaintance's name was Dulon Floyd, that he was an American who had been studying art in Europe for some years — "more years," as he said, "than he liked to confess to, for he felt that they were wasted."

"Come, now," said the earl, "that's a rather uncomfortable feeling to have, just as one is finishing his studies — just as he is — er — about to enter upon the practice of his profession. Are you quite sure that you are not underestimating the advantages which you have enjoyed?"

"Possibly I am; but my position is a singular one. If I go home and reconcile myself to live away from art influences, I shall sink into a commonplace dauber."

"Oh! not as bad as that, I'm sure," said Lady Helena, who did not like this tone of discouragement.

"And if I remain abroad, where I can see grand pictures, and be inspired by a healthful art atmosphere, I must give up my country and my nationality — and — I don't think I am prepared to do that."

"Very commendable, I'm sure," remarked the earl; "and yet I should fancy that a painter would care less than members of the other liberal professions about country, patriotism, and all that sort of thing."

"Not so, in my case," said Mr. Floyd. "Besides, I don't interpret patriotism to mean merely a sufficient love for country to enable one to take up his gun in case of war; but it means much more. Now in my art patriotism is next to impossible. I am a landscape-painter. If I paint American landscapes as they are, my own people will not buy them. They prefer the French school, the methods of which are no more suitable for interpreting the landscapes of our Western world than they are for depicting the glories of a tropical woodland. Certain conventions have been established in art, and the public bows down before them. Now, I will not bow to these conventions, and so I am going home, in a rather dubious frame of mind, to try one or two experiments in art, after which, I suppose, I shall sink to be a railroad superintendent, or, possibly, a man of leisure — if not worse."

The earl looked significantly at his cousin. Here was their very first American chance acquaintance singing the old familiar European song of "frustration." Perhaps the New World did not differ so greatly from the Old one, after all.

"I am going West," continued Mr. Floyd, "as far as I can get; and I am going to paint, with as much truth as my education and my small modicum of talent will allow, whatever I come across that seems picturesque and pleasing. I am not going to be alarmed because the colors are different from those seen through English haze or under the gray French sky. I may go as far North-west as the Arctic circle before I return. I mean to paint my pictures in the open air, and to feel that I can claim for them that they are conscientious interpretations of nature. Then I shall take them back to London, and range them up in rows in my studio in Brook street, and perhaps try to get one into the Academy. Then you shall see how the critics will condemn them as unnatural in color."

"Brook street—capital location, fine neighborhood," said the earl, who began to feel that the young American might prove a not undesirable acquaintance.

"Yes," continued Mr. Floyd, with the slightest possible movement of his eyes in the direction of Lady Helena; "I tired of Paris; the winters are horrible, and since the war the natives scowl at strangers. In Venice I felt like painting; but I never painted. I used to like to stand on some dark flight of steps at night and call '*poppe*,' and go floating in a gondola, and the next morning I was sleepy, and didn't like to take up the brush. I have been but a short time in London. I *couldn't* paint there; I should make all my skies black, and all my trees would be wind-scourged and twisted. But perhaps London will be a good place to come to with pictures already painted; I mean, if you will excuse the commercial boldness of the term, that London strikes me as a good market. Only — I repeat — the critics will insist that the colors are unnatural, because they have never seen them. And then I suppose I shall see the folly of my experiment and wish that I had painted in a house boat on the Thames, or in the Scotch Highlands, or — or anywhere except in America."

"But — bless my soul! do you mean to tell me that Americans will not buy American pictures, painted by American painters?" cried the earl.

"Certainly they will, if those pictures are painted in harmony with European conventionalities of art; not otherwise. — Ah! that was a shock! You would better have the lady's chair moved a little this way. I think we can drop art as a topic, and pay some attention to our surroundings. They seem to claim our attention."

Dulon Floyd was a noticeable young man, slender, refined and alert; his tall figure bent naturally into graceful and supple attitudes, for which reason he was frequently accused of "posing." His hair, which was thick, had an erratic way of tumbling down at odd minutes over his broad, white brow; and when he was excited he had a slight lisp in his speech, which was thought by his male friends to be a blemish, and by the ladies to be "positively charming." He was older than he looked — older than he felt; he miscalculated the value of his own experience, and was apt to bestow an exaggerated importance upon that of others. At thirty he was tired of Europe, having wandered up and down in it for five years. He had a small income; not enough to live on without work; but he would have been unhappy as an idler. At this especial period of his life he was weary of art, yet anxious to cling to it, seeing nothing else which offered the smallest prospect of reward for the trouble of living. His father and mother were dead; he was alone in the world; for the one kindly old lady who claimed, as his mother's sister, relationship with him, could hardly be said to live in the world; she was a Quaker, and resided in Germantown, near Philadelphia. To that tranquil community Mr. Floyd proposed to pay a visit; after which he was to set forth on his experimental tour.

Just as the earl was lighting a fresh pipe with a "Vesuvian," which, as Lady Helena declared, was "an odious chemical smelling thing," Captain Jobson reappeared, coming down among them in a burst of spray, like an ancient Triton.

"Little girl all right," he said. "I told her my

shark story that I keep on purpose for small girls in trouble. It never fails. She forgot all her own woes in sympathizing with the dreadful tale of the seventeen Malay children swallowed by one hungry shark. There's an old woman very bad in the steerage, doctor, and I have been to see her. She can't last long."

"I must go to her at once," said Mr. Floyd, jumping up and bowing to the earl and Lady Helena. "It's my poor Norwegian."

Lady Helena's eyes followed him.

CHAPTER V.

ATLANTIC NIGHTS.

Mr. Floyd was seen no more by Lady Helena or the earl or Captain Jobson until nine o'clock in the evening. In the meantime Lady Helena had had an experience. She had been down to the saloon to lunch, and, escorted by the captain and the earl, had even walked the whole length of the pitching deck twice or three times. She had sent consoling messages to Lady Offast, recommending her to gather up her courage, and to come out where she could feel the glorious sea air; but Lady Offast did not come. That shining member of the British aristocracy had determined that she would not leave her berth until the "Athabaska" dropped her anchor. She had become possessed of an insane fancy for a raw onion as the only thing which she could "nibble" in the intervals of her sea-sickness; and with this onion and Edmond About's novel, "Tolla," she was seeking to divert her attention from her woes. For many weeks thereafter the works of the sprightly French romancer were inseparably associated, in her imagination, with the pungent odor of the humble and much-abused garden vegetable.

Lady Helena fancied, as she sat in her deck-chair an hour or two after lunch, that she might congratulate herself on complete escape from the disagreeable malady. "There couldn't be anything worse than this, could there, Captain Jobson?" she queried, and she thought that the captain smiled rather oddly as he remarked that it was "coming on to blow." Her gaiety was very noticeable, and she manifested a disposition to enter into discussion on a great variety of topics; but she found it odd that nothing interested her long. A few hours before she had believed that no spectacle could be finer than that of the tossed and tormented water, with its innumerable and indescribable hills and valleys and ridges; but now she thought it was becoming monotonous. Furthermore, the odor from the smoke-stack had become very disagreeable; and an iron band seemed suddenly to have been placed around Lady Helena's head. She closed her eyes, but opened them again at once, for the darkness alarmed her. The worst of it was that she could not — try as hard as she would — concentrate her attention on anything. A sailor went by her hurriedly, and incautiously brushed against her garments. This appeared to bring things to a climax. A million stars danced before her vision, and she felt cold to the marrow of her bones. If the "Athabaska" would not reel so!

"You are pale and tired," said Captain Jobson, in a fatherly tone. "Perhaps it would be well not to sit here any longer just now." And, although she could hardly see him, she held out her hand in his direction, saying, faintly, "I fear I am going to be ill. It is very provoking; the sea is so pretty!" Then another chill overtook her; she had a vague sense of half-suffocated helplessness, and of being borne along as if flying through the air; and then she knew nothing more until she found herself in her cabin, lying on the sofa, with Jenks bathing her brow with cologne water.

Here she remained, much annoyed at her own weakness, until she heard the first gong for dinner resounding through the various aisles of the ship. Then she rose up resolutely, ordered Jenks to arrange her hair, and, to the maid's surprise, announced her intention of going in to dinner. The maid was aghast.

"It will never do, my lady," she said; "when

you was took you was worse than Lady Offast, and now here you are venturing out again"— "Silence!" said Lady Helena, "and choose me something becoming to wear;" and Jenks obeyed with astonishment and trembling.

Lady Helena met the earl and his two American companions at dinner. She was very pale, with a resolute frown which she had inherited from the old duke, her father, and which was strongly marked when she was very much in earnest. She had made up her mind that she would not succumb, and the earl was so pleased with her pluck that he exercised his ingenuity in ordering, out of the gross and ill-arranged plenty of the steamship fare, a really admirable little dinner. A glass of clear cold champagne revived the girl, and she managed to eat the wing of a bird and a bit of wine-jelly; after which substantial meal she declared herself quite ready to go on deck again. The captain and the earl exchanged glances. The weather was evidently more severe, as indeed Lady Helena could guess from the jingling glass and occasional crash of plates and bottles, and from the sombre dashing of the vast masses of water against the ship's sides.

They decided, however, to go on deck for an hour.

"To-morrow it may not be comfortable there," said Captain Jobson.

Lady Helena was once more warmly wrapped up, and, followed by her three cavaliers, she was climbing the broad staircase, which looked quite magnificent under the glare of the electric lights, when she met Mr. Floyd. He took off his hat.

"The old woman is dead," he said.

"Bless my soul! What old woman is that?" cried the earl, who had already forgotten the little story about the Norwegian family, which Lady Helena had rather vaguely told him. Mr. Floyd accompanied them to the door opening on deck, telling them of the sad scene which he had witnessed; of the heart-rending grief of the old man, and the despair of the pretty daughter.

"Let me go to her and comfort her," said Lady Helena, impulsively; "I am sure it is my duty to do so."

"You forget, cousin, that you are not strong," said the earl; "besides, it is risky walking about to-night; is it not, Captain Jobson?"

"Not on an errand of mercy, perhaps," said the captain, who was fond of sensations, and who was strangely pleased with Lady Helena's demand. It was accordingly decided that when Mr. Floyd had taken some refreshment, and recovered somewhat from the fatigue of his volunteer watch with the humble, stricken family, he should come for them, and they would visit the girl and her father. With this mission in view, Lady Helena felt her own illness rapidly vanishing, and she was becoming quite brave again by the time that Mr. Floyd's voice was heard calling out to know where they were. She wondered if he had discovered their names, for the earl had not taken the trouble to give them in return for Mr. Floyd's prompt courtesy in introducing himself in the morning; and she noted that he alluded to them as his "English friends." His voice was enough to identify *him* anywhere; there was none other like it in all the world, she was sure.

"Think a moment, cousin, before you undertake this excursion among those common people," said the earl. "If anything unpleasant should come of it I should never forgive myself. This is not like visiting among the tenantry at Branley, and this ship is reeling famously. On the whole, I don't think you can go."

"Cousin," said Lady Helena, giving a little pull at the hood of her water-proof and settling it firmly about her pale face, "I am going. And that is all there is to be said about it."

"Oh! very well; then if you are laid up in New York with broken limbs, while we are enjoying the splendors of the great excursion, you must not blame us."

"Shall I show you the way?" said Mr. Floyd's voice, and she gave a little start, and looked up at him as if almost indignant at the unceremonious nature of his question. But secretly she was pleased; besides, she could not say that the question was not addressed as directly to the earl and the other gentlemen as to herself.

"If you will be so kind," said Captain Jobson, who seemed much interested in the matter, and before Lady Helena realized her position, she was moving along the deck, leaning on Mr. Floyd's arm. The earl came grumbling behind her through the blackness, for it was now eight o'clock, and a very dark night. Out of the obscurity through which the "Athabaska" was working her way, came an occasional phosphorescent flash; and the swish and roar of the waves seemed to make a kind of rude melody, which kept time to the beating of the propeller, with its round-about, round-about, forty-three, forty-four, "forty-five to the minute," said the captain, as they went through the companion-way; "that is fine for such lumpy weather."

"Lumpy weather is good," said Mr. Floyd, and he laughed melodiously.

On steamships of the class of the "Athabaska" the steerage passengers are placed aft, in a location which in the ships of other days was thought desirable for passengers of the first class. In order to reach the place where the inconsolable Norwegian girl was bewailing the death of her mother the party had to pass through a long aisle lined on either side by the state-rooms of saloon passengers, then to open a door, and, crossing a little hall, to come out upon an enclosed space on the lower deck. Here, grouped around a closed hatchway, in defiance of the treacherous waters which now and then came to drench them, were twenty or thirty emigrants, —Irish, Swedes, Norwegians, North Germans, —all hardy folk, not afraid of the weather, but a little tamed by the boisterous motion and the novelty of their situation. Captain Jobson stepped briskly ahead as they came into the open air, and took up a position where "he could warn them if there was danger of a ducking." Lady Helena thought nothing of this danger. Indeed she did not realize its gravity, and she looked with interest and wonder at the spectral masts above and the black lines of the deck rail, beyond which was — chaos. As she gazed upward, Mr. Floyd looked down at her pale, resolute face, and a quick smile darted from his eyes to brow and lip, and transfigured his manly features. It was the gratified smile of one who, after long and vain seeking, has suddenly discovered a treasure.

"There they are," he said, in a whisper, pointing to a dark mass at the edge of the hatchway.

"No," said Lady Helena, "surely not there — lying on the rough boards."

"Yes, there they are, father and daughter, clasped in each other's arms, and heart-broken. There they have been ever since the surgeon told them that all was over, and since the poor old mother was taken from them, to be prepared for burial to-morrow. I think I never before saw such an exhibition of intense grief."

"God bless my soul! Poor things! They must be wet to the skin," said the earl. "A little brandy, now, would do 'em good."

"No," said Mr. Floyd, "they take a rude comfort in their misery." He stepped forward, and bending over the twain, shook the old man's arm.

Father and daughter turned upon him faces stupefied by anguish, and, seeing the group of visitors, they shook their heads feebly, and made signs they wanted nothing. "But," said Mr. Floyd, in German, to the father, "here is a fine lady who wishes to do something for your poor daughter. Will you not allow her?" The old man answered, querulously, "Let us alone. God has deserted us, and we don't care to live."

"Nonsense!" said Floyd; "you must not be cast down; it is your duty to live." And, in his anxiety to convince the old fellow, he knelt on the wet deck and tried to arouse him from his stupor. Just at that moment the girl uttered a slight moan, and, overcome by sorrow and excitement, fainted, her noble head falling heavily on her father's breast. "Heavens!" said Floyd; "is she dying, too?"

He spoke louder than he meant to do, and a moment later he was surprised to see Lady Helena on her knees beside him, raising up with delicate skill and firm strength the fair creature, and administering to her a restorative taken from the pocket of her water-proof. The "Athabaska" felt constrained just then to give one of her most treacherous lurches. Captain Jobson gave a warning shout; but Lady Helena would have been thrown down if

Mr. Floyd had not steadied her with his arms. She did not shrink away from him, and, when a second shock and leap came, he held her again, while she held the Norwegian girl. The earl began to feel that it was his duty to interfere; but he was too uncomfortable to stir much. Lady Helena now began to issue commands, and Colonel Hodges was despatched for the doctor, Captain Jobson for a certain cordial, about which Jenks could give information, and the earl for a Scotch plaid. Mr. Floyd admired the clear precision of these orders, but dreaded lest she should send him somewhere. He was sure that he preferred to remain where he was.

"You are very brave and kind," he said, moving away from Lady Helena, after the lurching was over, and looking admiringly at her.

"Not at all," she said, coldly. "This is only duty, I am sure. The girl is ill, and must be sent below. I wonder that the officers allow these people to be out in such weather."

"This is not considered dangerous," said Mr. Floyd; "and the officers have a theory that a few duckings do the passengers good. Shall I help you to arise?"

"Thanks; not until they return;" and she waved away his proffered hand and busied herself with the reviving girl, while the ancient father, now pretty well aroused, rocked and moaned.

Presently all the messengers returned, and the girl, enveloped in blankets, was taken up in the arms of two stout sailors and carried to shelter. Before going she seized Lady Helena's hand and kissed it repeatedly; then placed her own hand upon her heart, as if to hint at the agony that she felt. Lady Helena had regained her feet alone, but all at once she leaned heavily against Mr. Floyd, and he caught her in his arms to save her from a fall. "I think I have presumed on my own strength," she said; "I feel giddy" —

Mr. Floyd felt himself gently set aside by the earl.

"Helena, it is late and rough weather, and you will repent this zeal to-morrow. Take my arm and let me guide you to your state-room."

"Ugh! — no — not that horrible place; Captain Jobson, may we not stay on deck a *little* longer?"

"Yes — yes, plenty fresh air — get used to motion," murmured the captain — and the earl succumbed. But he frowned a bit when Mr. Floyd took a seat with them on the darkened deck, which was now deserted save by a few veteran travellers. For a moment he meditated some stratagem to get rid of the young painter; then something told him that such a movement was unworthy of him. Next he remembered Lady Offast; his conscience smote him, and he hastened away to see how she was getting on, promising to return speedily. On his way back he looked into the smoking-room, which seemed decidedly cosey, and he lost himself in a sprightly conversation over a cigar with an American gentleman, who asked him "if he crossed often," and "which line he liked best."

Floyd and Lady Helena felt, after their joint attentions to the bereaved girl, as if they had been friends for a very long time. Each was touched by the display of kindliness and sympathy in the other's character; and from gossip about the Norwegians, and the sombre story of the aged mother's death among the rude but pitying pilgrims bound for the New World, the young people drifted into talk about themselves. They forgot the Atlantic and its ravings in the darkness; their thoughts were in Paris, in Venice, on the Splugen Pass, or on the green slopes of Normandy. Not a word was said which could imply anything more than the most ordinary companionship of travel, and yet the two perceived that there was a secret bond between them. All at once Lady Helena remembered that it was getting late, and, leaning on Captain Jobson's arm, she departed, bidding Mr. Floyd good-night in such an indifferent manner that he became quite wretched, fancying he had unwittingly offended her.

"Very charming woman! — original, delicate," said Captain Jobson, when he returned to the deck, and found Mr. Floyd musing, and straining his eyes at the darkness. "Best blood in England."

"So another gentleman told me," said Floyd, carelessly. "She talks well, and, without constraint, for an Englishwoman. But you see that I startled her by asking her to attend the funeral to-morrow morning. One never knows where to draw the line with these people."

"Hum!" thought Captain Jobson; "the young gentleman is not so deeply interested after all."

Yet he *was* interested — far more so than he would have been willing to confess; and the next day, although he felt a little hurt and annoyed that she did not come on deck just before dawn to witness the sea-burial of the old woman, he managed to spend two or three hours in Lady Helena's company. But this time it was not in the open air, in full view of the tossing waves. The sea was running furiously high, and none but the most adventurous braved the terrors of the weather. Lady Helena was ensconced on a sofa in the passage-way to the lower deck; and, despite the cold wind which came boisterously to trouble her every few minutes, and occasional terrifying bursts of water through the door opposite her couch, she protested that she was quite comfortable. But there were lines of pain in her face, and she avoided the subject of breakfast and luncheon in a manner which showed that they had lost their charms for her. She gave Captain Jobson and Mr. Floyd amusing descriptions of the consternation of poor Jenks, and, had it not been for the sudden arrival of the earl at an unexpected moment, she might have favored them with an account of Lady Offast's phenomenal devotion to the onion and to Edmond About.

CHAPTER VI.

REACHING MANNAHATTA.

THE "Athabaska" weathered the gale, and doubtless would have encountered without danger twenty such commotions. Yet there was one night when the laboring of the huge monster in the mighty hollows of the sea was so painful that all trembled, and even the stewards, who had been to sea in everything from a cockle-shell to the "Great Eastern," murmured apprehensively. To the storm in due time succeeded comparative calm, which had a marked influence on the nerves of the countess and her maid, and gave the former a taste for something more substantial than the ethereal onion and the vaporous About. The sun condescended to appear on the first occasion when Lady Offast presented herself on deck; and this so flattered her that she declared she "enjoyed ocean travel when there was not imminent danger of going to the bottom, you know." On the beginning of the seventh day the passengers talked of seeing land, and Captain Jobson prophesied the exact hour at which the "Athabaska" would drop her anchor.

"Do you think," said the earl, "that we can get a train for Minnesota the next morning? I'm told that there's very little to see in *New* York." The earl invariably accented the *New* as if quite determined to have it understood that there was an *Old* York in his beloved country, and that that fact must under no circumstances be forgotten.

"I'm astonished," said Captain Jobson, to whom this remark had been addressed. "We think New York a very beautiful place; and you would hardly find it convenient to leave before you have rested a few days."

"But are not the Irish" —

"As yet they do not outnumber the Americans," said Captain Jobson, with a twinkle in his kindly eyes. "And where our English cousins get the notion that New York is Irish in aspect I cannot imagine. It is as little Hibernian as it is — English. It reminds you of Naples and Trieste and Rotterdam and Havre and Messina and Antwerp inextricably mingled, with just a bit of Hong Kong or Canton thrown in. When I was in Manilla in 18 — But never mind that. I know there was a corner of Manilla that reminded me exactly of a nook on Canal street."

"And do you think it will be necessary to get out white flannels, and wear a straw hat, and all that?" inquired the earl, with some apprehension. "And umbrellas? Do you know that my stupid man put all my umbrellas in a place where they were broken by the steward, who seems to have danced upon them on the rough night? Can you imagine such an idiot? Can one get something that will answer in the shape of an umbrella in New York? I suppose that in the provinces it would be quite out of the question."

Captain Jobson turned away to hide the laughter in his eyes, but Mr. Floyd, who was promenading the deck with Lady Helena, and who chanced to overhear these inquiries, stopped short.

"I have an uncle," he said, "who has the misfortune to be in trade, and he makes a business of exporting umbrellas to Great Britain. They are all marked with English trade-marks, so that, if it unhappily becomes necessary for you to purchase one, I don't think that any one will ever find out that you are not carrying a veritable British one. But why have an umbrella? A sunshade is much more useful at this season of the year."

"God bless my soul!" said the earl, with much warmth, and he turned so suddenly away from Lady

Helena and her escort that the former laughed merrily in spite of her efforts to control her mirth. The earl was annoyed. This was not the first time that he had had reason to believe that the young American was laughing at him. And it was especially hard, in view of the tremendous efforts which he made to come down to the democratic level and to act in American fashion. So he lit his pipe and walked off, fulminating wrath against "Mr. Dulon," as the youth was now called by most of the members of the party. "What do you think of that young fellow?" the earl inquired of Colonel Hodges, whom he found leaning over the rail and peering America-ward, as if he were very anxious to arrive.

"Well, sah," said the colonel, after a moment's reflection, "I think he needs taming. He wants the originality taken out of him. And by and by a crisis in his life will come along and reduce him, sah, to the level of a right sensible fellow. Unless — unless he falls in love."

"In love — in-deed! Why, whom should he fall in love with?"

"His ideal, when he meets her," answered the lean colonel, daintily scattering the ashes of his cigar upon a slowly descending wave. "He is sure to have one, and nothing could keep him from possessing it if he once got the fancy that it truly belonged to him."

"Hum!" said the earl; "you don't think, for instance, that he might try to find his ideal on board this vessel, do you?"

"Well, I really had not given the subject much consideration," was the lazy answer.

The earl was now more ruffled than before. The colonel's answers confirmed his own suspicions — that Mr. Dulon Floyd was making love to Lady Helena, and that that gentle personage did not look upon his overtures with dislike. No, on the contrary, she welcomed them. Was she not always — now that she was well once more — pacing the deck with the youthful painter, or listening, while seated in the comforting shadow of the smoke-stacks, to his gay stories of student life on the Continent, and to his somewhat cynical comments on European politics and society?

"The little radical!" said the earl; "I believe that I could have liked that fellow if she had not allowed him to pay court to her; but now — I'm very certain that I don't." And he speculated, as he smoked, on the means of making their parting in New York a permanent one. Mr. Dulon evidently was not one of the guests invited on the great excursion, but the earl had heard Captain Jobson telling the youth about it, and he suspected the old mariner of a secret complicity in a plot to get Lady Helena entangled in the meshes of what he certainly would have regarded as a *mésalliance.*

Yet he would say nothing to the countess about it, for it seemed to him quite possible that that excellent personage might allow herself to be brought round to her cousin's views. "Lady Helena would not even need to state what she felt," he mused; "those two would understand each other without a word."

While he plotted the day waned, and a little scudding storm came to warn them not to be too confident as to their own prowess. Then the sun came out, a rain-dog showed his head on the horizon, and finally there stole around them a ghostly twilight, so still and solemn that the earl might have been frightened at it if he had been endowed with the smallest modicum of imagination. There were at least two persons on board the "Athabaska" who did appreciate to the full the shadowy and almost religious silence through which the ship sped onward. Mr. Dulon and Lady Helena walked the damp deck until Jenks came to cough discreetly in the neighborhood of the young pair, and they enjoyed to the utmost the beautiful spectacle of the sea rolling up its lazy phosphorescent waves as if to caress the ship's sides, and then calling them back again into the shade, with siren-like whispers and murmurs.

"I wish we might go on forever so, in just such shadow, in just such a delicious humid air, and over just such a strange sea," said Mr. Dulon, waxing poetical.

"Ride, ride together — forever ride," quoted Lady Helena, gayly. "Browning put that idea in your head, I fancy."

"No, it was not Browning," he answered, with a certain simple sincerity which left no sort of doubt in her own mind as to whom it really was.

Presently the moon arose and silvered the waters, and just as Jenks was coughing somewhat impatiently, for the last time before leaving Lady Helena to incur the anger of the earl, her protector, a spectral sail was seen, gliding along, as if afraid of being seen.

"Ho!" said the earl, suddenly appearing on deck, "that must be the pilot, at least, so says the first officer. What! cousin, you here, at such an hour? I'm surprised!"

"And why, cousin, should you wish to deprive

me of seeing the pilot come on board? I'm sure it's not your custom to be so very unamiable!"

The earl had already lost his temper, but his wrath at Lady Helena's mild defiance was nothing to the ebullition which he could not suppress when Mr. Dulon took him by the arm, saying, pleasantly:

"Let us all step over to this side and get a good place before the other passengers begin to crowd. The pilot cannot be on board for twenty minutes yet — if this out yonder happens to be his boat."

"Confound it!" said the earl, wrenching himself free. "I suppose you will allow me to choose a place for myself."

"Why, certainly, there is plenty of room, as you see;" and Mr. Dulon made a sweeping gesture, which clearly intimated to the earl that if he were not satisfied with such room as could be found on board he would not be troubled to discover seclusion in the seemingly illimitable wastes of moving water around them.

Lady Helena was a trifle shocked; she was accustomed to see her cousin treated with more deference; she felt that in some way the young American had lost his own dignity, and she was quite angry with the earl for having spoiled what she was beginning to believe a "divine evening."

She saw the pilot scramble on board, and was treated to all the latest English news from the "New York Herald," a package of the latest dates of this popular journal being handed to the earl by the purser.

"Jest let me have a look at one of them, captain, will ye?" said a Western passenger, coolly taking one of the papers from the earl's hands. If the family portrait of the earl had been painted shortly after that occurrence, it would have seemed apparent to future generations that his lordship had been of a decidedly apoplectic temperament.

. . . .

Next morning the earl came to knock at Lady Helena's door. "Come, cousin," he said, "here's land, or a huge whale, or something ahead. I say it's a whale; but the others laugh. I regret to say that the other members of my family are too lazy to turn out. Come!"

It did look rather like a whale's back, thought Lady Helena, as, half an hour afterward, she stood taking her first view of the American coast. And oh, how warm it was! The earl had mounted a superb Panama, which gave him the air of a West Indian planter of British descent. And Lady Helena was inclined to laugh at this, until she discovered the warmth and what she was pleased to term the general lifelessness of the air. "Surely the atmosphere of Liberty is not very inspiriting," she ventured to observe. "What must it be on shore?"

"About 109° this morning," said *the* voice behind her; and Lady Helena, in spite of her well-trained English nerves, started violently.

A delicate shimmer of heat seemed to overhang everything: the low and rounded shores, with their picturesque villas and tinder-box houses, as the earl called them; the vast strip of beach, studded with gaudy hotel-palaces; the innumerous tiny craft which went bellowing and puffing into every nook and corner of the bay; and, beyond, majestic under the morning sunshine, the colossal bridge which unites two enormous cities. Yet there was no lack of life, because of the heat. The animation was as brisk and merry as the movement of Liverpool was solemn and measured.

"Ugh!" said the earl, pulling off his straw hat and using it as a fan, "now we know why the Americans drink so much ice-water."

"No," said the young painter, "if you will excuse the observation, you have not found out the real reason for that yet."

The earl's dislike for the young painter was presently modified by his natural good manners and his sincere desire to be agreeable to all around him. After two or three more tilts at each other the twain declared a truce, much to the relief of Captain Jobson, who was beginning to be very uneasy. As to Colonel Hodges, he assumed an indifference to anything which concerned Mr. Dulon, and busied himself with doing the honors of New York for his aristocratic friends. As the "Athabaska" was slowly warped into dock the good colonel pointed out the various objects of interest. Lady Helena admitted that she was grievously disappointed in the appearance of the American metropolis.

"Why does the dirt lie an inch thick on your wharves? Surely a country which boasts that it draws the nations of all the earth to it ought to keep its threshold clean." And Lady Helena disdainfully contemplated the grimy planks under the cheap dock-shed, and made a little gesture of shuddering disgust at the filthy pavements, and the general aspect of neglect and decay.

"Fact is," said Captain Jobson, — who was a good patriot for a man who had spent most of his life away from home, — "fact is that all the nations of the earth contribute to make this litter. The poor folks have been coming so fast, especially from the British islands, for the last generation, that New York hasn't had a chance to sweep up."

"Hum!" said the earl. "A poor excuse is better than none. But I don't think you will claim that these wretched piers compare very favorably with our splendid docks in the Mersey"—

"Question of time, sir, question of time," interrupted the old captain. "Some day New York will be all ringed around with marble quays and granite buildings for customs and emigrants, and all that sort of thing. Now, on the whole, don't you think it is more encouraging to have wooden piers, somewhat the worse for wear, and to be receiving immigrants from all parts of the world, than to have stone docks and other splendid facilities which only serve to make more easy the departure of your own people who are quitting their homes because they cannot make a living in them?"

The earl remarked, in a distant way, that he had always heard it said that the Americans were the most susceptible people on earth, and that he dared say that observation was correct. They had an explanation, he believed, for every one of their shortcomings, and insisted that even their "failings leaned to virtue's side." As for himself, he should not hesitate to make comments on what he saw, and should expect now and then to be brought up with a round turn, American fashion, don't you know, if he were considered too aggressive.

"Well," said Captain Jobson, whose eyes seemed to twinkle with a keener light than usual, now that he was beneath the brilliant blue sky of his native country, "Americans have done so much that when they are criticised because they have not done more, they consider the critics unreasonable. When I first sailed out of this port in the 'Invincible'"—

"Built of mahogany," chimed in Lady Helena.

"Your ladyship is right. When I first sailed out of this port in the 'Invincible,' New York was as far behind the city of to-day as Macao is behind Liverpool. And, considering that they have been overrun with visitors here, they certainly have done wonders."

The earl was not listening very carefully, for his attention was attracted to a craft which he saw hovering near the steamer, and from which came sounds of revelry. This craft was a small cutter, such as is used in the revenue service, and underneath a canopy on its deck was spread, on little tables, an appetizing display of viands and potables.

Half-a-dozen young men, with very red faces, and with a general appearance of having been out all night, walked to and fro between these tables tooting upon tin horns. On a white canvas placard stretched across a door-way were these words:—

"SHIP AHOY! IS JIM SIMMONS AND BILL O'BRIEN ON BOARD? THE PRANCING ELKS HAS COME OUT TO WELCOME THE BRAVE BOYS HOME."

While the earl was gazing with intense curiosity at this singular steamer two tall and bony men came hurrying to the "Athabaska's" side, and shouted a welcome to the "Prancing Elks," who at once set up a series of blood-curdling yells, interspersed with frantic tootings on their detestable horns. The tall and bony men had been often remarked by the earl during the voyage for the pertinacity with which they adhered to the game of "poker," and to a certain kind of drink denominated a "John Collins." It was now easy to identify them as the "Jim Simmons" and "Bill O'Brien" concerning whom the "Prancing Elks" demanded tidings. The boniest of the twain, leaning over the rail, shouted out, "Why didn't yez come down to quarantine, b'ys? Sure we was dressed and waiting to go off wid yez."

"The captain wint on the spree, Jimmy, and didn't start early enough. So whin we seen the 'Athabaska' comin' up the bay, we put about to wait for yez here, and whin yere in dock we'll take yez up river to the head-quarters. They's a meetin' appointed for this evenin'."

"Have ye heard the news, Jimmy?" shouted another "Prancing Elk," who seemed to have encouraged hilarious enthusiasm over the arrival of the bony men to that extent that he was perilously near the verge of insanity. "The dynamite fund is complete, and operations is to begin nixt wake!"

"Hould yer whist!" said Jimmy, turning uneasily around to inspect his fellow-passengers. "Murderation! will we never get off of this?"

"Can you tell me"—said the earl to a young man who had come on board with the doctor and the customs officers, and who was surveying the scene with an evident air of amusement—"can you tell me what all this absurd clamor means?"

"Welcoming home the dynamite delegates, sir," answered the young man, with a quick look at the earl. "I've just got all the particulars, and you'll find them in the 'Evening Flail.' These gentlemen who came over with you belong to an Irish-American patriotic society called the 'Prancing Elks,' and they have been to England to inspect various places where it is thought that dynamite could be used to advantage, as a means of coercing British opinion. The 'Prancing Elks' used to be a social organization, but since the severe measures were decided on, it has been the head and front of the dynamite movement."

"It is not strange, then, that they are so impulsive this morning," said Mr. Dulon, who had strolled up in time to hear question and answer. "Just fancy being the head and front of a dynamite movement! It gives one a fine sense of motion."

The earl bestowed no attention on the young painter. He was altogether too preoccupied with what the new-comer had told him. "God bless my soul!" he cried. "Do you mean to tell me that these wretched creatures have been deliberately spying about Great Britain to see where they can best injure us, and that there is no Government agent here to arrest the rascals on their return? And the United States pretends to be a friendly power! 'Prancing Elks,' indeed! Then I was not misinformed by the person who told me that the Irish are getting complete control over here?"

The young man smiled, and glanced at the passenger-list which he held unfolded in one hand.

"If Great Britain never encounters any more serious enemies than the 'Prancing Elks,' she will not be in mortal danger," he said. "Can you tell me, sir, if you please, where I shall find the Earl of Offast?"

The noble gentleman bit his lips. He had the national allowance of shyness; and, furthermore, he felt that this youth did not approach him with a sufficient amount of fear and trembling. At last he said: —

"I am the gentleman for whom you are looking," and at the same time he moved away a few steps, as if anxious to terminate the conversation.

"Ah! Much obliged. Then will your lordship allow me to ask a few questions with regard to English sentiment on this dynamite matter? It will make an excellent *pendant* to my article on the arrival of those fellows yonder," pointing rather scornfully at the bony men. "Of course your lordship would prefer to express yourself to the representative of a respectable organ like the 'Daily Flail' rather than to" —

The earl now had an opportunity for which he had been impatiently waiting ever since he left

England. Here, at last, was the interviewer — the scourge of travellers, the dread of newly-arriving British aristocrats. Many a time the earl had smiled grimly as he thought how he would crush the presumptuous Yankee scribe who should venture to approach him. So now he stepped back still farther then before, and, clearing his throat and making his voice as big as possible, he said: —

"No, sir, *no!* You are quite wrong — er — d——n it, sir — quite forward in presuming that I desire to appear as a pendant to a trashy lot of Irish dynamiters in any species of print whatever! And I — er — I am quite at a loss to discover how — er — how you manage to present yourself — er — to me without a proper introduction."

While the earl was thus fulminating his wrath the young man was reflectively chewing the end of his pencil. When the outburst was over he smiled wickedly and said, "Your lordship couldn't have given me a better interview if you had tried harder," and was gone.

What with rage and the unaccustomed heat of the day the earl felt quite faint. He fanned himself vigorously with his Panama hat, and was still muttering contemptuous expressions about the recklessness and unfriendly indifference of the

"States," when a new series of yells from the "Prancing Elks," and a grating sound accompanied by the straining of ropes, announced that the "Athabaska" had been safely docked. And now Captain Jobson and Colonel Hodges came hastening with offers of assistance at the "Customs." The countess and Jenks and Lady Helena were soon standing on the wharf in the grateful shade, and, while the earl was personally superintending the disembarkation of his voluminous luggage, Mr. Dulon Floyd made his appearance at Lady Helena's right hand. The stately young English lady blushed faintly and seemed a bit annoyed. She felt instinctively that he was about to say good-by, and it seemed quite heartless of him after all the pleasant conversations that they had had on the much rolling "Athabaska," thus to leave them unceremoniously. But she misjudged the painter.

"I dare not say good-by to the earl," he said, smiling, "for he is in a rage at me and at everything American at this minute. I will ask you to intercede with him for me, and may I have the honor of calling upon you before you leave New York? If you do not feel like according me a few minutes during your stay here, perhaps we shall meet in the West."

Lady Helena gave him her hand, and referred him to the earl for their address. "It is a hotel with an odd name," she said, "and I am sure we shall be glad to see you if you can find us out." The countess frowned, but Lady Helena's eyes sparkled, for she was now convinced that the painter intended to join the excursion. She could not deny that the thought of a definite parting from him would have appalled her.

"It must be the Brevoort," said Mr. Dulon, reflectively. "English people have a passion for the Brevoort."

"That sounds like it," said Lady Helena.

"That is it, m'm," said the incautious Jenks, who secretly adored Mr. Dulon, and who had already perceived Lady Helena's decided liking for the young American. Upon that the painter took his leave, and went to look after his trunks, promising to call on the second day of their sojourn in the metropolis. After what seemed to the ladies an interminable period of waiting, Jenks was summoned to produce the keys. In a few minutes the earl came to them quite radiant.

"Very handsome," he said. "Our old friend Captain Jobson just mentioned who we were and our boxes were not opened."

Had the earl known that his exemption from the annoyances of the customs was due to the fact that Captain Jobson was an old port officer, and, with his usual felicity, had unearthed in the examiner detailed to the earl's luggage, an ancient colleague, he would have been less exalted. But Captain Jobson prudently kept his secret, and presently the servants were despatched to the Brevoort with the *impedimenta*, while the party of distinguished travellers chartered a carriage, driven by a Hibernian gentleman who looked as if he might belong to the order of the "Prancing Elks," and were taken over to Broadway that they might get a striking first impression of the colossal movement of the American metropolis.

"Well," said the earl, after they had seen Broadway, "there certainly is nothing in London like it. I don't say that it is the volume of the movement which impresses me; it is its character. Here it is hot enough to roast apples, and every one is moving along at a brisk trot. Even the ladies seem to be in haste. And then — it — er — it looks metropolitan. I — er — fancied — don't you know? — that it would seem colonial."

The ladies were not so frank and enthusiastic as

the earl. They thought the Rue de Lafayette in Paris finer than this much-vaunted Broadway. Besides, they said the sun made their heads ache. That they were overwhelmed by the heat was not very wonderful, as they were still wearing the seal-skin jackets which they had found comfortable on the "Athabaska."

"By the by," said the earl, as their carriage turned into Eighth street, "what became of that young painting feller? He was not a bad sort; shouldn't have minded seeing him again." Like a true Briton the earl liked Mr. Dulon because the latter had "stood up" to him.

"He asked permission to call," said Lady Offast, "before he bade us good-by."

"Oh, did he?" And the earl looked very sharply at his cousin. "Then let us hope that he will come at once, for I am resolved not to pass more than thirty-six hours in this fiery furnace."

They found the Brevoort very comfortable and homelike, although the earl was enraged at the waiters who were summoned to his private dining-room, and were requested to furnish forth half-a-dozen indigenous delicacies — all of which happened to be "out of season"—for his evening refection. "No oysters in August—no terrapin just now—no canvas-backed ducks. God bless my soul, man! Do you think I have come all the way from London to dine on an *entrecôte à la Bearnaise*, and to drink Burgundy and Bordeaux?" He dined well, notwithstanding, and next morning he allowed Colonel Hodges, who appeared at ten, quite miraculously gotten up in cool linens, to take him down-town by the "Elevated Road." Lady Helena solicited and obtained the favor of accompanying them; but the countess declared that she still felt the motion of the ship, and passed her morning in taking cool baths, and in adjuring Jenks to prepare plenty of "thin things" for the excursion.

On the way to the "L," the colonel put into the earl's hands a copy of the "Evening Flail" of the previous day. In this bright paper was a long interview with the "noted Earl of Offast" on the subject of dynamite outrages. The noble earl, said the interviewer, was accredited with a special mission from his government,—a mission closely connected with recent political, not to say Anglo-Irish, events; and the results of his visit would even be seen, unless some of the dynamiters, like the

"Prancing Elks" or the O'Galligan Muster party should adopt radical measures with regard to the distinguished member of the House of Lords.

"This is infamous," said the earl, mopping his brow. "When I said nothing at all to the feller! And now, I suppose, we shall have all the 'Prancing Elks' charging down upon us!"

CHAPTER VII.

DOWN-TOWN.

Lady Helena would have faced lions rather than own that she was afraid of anything; but after she had climbed the narrow flight of stairs which led from the street to the elevated-railroad station, she was forced to admit to herself that she was dizzy and a trifle alarmed. How *could* this railroad be secure? There was nothing to prevent the wretched passengers from being cast headlong into the street, among the horse-cars and the swarms of women and children. And what a fate it would be, to be crushed under one of the falling cars! It was really too dreadful! But all at once a tiny locomotive came humming along, drawing two or three pretty cars, into one of which Lady Helena stepped because the earl and Colonel Hodges did so, and because she would not speak out her fear. These "carriages," as she called them, were of a novel type to her, and she examined them curiously, while the earl sat down and refused to stare at anything, being anxious to convey the impression that he had been doing things in "American fashion" all his life. Here you entered the carriage by a door at the end, opening upon the platform, on which stood a youth of resolute mien, who stared you out of countenance, and shouted the names of stations in some language which Lady Helena was quite certain she had never heard before. Perhaps this was a foreigner, who was allowed, by the kindness of a people of superior education, to cry the stations in his own language until he had learned that of his adopted country. There were no separate compartments for different classes, and although Lady Helena expected to be horrified at this, she was not. Every one who came in was clean and decorous; the workman and the gentleman did not seem to offer so extraordinary a contrast as in London. It was not that there was something lacking in the gentleman, but it was apparent that the workman was gaining on him, and would one day be alongside him in the social race. This was quite wonderful, and, while Lady Helena did not analyze her impressions at that moment, they were none the less definite and distinct. In the long aisle through the centre of the car people came and went with a recklessness which she considered astonishing. They did not wait for the train to stop, and each one seemed anxious to get ahead of the other, as though it were a habit which he had inherited, and which he kept up even when it was not of the slightest use.

When she had got courage enough to look out at the window Lady Helena was pleased and fascinated. The locomotive seemed to be on friendly terms with the occupants of all the "second story backs" along its route; and it poked its friendly nose into many an odd corner so near to pale-faced tailors sewing on benches, or bevies of pretty girls making pasteboard boxes, or bilious compositors daintily distributing type, that any of them might have petted the puffing little creature on its back and have said to it: "There you are again! Always at it, and never tired!" Now it skipped around a corner, and came into a still close, where Flemish and Dutch women were ironing before open windows, and cackling to each other in high-pitched voices; now, emerged upon a long line of straight track, flanked on either side with mighty buildings which cast shadows on the train; and now went half-timidly through a sinister court where evil men and women were leering from dirty doors and soiled sills; where the odors of beer and strong liquors were on the air, and where, in the streets below, there was ponderous rumbling of drays and incessant clinking of horse-car bells. The heat was as great as on the preceding day, and Lady Helena, hot and uncomfortable in her walking-dress, which was considered just the thing for an English August, quite envied the workers in the cool, half-darkened rooms of which she caught glimpses. From what she saw on this journey " down-town " she gathered the opinion that New York is filled with small industries, carried on in nooks and cocklofts by industrious foreigners. She felt certain that she had seen into the workshops of a hundred inventors, and at least a thousand small artisans, before Colonel Hodges and the earl called to her to accompany them. And she declared afterward to the countess that she had never seen anything more picturesque and entertaining than this panorama of gayly colored house walls, pierced with innumerable windows, out of which peeped every variety of human visage, and the whole " lighted up by a sunshine that was quite fantastic, I assure you."

They left the train at a small station not far from the North River, which Lady Helena could see gleaming in the distance; and the earl, after he had blessed his soul and sought in all his pockets for his ticket, remembered that he had deposited it in a glass receptacle on entering the up-town station where he had embarked. As they went downstairs, and through the crowded and dirty streets to Broadway, Colonel Hodges moralized on the mission of the elevated roads in New York.

"They will really have an important influence on city politics," he said.

"But I thought the Irish had entire control," interrupted the earl.

"The demagogues who handled the ignorant Irish vote, sah, had complete control of New York for a time, simply because the mass of business men, the merchants, the bankers, the financiers, did not reside in the metropolis. When five o'clock came there was a general exodus to towns ten, twenty, or thirty miles from New York, where the business men had established homes, preferring the inconvenience of daily travel to the expense and dirt of the great city. Now the quick transit by the 'elevated' is making it easy for all these people to live in town, and they will soon take the government of this vast community out of the hands of the roughs."

Thus spoke the good colonel, who voted the Democratic ticket when he was at home, but whose clear vision had detected the influence, potent, though silent, that the "L" is wielding in the island of Mannahatta.

On Broadway there was a breeze, which had come straggling up from the bay to disport itself for a few minutes among the throngs of nervous and dejected-looking men, and pale and tired women.

"Ah! this is something like," said the earl. "It's the first time I've felt like drawing a deep breath since I left the ship. I was about to say that I must decline to walk about much longer in this intense heat."

"Ah! beautiful day! lovely climate! reminds me of Manilla! Hope your ladyship is quite well," said a familiar voice; and Captain Jobson came hurrying down from the steps of the Astor House, which ancient and reputable hostelry they were just passing, and was warmly greeted by Lady Helena. "Charmed to meet you, I am sure," continued the worthy captain, bowing to the earl, and saluting Colonel Hodges with a familiar "*How* are you?" "What courage, to be on foot, in the most crowded street in New York, on such a baking day! I guess your ladyship never took a walk down past the Mansion House and into Lombard street, in London?"

"Well, no," said Lady Helena, smiling, "I don't

think I was ever east of Temple Bar more than twice in my life. But travellers are not bound by any of the conventionalities which prevail at home, and I am *so* curious to see Wall street. There are days when my cousin can talk of nothing else. He has so many American investments, you know."

"Funny place, Wall street," said the captain, with a grimace and a shrewd twinkle in his eyes. "They say here that a man is not fitted for serious business until he has made twenty-five thousand dollars in Wall street—and lost it. Full of mischief, the street is—full of mischief! Talk about the wrecks on the ocean! Why, I've circumnavigated the globe three times, and been around the Horn in voyages innumerable, and crossed the Pacific in a ferry-boat, and here I am, unhurt and happy! But out of a hundred men who go cruising in Wall street, ninety-nine are wrecked."

"Is it so dreadful as that?" said Lady Helena, who had the most implicit confidence in anything that the captain said.

"It is a street of gamblers. Two-thirds of the men in it are too lazy to employ their energies in industrial enterprises, and in legitimate trade, in which they might make secure fortunes. They prefer the excitement of speculation, and the tricks and turns of stock gambling, rather than honest exertion. When one man is ruined there is another — er — idiot to take his place, and so" —

"What furious moralizing!" said the earl. "You will frighten us before we reach this celebrated street."

"I beg your pardon," said the captain. "Every one has to learn his Wall street for himself. As the colonel is an excellent guide, perhaps I can be of no further service to you."

"Oh, go with us, by all means," cried Lady Helena, and so Captain Jobson took the lead, piloting them in miraculous fashion through the hurrying crowds, and over street-crossings where interminable lines of teams were waiting, and so on until they came to Trinity Church, peaceful and impressive in its old-fashioned beauty, surrounded by its ancient tombs. At the captain's suggestion they went up to the belfry of the church, and looked out over the island city, and the broad rivers, and the great bridge stretching away to Brooklyn, and the islands in the harbor, and all the quick glad boats and ships coming and going on the blue water.

"It is as pretty as Venice from the Campanile," said Lady Helena; "and there is a magic about this translucent sky which I cannot explain to myself. It seems to invest the most commonplace objects with beauty. Look at that group of barges and lighters just at this side of the bridge. Is not that a complete Turner effect? I am sure if the great painter could be here now he would point triumphantly to that as a justification of his work. And how far away the sky seems! Now in England there are days when we feel like stooping for fear our heads may brush against the clouds."

"Now, cousin!" said the earl.

"But I am sure you will admit, cousin, that there is a kind of intellectual intoxication in this exquisitely clear atmosphere. I feel at this minute, looking down over New York and its tributary ocean and rivers, as if I could engage in all sorts of enterprises — as if there were nothing that I could not undertake, and succeed in! I feel the propulsion of the climate, the desire to go ahead, the restlessness of those gamblers that the captain has just told us about."

"Come away, my girl," said the earl; "you will be giddy if you remain longer here. Can we see Wall street?" he inquired of the colonel.

"There it is, at your feet," said Colonel Hodges, pointing to the crooked and unimposing avenue where so many fortunes are annually made and lost.

"Ay, is that it?" cried the earl, putting up his eye-glass. "Dear me, it looks much like any street. And what is that vast edifice looming above all the others? It is like an unfinished wing of some colossal palace."

"That," said the colonel, "is a sign of the times. A hundred years hence New York's business sections will be filled with buildings like that one — each ten or eleven stories high. The elevator, the telephone, and the telegraph, have revolutionized the mode of construction here. There is room on this small island for a population as large as that of London, when this new mode is fully adopted. And now, if you wish to pay your compliments to the gentleman who has invited you to join the excursion, it is to the top of that structure that we must go."

"God bless my soul!" cried the earl, with even more than usual warmth; "climb to the top, after this journey into Trinity belfry, and on this hot day? I must respectfully decline." Then he added, a trifle stiffly, "I fancy it will do if I send my man with our cards."

"'Twould be better to go," said the captain. "You will find the journey up less difficult than you imagine." A few minutes later they were in one of the entrance halls of the Mills Building, and Captain Jobson piloted them to a door opening on the elevator shaft. While the earl was contemplating this, an elevator came down like a comet. The door flew open, an Irish-American voice said, "Goin' up?" the captain answered, "Top," at the same time hurrying the company into the ambulatory box. The door shut with a soft click, and the passengers spun skyward with vertiginous rapidity. Before the earl could realize where he was, he, with the others, had been dislodged from the elevator by this phenomenal boy, who was half-way down again in twenty seconds.

"Here we are," said Captain Jobson.

He led the way into an anteroom, and the visitors sent their cards to the manager of the excursion, who presently received them with quiet courtesy, and gave them many tickets and much information. "We are glad," he said, "to have so distinguished a gentleman as the Earl of Offast with us on the occasion of the driving of the golden spike."

"The golden spike!" said Lady Helena. "What is that?"

Then the manager proceeded to explain that the completion of so important a transcontinental railway line as the Northern Pacific was, in some respects, the most striking event of the year; and that the ceremony of laying the last rails in presence of several hundreds of invited guests, chosen from the *élite* of European and American society, would be marked with as much splendor as possible. The last spike driven into the last tie to hold down the last rail would be of fine gold, and to it were to be attached telegraphic wires, so that the blows of the hammer might be heard north, south, east, and west. The ceremony would take place in a pretty valley in Montana, and would, the manager thought, be a memorable affair. He had that very morning arranged for having it reproduced in painting by a talented young American painter, who had been for some years residing abroad, Mr. Dulon Floyd.

Lady Helena changed color and the earl scowled. There was no longer any doubt that "Mr. Dulon" was to be a member of the excursion party. It was annoying. The youth was presumptuous. The earl cut the conversation short, breathing more freely after discovering that a "private car" would most probably be put at his disposition, and that the excursionists were to leave New York two days from that time.

"And to think," he said, "that we have a journey of fifteen hundred miles to undertake before we reach the point at which the excursion begins."

"Yes — in Minnesota," said Colonel Hodges; and at mention of Minnesota Lady Helena opened her eyes widely.

"Do you mean to say, colonel," she inquired, "that Minnesota is fifteen hundred — miles — from the city of New York?"

"Quite so, your ladyship."

She said nothing more for some moments, as they followed Captain Jobson through the labyrinthine corridors; but at last she observed in a low voice to her cousin: —

"Do you know that I thought Minnesota was some charming little place close to New York? The name sounds so diminutive and pretty." Little she knew about the Great North-west.

And now Captain Jobson led them up a flight of stairs, and, to their amazement, ushered them into a cool and airy restaurant, from the windows of which they could look out over acres of flat roofs and on the tall ships coming and going, and on the wharves, to and from which the white ferry-boats were darting like playful monsters. Lunch was ordered, and the earl, as he quaffed a glass of ice-cold champagne, leaned back in his chair and closed his eyes with infinite satisfaction. The truth is that this was the first time since he had seen the "Evening Flail" that he had felt quite secure from the "Prancing Elks."

At a neighboring table sat a large, fresh-faced man, somewhat expansive in demeanor as well as in person. Captain Jobson called the earl's attention to him.

"He is going in a minute or two, and when he is gone I will tell you a tale, as you say in England, about him," said the venerable navigator.

The fresh-faced man soon departed, after carefully looking over the earl and his friends, and when the door had closed behind him the captain said:—

"That is a gentleman who has something to do with investments in Wall street. I dare say you have never seen him in London?"

The earl declared that, to the best of his belief, the fresh-faced man was totally unknown to him.

"He is the enterprising gentleman," continued the captain, "who went over to London to see what he could do for the fortunes of a railroad stock somewhat famous; you probably remember the Warsaw, St. Mary, and Atlantic preferred, which is now, and has been for some years, in the vicinity of thirty. It can't get above it. The enterprising gentleman arrived in London anxious to do a stroke of business, and after due investigation he thought it important that he should be introduced to the Duke of Mellingford, Sir Harry Carnes, and several other noblemen, who had a little syndicate of their own and were not averse to trying American things. Cute feller, wasn't he? So, by and by, he discovered that the Duke of Mellingford was having his portrait painted by Miss Warlock, an artist of distinction. Away he went and secured an introduction to the Warlock and gave her a commission to paint his portrait. He talked so well and told so many amusing stories, especially about railway stocks and bonds, that the Warlock could not refrain from repeating some of them to the Duke of Mellingford, who was duly amused by what this American millionnaire had said. After a time the R. M. noticed the duke's portrait; said it was a fine work; that he had heard that the duke had a remarkable collection of paintings in his town residence. Could Miss Warlock secure him the privilege of seeing these paintings? She would be delighted to do so; at next sitting asked duke, and duke consented. So the enterprising American went to visit the gallery in the duke's house with a card of admission from the duke himself. After he had looked at the art treasures, he took out his card with a flourish, handed it to the servant and begged him to give it to the duke with his compliments and thanks. Then he retired.

"Some time after he was gone the servant found on the gallery floor a telegram without its envelope. He picked it up and took it to the duke, who thought it might belong to him, and read it. But the telegram was directed to the American, and ran thus: 'Important and immediate. Great rise in Warsaw, St. Mary, and Atlantic preferred imminent. Don't part with any under ninety.'

"The duke was punctilious, and regretted that he had read the telegram. He got into his carriage and went to Miss Warlock's studio. 'Look here,' he said. 'Your American friend has let fall this telegram in my house. I have inadvertently read it; it's very important. What's to be done? Will you send it to him, or ought I to send it to him? It's about a stock and'—

"'Oh, probably the shares of which he is always talking; such a splendid thing, the Warsaw!'

"'That's it,' said the duke; 'then it's a good thing, is it?'

"'Magnificent, from what I hear.'

"'Do you think he would let *us* into it?'

"'I'm sure I don't know.'

"'Then if you will kindly return him the telegram; — but he must know I opened and read it by mistake.'

"'Without doubt.'

"So the lady painter returned the telegram. The American gentleman called and went into ecstasies over the duke's high-bred punctiliousness. He must call on the duke and return his personal thanks. He did so. The duke, in due course, invited him to dinner — and — the American gentleman, in three weeks' time, placed an hundred thousand pounds' worth of 'Warsaw, St. Mary, and Atlantic preferred,' at *ninety*, with the duke, Sir Harry Carnes, and others of the little syndicate. Then he was suddenly recalled to New York, and meantime the shares remain lovingly near to thirty."

The earl laughed heartily. "So the duke was 'done,' was he? Well, he must serve as a warning to others, I suppose."

"Really, Captain Jobson," said Colonel Hodges, "really, sah, I fear your 'tales' are not calculated to give our English friends confidence in American securities."

"Oh, for that matter," said the earl, "there would be no amusement in investing if one were not taken in now and then. The fun consists in learning to choose between securities and insecurities."

"That's the true Wall-street spirit," said Captain Jobson.

"It's in the very atmosphere, I assure you," added Lady Helena.

After their early luncheon the travellers descended to the street, and Lady Helena returned in Captain Jobson's care to the Brevoort, while the earl and Colonel Hodges went on to see the lions, the bulls, and the bears of Wall street. When the earl was shown the place where Washington was inaugurated as first President of the United States, he said he believed that Washington came of a very good family, and that he had often heard him spoken of as a clever soldier and a clear-headed patriot. The colonel felt strangely disturbed at this; it seemed somehow to bring Washington, as it were, down to yesterday, instead of leaving him, surrounded by the halo of immortal renown, in a remote and glorious past, where his every attribute was poeticized.

CHAPTER VIII.

DUE WEST.

WHEN Lady Helena reached the hotel she was a trifle annoyed at finding Mr. Dulon Floyd's card and at learning from the countess that he was not likely to call again before his departure for the West.

"A rather audacious young man, my dear," said Lady Offast. "He was quite certain he should meet us at some point on the excursion, in any case at the ceremony of — doin' what did he say, Jenks?"

"Drivin' the last spike, my lady," said the maid, who had been making numerous inquiries of her own concerning this far westward journey, and who, having discovered that no danger was to be apprehended from Indians, and but little from white banditti, began with zest to enter into the spirit of the thing. "It's when the workmen comin' from the West meet them as is comin' from the East, and they lay the last rail and drive in the last spike. And the gentleman said he was goin' to paint it; —

though why a last spike should be painted, I carn't think, which" —

"That will do, Jenks. Chattering creature!" observed the countess, after the maid had left the room, "I fancy she is acquiring some of the detestably rude habits of these horrible American domestics. I don't know why they call them American, I am sure. Of the servants here seven have a rich Irish brogue, three of the maids on this floor are French and two are German; but they have such ways! And they seem to think they are conferring a favor on me when they bring me anything or go on an errand. It's really quite dreadful. Well, my dear, I trust you have enjoyed your outing. Your face is flushed and your eyes are quite dull. You must not run about so with those men, Helena; they will wear you out."

"O cousin! I enjoy it. Ah, what exquisite flowers! Where could the earl have found them?" and the girl bent delightedly over an enormous bouquet of rich blossoms, as fresh and as fragrant as if they were still springing from their native beds, and a summer rain had an hour before fallen on them.

"The flowers!" said the countess; "ah, yes! I had forgotten them. They were sent by Mr. Floyd shortly after he called, and were 'for the ladies.' The 'ladies,' if you please, Lady Helena. It appears that it is quite the correct thing, and that we are not to consider it at all extraordinary."

"I think it is very charming," said Lady Helena, dreamily caressing the petals of the roses and plucking at the violets.

"But, my dear girl," cried the countess, impetuously, "to speak quite plainly, do you think it proper that this unknown person — this Mr. Floyd — a mere painter — should be encouraged to believe that his attentions are — are desirable? Really" —

"His attentions do not offend me," answered Lady Helena, rather coldly. "I have always found them in excellent taste. How hot it is in this room! and my head aches. I wish we were already on our way to the West."

"So do I," sighed Lady Offast, "but my packing is not half done, and Jenks is lazy. She says 'it's the 'eat.' It *is* hot. And these carpets! I want to have them up. I feel half stifled. I believe I shall have to drink ice-water."

. . . .

It *was* hot. Even the New Yorkers, who pass their summers in decrying the torrid temperature of Philadelphia, were compelled to own that for once it *was* hot. The very paving-stones on Fifth Avenue seemed ready to crack open. The mansions on either side of the celebrated street were like a collection of colossal tombs, so completely had "light and life" gone away from them. Young men with fans in their hands and with white sun umbrellas held above them went by cautiously, as if fearful that any excess of effort might result in sunstroke. The horses drawing the drays or vans which now and then strayed into Fifth avenue had little caps on their heads, giving them a grandmotherly aspect which was irresistibly mirth-provoking. As for the drivers, they had followed the time-honored Irish-American custom of drinking as much whiskey as they could hold at an early hour, so that they might "support the hate," and the result was that they sat on their lofty seats with but insecure majesty, their heads swathed in wet handkerchiefs and their broad faces blazing with the fires of bad alcohol. They were pitiable spectacles. There was no air. One felt an almost uncontrollable desire to go down to the water's edge and to get into the first craft that one found at a pier, and to push off in pursuit of a fresh breeze.

"How can it be possible that New York is an

island!" moaned the countess. "There are no island breezes here." In the house, although the blinds were down and the Brevoort seemed for the nonce to have neither flies nor mosquitoes on its conscience, the temperature was not much more comfortable than out-of-doors. A walk across the room brought out the beady perspiration on the brow. Stooping to pick up a book which had fallen to the floor gave one something unpleasantly like apoplectic symptoms. The process of dressing was most irksome, and one looked forward with a shudder to the airless night which was to come. The countess was sorely puzzled, because she had searched over half Paris and London for their garments for wearing in the "States;" and now that she had brought them where they were to be worn none of them seemed cool enough.

When the earl came home, an hour or two after Lady Helena, he informed the ladies that he had received numerous invitations to country-houses on the Hudson, at Newport, and elsewhere, but that he adhered to his determination to start with the first section of the excursion. "To-morrow evening let everything be ready," he said. "We start at nine o'clock from the Grand Central Station," he concluded, reading from a printed card, "and I suppose we shall stop only to breathe once or twice before we reach Minnesota."

"Will it be more than one night to Minnesota?" timidly inquired the countess.

"Several nights, several, and all in sleeping-cars," answered the earl, firmly; "so prepare for your martyrdom, and don't look at me in that tearful manner."

"Anything—anything," murmured Lady Offast, "to escape from this horrible heat."

At eight o'clock on the following evening the earl arrived with his ladies at the Grand Central Station and paid the hackman his exorbitant fare without a murmur. The earl had prepared himself for the fray; his blood was up; he was ready to encounter American eccentricities innumerable, and not to be dismayed. On this very evening he was anxious to do things in "American fashion;" and to that end he had instructed his valet, who seemed quite incapable of understanding the ways of the New World, to stand aside and let him manage the luggage. The valet grinned and thought that it would be rare fun; and so indeed it was.

Neither Captain Jobson nor the colonel had yet arrived, so the earl, having seen his seven trunks and his numerous hampers, sacks, gun-cases, packages of fishing-tackle and his saddles and harnesses in crates and baskets all bestowed upon a long counter, which reminded him of the Bureau of Customs at Charing Cross, strolled up, and, placing his hand on one of the objects, said to the person behind the counter:—

"Now, my man, just see that all these things are properly labelled for Saint Paul—for the excursion—the big excursion—don't you know? And look sharp, please."

The personage thus addressed was a colossal Irish-American, who might have served as a model for Atlas or Hercules. His round head and good-humored face inspired confidence; his massive limbs and vast breadth of shoulder solicited physical respect. He was neatly, even somewhat expensively, dressed; underneath his blouse was a shirt of excellent linen, and a gold button shone in the collar which he left open to display the symmetry of his neck. When the earl spoke, thus for the first time in his life descending far enough from his dignity to look after his own "luggage," this Samsonian porter was engaged in a political discussion with a friend nearly as burly as himself, and so he seemed not to have heard the Englishman's observation. Suddenly, however, he turned to the long pile of luggage, and placing one huge hand on a piece of it, said, unconcernedly, and as if it was a matter of profound indifference to him: —

"Where dy'e want all this to go, boss?"

"This — er — this is my lug — baggage — er — and I want it labelled for St. Paul. I am going on the excursion — leaving by the New York Central at nine o'clock — er. I think I told you all this a moment — er — ago."

The Colossus continued to ignore the earl, and his criticism evidently produced no effect. For some reason that he could not define, the earl felt his blood beginning to boil; and while the Milesian porter dragged away piece after piece of the *impedimenta*, he reflected as to what manner of reproof he should administer to him. But his first temper was nothing to his last, when he heard the huge fellow say to his companion, in tones perfectly audible at some distance: —

"Jim, here's another of thim foreign dukes immigratin'; and this is his museum. Begor' it's a big one!"

After a time he strode forward, threw down a handful of brass checks and said: "No extra baggage to pay. Orders from excursion. Saint Paul. That's all right. Thim's chicks to claim yer baggage wid. We don't give no labels in this country. Stand out of the way a little, plase, and let that gentleman put that trunk upon the counter." Leaning over, he moved the earl a bit to one side, placing his heavy hand familiarly on the nobleman's shoulder.

The earl leaned against the counter for support, and with trembling hands picked up his "chicks." Then he extracted a silver dollar from his waist-coat pocket, and laid it before the man. "That is for your trouble," he said, haughtily, "although I really"—

"Never mind the trouble, boss," said the fellow with a saucy grin; and pushing back the money, "We don't take our wages in sections; we git 'em paid riglar once a month;" and turning with alacrity to the new-comer, he sang out, "Next."

"I—er—I should like to know your name—er—if you have got one!" shouted the earl, his face flushed with rage. "I should like to complain of your—er—your infernal insolence, and to find out whether or not your employer sanctions it. I—er—I never was so treated in my life."

"Better write to the 'Times,'" said the Colossus, with indescribable impudence, at the same time handling a large trunk as if it were a doll-house.

The earl dared trust himself no longer. He turned away, clenching his fists and murmuring: "This is intolerable! I could have stood it if the fellow had been simply insolent — but when he tried to patronize me! That was a little too much!" He refused to tell the ladies the cause of his anger, and had hardly begun to cool down by the time Captain Jobson and the colonel had arrived. The captain at once took charge of the convoy, went, much to the earl's comfort, and verified all the checks which the Colossus had so scornfully given, and reported that a silver dollar, which the baggage man would not take, for reasons best known to himself, still ornamented the "counter."

"Then let it lie there till it rots," said the earl, growing red again, and forgetting, in his heat, the imperishable quality of precious metal.

. . . .

The splendors of a palatial "Wagner" car, with a drawing-room, which the English party succeeded in securing for their journey to Chicago, contributed somewhat to restore the earl's equanimity, and he was further aided in cheerfulness by the kind offices of one of the managers of the excursion, who was attentive without being oppressive, and who seemed to fit in so completely to the earl's particular groove that it was quite refreshing. The much-tried nobleman forgot the dynamiters, the "Evening Flail," and the liberties it had taken with his name and fame, and turned his attention to sporting topics and to the ever-interesting subject of investments. The countess was cross and sleepy, and required Jenks's constant attention; and Lady Helena, finding that the main saloon of the great car was almost empty, went forward into it, and ensconced herself in a comfortable seat, where she could look out at the windows. For hours she sat there, despite a message from Jenks that she was "to come to bed forthwith." She saw the wide Hudson gleaming under the bright August moonlight; she was startled and amazed at the numbers of large towns, all seemingly old and staid and not particularly different from those she had left behind in Europe; and gradually a kind of enchantment took possession of her senses. It seemed to her that this journey was to be a very important episode in her life; that mingled delights and pains were coming to stir her heart as they had never come before. She felt a strange indisposition to remain in the company of her cousin and his wife, and she sighed for something she could not define. Perhaps, if she had been able to define it, it would have been nothing but a voice.

At last the earl came through the car, at a very late hour, having been engaged in a long conference in the smoking compartment with Colonel Hodges, Captain Jobson, and others of the company, and he ordered the romantic young lady to bed. Next morning, when she was ready to appear again, she found the train was whizzing along through salt marshes; that the air was cool and keen, and that the conductors at the stations shouted out classical names belonging to some of the magnificent towns of antiquity, but now applied to new collections of houses in this strange district, which seemed full of the most kaleidoscopic changes. Syracuse and marshes were succeeded by noble valleys filled with farms and sylvan glades, through which a peaceful canal was bearing on its bosom fleets of odd-looking boats which reminded one of Holland, as, indeed, did many things in this part of the Empire State.

Lady Helena was so startled by the black man who persisted in standing beside her chair, and whispering confidentially into her ear at the stations where excursionists took breakfast, that after she had given her order, she said, faintly, "Go away, please." He retreated to the wall with a heart-broken look, but finally returned timidly, and once more, placing his enormous lips down near her tiny ear, said, "Excuse me, lady, but I des want to know if you like some buckwheats? Dey's mighty good!" At this her repulsion vanished, and, glancing at the earl, who had often had "buckwheat cakes" on his own table in London, and who acclaimed them as one of the chief delicacies in the American *cuisine*, she burst into a merry peal of laughter, and ordered the savory compounds to be brought, rewarding the African with a silver coin, which he pocketed with an obsequious grin.

"The best servants in the world," said Captain Jobson. "The darky is without his equal. Had a French darky on my ship, the 'Invincible,' as a cook. He was a master of his art. My first officer always tasted everything prepared for the crew before it was served out of the galley. When we came into port, and some of my men tried to desert on the ground that the food was bad, I had 'em up before the local magistrate. 'I will show Your Honor,' I would say, 'my bill of fare for my crew.' Then my black cook would come forward and explain the items. Result: the magistrate would say, 'Captain Jobson, I would like to go with you as a passenger, just for the sake of enjoying that bill of fare;

and if these men insist in their wish to desert such a home, why, I think we shall have to give them a month's hard labor apiece.' So then I would take them all back to the ship, with the black cook bringing up the rear. Fact."

"You are wrong about the negro, captain," said Colonel Hodges. "The Chinaman is the ideal servant."

"Dirty pagan!"

"Not at all. Cleanly beyond expression, and not to be improved on, sah, as a servant. Our Irish friends hate him so bitterly because they know that there is no competing with him."

The countess thought there were no servants like English ones; and, as no one wished to discuss the point with a lady, this topic was set aside. Presently the party rolled away again, and now the "West" seemed to have begun. The fields were rough and but half-cultivated to European eyes, and everywhere building and digging were going on as if the residents had but recently arrived. They skirted the smoke of Buffalo, after dining amid more black men in the railway restaurant there, and in the afternoon the great inland lake, with its miraculous water, which changed color at the touch of every breeze, and its straggling white sails on windy horizons, amused them for an hour or two.

At Cleveland Lady Helena began to be tired, and to remember that she had not seen Mr. Floyd. Why was he not with the excursionists? Her heart would have been lighter had she known that he was rushing Chicagowards by the Pennsylvania line, and that his only thought was for her.

"What is Cleveland celebrated for?" asked the earl.

"Cleveland," answered Captain Jobson, "produces the best people in America; or, I should say, draws the best people to itself; and keeps them there. All the finer qualities of the new American race are crystallized here. Curious, isn't it? But so it is."

"It is quite remarkable," said the earl.

"Yes," sighed the captain, pensively; "my second wife is from Cleveland."

CHAPTER IX.

MINNETONKA.

"GOD bless my soul!" said the earl. "That is indeed most extraordinary. And do you mean to tell me that it often happens?"

"Quite common, I assure you, and is not thought remarkable in these parts," replied Colonel Hodges.

They were standing together on the platform of a private car in which they had just arrived at Minnetonka, — the rendezvous for all the excursionists; the point at which the grand journey through the newly opened regions of the North-west was to begin. It was a cool, fragrant September Sunday morning. The dawn was breaking with majestic slowness, as if it were sorry to disturb the exquisite revery of earth and lakes and forest and sky. After the long period of rattling and roaring and hissing noises, the rumble and dust and heat from New York to Chicago, and from Chicago to St. Paul, this idyllic stillness, this profound repose, these temperate lights of the awakening heaven were delicious. The earl was charmed. Everything pleased him. He felt that henceforward the excursion would be one long delight. Colonel Hodges explained to him that here they were in the centre of the noble lake region of Minnesota; in a land of green meadows and lovely glades, and bewitching forests filled with unsuspecting game — of azure-tinted lakes of wide extent, dotted here and there with acres of lily pads, and fringed to the very water's edge with pleasant green. In summer and autumn a restful land, much frequented and deeply admired by the sun-scorched citizens of New Orleans, who come thousands of miles up the "Father of Waters" to breathe the inspiring air and to bathe in the crystal waters. In winter a wild land of snow-clad spaces, with treacherous ice-gullies and dangerous roads; a land scoured and ravaged by the winds, buffeted and torn by storms, and visited by Arctic cold, but ever awakening in May into a sylvan freshness and verdure worthy of Arcadia when the world was young.

Four long trains had come to rest at the base of a slope crowned with an enormous wooden hotel, which resembled nothing so much as a number of old Queen Anne mansions, all set side by side, and then hooped together by a wide veranda, decorated with innumerous arm-chairs painted red and blue. The locomotives had "blown off steam" and were now silent, as if they were, like the human beings whom they had brought thither, holding their breath and gazing spellbound on the beauties round about them. The negro servants were unceremoniously tossing hundreds of hand-bags into the long grass where owners were expected to hunt up and claim their property. The earl had already expressed his opinion so frequently as to the Western domestic that Colonel Hodges took a wicked pleasure in calling his attention to anything which afforded a fresh illustration of the difficulties of maintaining a proper serving-class in a republic.

"It is every man for himself in this country," said the colonel. "Rank and title seem to produce no impression on the minds of these freeborn domestics." The colonel sighed as he thought of the servants in his own Florida "befo' the wah." "Now, do you see, my Lord, that gentleman struggling up the slope with a fat valise in one hand and an umbrella in the other? I mean the gentleman in the white hat and linen duster. You observe that he marches off alone without the smallest attention paid to him; and when he gets to the hotel he will stand before the counter and wait his turn and register his name precisely like any other member of the excursion."

"Yes," said the earl, looking puzzled.

"Yes, sah. Well, that gentleman is General Grant, once the greatest hero of his generation, and twice President of the United States. And may I call your attention to the tall personage behind him, likewise carrying a heavy bag — that one there, who just stumbled? — that is the late Secretary of State. Imagine two English dignitaries of that calibre caring for themselves in that off-hand fashion."

It was then that the earl uttered the "God bless my soul!" by which he was wont to express profound astonishment, and then he fell into reflection for a minute, after which he said: —

"It's because you haven't got the 'tip,' you know."

"I don't understand," said Colonel Hodges, puzzled in his turn.

"Well, if you had the 'tip,' don't you know, and had it well introduced, these servants would not be so disgustingly independent. At present they get wages, and are determined, like all servants, to do as little as possible for them. Give them insufficient wages, my dear fellow, and then fee them for every small service, and you will have no trouble in getting your bags carried, and your tables served, don't you know, in proper form. In these days, when every man is insanely anxious to be considered equal with every other man, the only way to keep servants in their proper places is to make them dependent on the 'tip.' General Grant could never have got where he is on that hill just now with that bag in his hand if you had the 'tip' system. One servant or another would have taken the bag from him some time ago, and would have made him pay at the top of the hill, so as not to interfere with the presumptive 'tips' to the hotel porters."

Colonel Hodges tried to explain how it was because of the very independence which it vouchsafed them that the serving-classes in America would refuse to accept any modification of the wages system; but the earl was obdurate, and insisted that it should be tried. The colonel had not the heart to remind the worthy nobleman of his failure in "tipping" the impudent railway porter in New York; so he suggested that when the ladies were ready they should all go to the hotel for breakfast and for rooms.

"I fancy," chuckled the earl, "that I am somewhat better provided here than our distinguished

American friends, if they are as careless of their comfort as you would have me think; for, when I learned at Chicago that we were coming here, I telegraphed for a suite of rooms, which I hope you and Captain Jobson will share with us." The earl thought this was a great unbending, and glanced at the colonel, who accepted with thanks for himself, to see if the effort were duly appreciated.

Presently the ladies appeared, declaring that a "private car" was as comfortable as one's own home; and the cheerful ancient captain also shone forth, bringing in his wake no less a person than the young painter, Mr. Dulon Floyd.

"I missed you in Chicago," said the young artist, shaking hands with Lady Helena, and betraying his agitation at again meeting her by nothing except a slight tremor in his voice, "and I was sorry, for I wished to show you some of the beauties of that mushroom city. I hope you — and your friends — were favorably impressed?"

Lady Helena said frankly that she did not like Chicago. She had expected too much, and had been grievously disappointed. There was nothing original about it, and the site was by no means picturesque, and the "elevators," as they called them, were hideous.

"I could not help feeling regret that a new Manchester or smoky Birmingham has been set down in the midst of the grand prairies," she said. "Has the Western mind no originality?"

The earl thought Lady Helena rather too severe, and reminded her that he had seen the finest stock-yards in the world during his stay in Chicago. "Never saw so many horned beasts together before," he said. "It was impressive."

"Cousin! Do we cross the Atlantic to see horned beasts? What we want to know is whether the men of Chicago have been able to build a fine city with the money made out of selling cattle and swine. And I say not."

"What severity!" said the countess. "I am sure Mr. Dulon — Mr. Floyd is quite shocked."

"On the contrary," he said, "I quite agree with her ladyship's opinion."

"Dear me! Now, I thought the Michigan avenue (she pronounced it *Mitchigan*) was rather fine."

"And so this is Minnesota!" said Lady Helena, dreamily, as she walked up the slope, side by side with the young painter, who assumed her escort as if he had been doing nothing but attending her steps for the past week. "It is very beautiful. How lovely are those ripples on the water; and these cool breezes, after the torture of those days in New York! — and," she added, with a merry twinkle in her eyes, "after those mosquitoes in Chicago — are like blessings."

"I have found a capital place in which to set up my easel — a perfect nook, on the shore of the lake; and if you would like to take a walk there after breakfast" —

"Mr. Floyd," said Lady Helena, "do you mean to say that you are going to paint on Sunday?"

"Is this the Sabbath?" cried the youth with a grimace. "I had forgotten it. But to-morrow we are invited to half-a-dozen civic receptions and banquets in the cities near here, and there will be no time. However, you will not refuse me the pleasure of showing you the nook, I am sure. This is the region that our poet Longfellow has so well described in 'Hiawatha.' The falls of Minnehaha are not far away, and the woods and fields are almost as primitive, as unsubdued, as when the Indians were the only inhabitants."

"Oh, how charming! Then this is the Hiawatha-land! And I, who thought that Minnesota was in the neighborhood of New York!"

The earl found his rooms ready for him, and

decided that his meals should be served therein, although the countess admitted that she was dying of curiosity to see the great dining-room in which twelve hundred guests could dine at once. It cost the earl an effort to invite "Mr. Dulon" to join the private breakfast party, but he did so, much to Lady Helena's amusement. She knew that he had *felt* her unexpressed wish, and obeyed it.

"Fun ahead for to-morrow," said Capt. Jobson, as he took his seat next the countess at the breakfast-table. "The members of this excursion are to be entertained by two cities to-morrow. These cities are rivals, and are only ten miles apart. Their citizens detest each other cordially. Each believes that the other is the only obstacle to its own development."

"Receptions are a bore," said the earl. "I shall take my gun and see if I can get any game in this vicinity while you are going through your two receptions to-morrow."

Captain Jobson amused the company with tales of the "Invincible" until breakfast was over, after which he took the earl down to the roomy corridors below to introduce to him, as he put it, some of the numerous American celebrities who had gathered there for the enjoyment of the morning cigar.

The earl yielded to the temptation of this extemporized levee. The countess began to busy herself with Jenks and the valet, holding them to a stern account for the disposition of the luggage. Colonel Hodges said the white wine had made his head ache, and that, as he had slept poorly in the train, he should retire for a nap. As fate would have it Lady Helena found herself alone with Mr. Dulon, and felt that that unabashed young gentleman was devouring her face with eager gaze. She blushed violently, and, arising from the table, walked to one of the open windows and looked out. The painter was beside her before she had recovered from the agitation which she could not explain. Where were the coldness, the haughtiness, for which she was renowned in London town? Where were those icy looks with which she had so often reduced to chaos the cleverly combined artifices of the aristocratic dandies of her social sphere? They would not come at her command, and this inability to compel them made her quite wretched. She bit her lips, and was so impatient that the manifestations of her temper did not escape the painter's notice. Truth to tell they alarmed him a trifle.

"If I ask you again," he said, timidly, "if I may claim your company for the walk of which I spoke, it is not to insist; perhaps you are wearied with the journey. But the day is so perfect, and the scene so splendid" —

Lady Helena looked around at him with a flash of resistance in her eyes. She was anxious to rebel against his power over her, but when she heard his voice, all her resolution to be independent, exacting, capricious, to lead him, vanished. She felt as if she were the passive instrument of his will, and as if, in case the enchantment lasted, she would soon take delight and find pride in being so subjugated.

"I will go," she said; "but you must promise not to sketch, for it is Sunday. I suppose you have many wicked Continental notions."

"It shall be as you wish," he answered, smiling. "I will not sketch; but I am sorry that I cannot, for the picture that we are to see is a rare one. Nature is not often in such mood as to-day."

Half an hour later they were strolling through the tall grass, with dozens of wasps "zooning" around them, and with the birds singing merrily and saucily above them. Lady Helena thought that these Western birds were strangely familiar, almost contemptuous for human beings. They had none of the shy, reserved, half-cynical ways of the English songsters, who seem instinctively to recognize in man a creature bent on their destruction or captivity. They soon came to a large garden, in which a lean man, clad in yellow homespun, and escorted by two fierce-looking dogs, was wandering to and fro, surveying the monstrous pumpkins which lay sprawling hither and yon at the ends of their parent vine. When he heard the new-comers' footsteps he looked up with that expression of mild melancholy always found on the face of the Western agriculturist, and waited to be accosted.

"We want to get down to the shore of the lake, if your four-footed friends will allow us to take the liberty of passing through your garden," said the painter.

"The dogs won't bite ye," said the man, with a homely grin, which was instantly grappled with and suppressed by the ever-vigilant melancholy. "Come meer, Tige. Keep round to the right. Path thar take ye straight down to the cornfield. Shortest way right through it." And he turned away, and recommenced his examination of the pumpkins, as if he had already forgotten the strangers' existence.

"The gardener is — very cool — and — unconcerned — is he not?" said Lady Helena, who was a little surprised that the man had not touched his hat, and come forward to show them the way, exacting thereafter a tribute of small coin.

"They are all that way out here," observed the artist, reading her thought.

They went on, Lady Helena's trim figure tightly clad in gray travelling-dress, flitting ahead through the tangled mass of vines and creepers, and among the scarlet poppies in the small oasis of waving grass. At last they reached a path hedged with blackberry bushes, where they could walk abreast. This path led up to a green wall, at sight of which Lady Helena paused, swaying her unopened parasol to and fro.

"I suppose you will find me very ignorant," she said, "but I really have not the slightest idea what this is that we are coming to now."

"That is the cornfield."

"And what is a cornfield? Surely that bears no resemblance to wheat, nor to barley."

"Oh, I had forgotten that you are a stranger to the rustling corn!" cried Mr. Dulon. "It seems so odd to think of you as — as different from ourselves. This is a field of maize — the Indian corn of which Longfellow sang so melodiously."

"Fancy!" said Lady Helena. And a strange smile came to transfigure her face — to chase away every trace of haughtiness, and to render her for a moment positively beautiful. "It is like a miniature forest," she said.

"A trackless, but fortunately not a very wide forest, into which we must venture in the spirit of true pioneers," said the artist, leading the way.

But Lady Helena hesitated; so Mr. Dulon turned around and held out his hand to her. "The forest is not enchanted," he said.

The girl seemed not to see his proffered hand. She uttered a low "Thank you," and stepped quickly in among the tall, green shafts. "What lovely, quaint whisperings and weird little sighs and murmurs!" she said, as for the first time she heard the gracious voices of Mondamin. "And what are these strange protuberances between these long sheaves? You must not laugh at me!"

She paused again, and he looked down at her admiringly as she stood flanked on either hand by the majestic Western cornstalks, more than six feet high. The tempered light that played on the bending and swaying sheaves cast a mellow reflection upon her clear-cut features. She bent her gaze on the ground and began to pry with the end of her parasol at a small stone near her feet.

"I am not laughing," he said. And indeed he felt more like crying, or like shouting. The magic of the sunshine, the madness of the pure upland breeze, the intoxicating aroma of the wild flowers and the vines and the fruity flavor of the corn seemed to have got into his blood. His emotions were passing beyond his control; his head was light; he felt drawn irresistibly toward the girl. But he reached up and broke an ear off from a cornstalk, and, stripping it of its symmetrical outer coverings, showed her the delicate silken tassels, and the pearly rows of kernels.

"This is the primal wealth of America," he said, with a little touch of pride in his voice. "This is the true gold mine, in which the earliest colonists found their richest treasure. Is it not beautiful?"

"It is very strange," said Lady Helena. "And did the Indians cultivate this?"

"They did, and heard in the rustling of the sheaves the voices of sprites and goddesses."

"As I seem to hear them now," said she. And she held up her hand, as if commanding him to listen. For the first time since they had started on the walk he noticed that this hand, unlike the other, was ungloved.

They were standing close together, with the

sheaves brushing their garments. As Lady Helena lowered her daintily jewelled hand the artist took it in his own two honest palms, raised it to his lips, and kissed it.

Then a great shudder of joy appeared to run through all the sheaves, and it seemed as if they murmured in unison some strange incantation in an unknown tongue.

CHAPTER X.

THE RIVAL CITIES.

Lady Helena was not angry with Mr. Floyd, but she was vexed at herself because she was not angry with him. The moment after the kiss had been stolen the young painter looked as if he were ready to sink into the ground. He was still at that happy age and stage of worldly experience when one can blush, and a rosy color invaded his cheeks, and mounted even to his brow. He did not know what to expect; a vague fear that Lady Helena would suddenly turn around, make her way out of the cornfield, and go back to the hotel alone, took possession of him. He stood, helpless and absorbed in thought, before the object of his adoration. Heaven alone knows what turn matters would have taken had not the sound of something moving through the corn suddenly been heard.

"Ah! what is that?" said Lady Helena, looking a trifle alarmed. "I hope those dogs are not coming after us! Or suppose it should be a bear?"

Mr. Dulon laughed heartily, and all at once saw

his way out of the situation. "It certainly is an animal of some kind," he said, glancing at her to see if she were really frightened. "The steps are too heavy for those of a man."

"Do you *think* so?" she said, grasping her parasol nervously with both hands. "Fancy! It would be romantic, would it not, if we should encounter a bear? Cousin would never forgive us for not having invited him to accompany us, if he discovered that he had missed a chance for a shot." Her voice faltered a little, and she looked up at the painter with a shy, questioning gaze, her face faintly lighted by a dawning smile, which completed the fascination. The lumbering steps came nearer. The young man almost hoped that it *was* a bear, that he might do valiant battle for his lady-love.

But it was nothing more dangerous than an old horse, who had slyly found his way into the field, and who wore upon his battered equine features that half-humorous, half-cynical look which horses always wear when they know that they are doing wrong. The venerable thief had a green sheaf in his mouth, and was evidently enjoying to the full the Arcadian coolness and abundance. He paused as he saw the young couple, and Mr. Dulon could have sworn that the brute winked at him.

Lady Helena laughed now, and so merrily that the painter felt reassured, and even carried his re-awakened presumption far enough to ask her if she would take his arm until they got by the horse. But this she flatly refused to do; and just then the animal turned round about, and went away from them, trampling down the corn, and laying up fine store of wrath against himself when he should be caught. So the two went silently through the verdant odorous alleys until they came to the side of the cornfield next to the lake, and passed along a pretty slope to a tiny grove on a bluff overhanging the water. Here Mr. Dulon pointed out the scene which he had desired to sketch; and while they were contemplating it, they sat down on a rustic seat beneath one of the trees.

"But this is not at all like what I fancied Minnesota to be," said the girl. "I thought that there would be steep hills, with tremendous torrents brawling down between them, don't you know? and tropical foliage (I am sure corn is not tropical), and plenty of Indians in scarlet blankets; — and a profusion of wigwams; and broad-hatted men. Now, this — is — is — like any other part of the world; with some not very striking exceptions, is it not? That tranquil lake might be Windermere, or Coniston, might not it?"

"Yet you shall soon see wonders," said Mr. Floyd, who did not exactly like these observations, because they sharpened the sense of disappointment which he himself felt. "We are promised views of wheatfields vast as some of your European seas; processions and dances by picturesque and presumably ragged and dirty Indians; a trip across the *Mauvaises Terres* of the old French trappers and voyageurs, lands where the fantastic cliffs and buttes and projections are girdled with crimson and overstrewn with volcanic scoria; where the great veins of coal, which have been smouldering for generations, look like fiery serpents crawling across enchanted land; where whole forests, turned into stone, will astonish you. And then we shall come to the wonders of the Yellowstone, the mysterious land where that wily diplomat and warrior, Sitting Bull, marshalled his braves, the irreconcilable Sioux, and entrapped the flower of our cavalry"—

"Really, Mr. Floyd, you are becoming quite enthusiastic and poetical. Those are the things that we came to see; but where *are* they?" And Lady Helena looked around her as if she expected to find them springing out of the ground, obedient to her ladyship's command.

"We must go to them; they will not come to us," said the painter, "and I am as anxious as you to push on. But I fancied that I had observed an indisposition on your ladyship's part to devote the Sabbath to secular pursuits."

"Sunday still makes itself *felt* here," she answered. Perhaps if we were in some place like these *Mauvaises Terres* that you speak of, we should have a new set of sentiments suitable for the savage nature of the locality."

"Then am I to understand that you think Sunday is only a prejudice, as the Frenchman said of the rain? In other words, that if you choose to maintain that it does not exist it has no existence?"

"Sunday is a necessity of civilization, Mr. Floyd. Can you not imagine places where all days are days of rest and where a Sunday would be an absurdity?"

"I wish I had not told you that I thought of sketching to-day," said the painter, smiling, and rising from his seat.

"That you might have stolen away and guiltily done the work, I suppose," she said. "Wait until we reach the Yellowstone. I am certain that there are a hundred lakes like this in the world."

"And I am sure that there will never be a hundred days like this in the world," said Mr. Dulon, standing in front of Lady Helena. "It is the pearl of days for me — more beautiful than any that I have ever known, because" —

"Oh, look at that deliciously ugly toad hopping through the grass!" cried Lady Helena, jumping up. "Isn't he a love? Did one ever before see such entrancing homeliness? He is what Lady Offast would have called, before I weaned her from the lean æsthetic school, too unutterably tender, too divinely sublime." She overtook and halted the squat and blinking creature, and caressed its knobbed back with the end of her parasol.

"Shall I capture him for you?" said the painter, who saw plainly the feminine ruse, and who began to comprehend that a strange inspiration was carrying him on to dangerous lengths. So he subdued his impetuosity, and exerted himself manfully to be entertaining and to make Lady Helena forget the little adventure in the cornfield. They walked along the shore of the lake until they came to the uncleared forest, and then, skirting the cornfield, they went up through sweet meadows and in and out among the poppy-fields for more than an hour, regardless of the heat which had at first so dismayed the English girl. Then they found themselves among the excursionists; and presently Lady Helena signified her desire to return to the hotel.

When Mr. Dulon took off his hat as she tripped up the wooden steps of the veranda, he felt that his action of that morning had in some way raised a barrier between them, and he went away to smoke a gloomy cigar and to grumble at his own folly.

In the late afternoon he went across the lake with two or three hundred noted Germans and Englishmen, and as many more prominent Americans, on a "steamboat excursion;" and he saw neither the earl nor any of the earl's party again until the next morning, when the whole company was to start on its visit to the "rival cities."

"No," said the earl, as he came down the dewy slopes to the train, "I am not going to be received by the rival cities, and the countess is to remain at home getting courage for our start at midnight. As for me I intend to go and shoot something." And he smiled benignantly on the crowd of Americans who themselves were grinning at this last remark.

"Dreadful man!" said Lady Helena, who had

just come down, escorted by the captain and the colonel, and becomingly attired in a new travelling costume which had cost a pretty penny at Lambert's, in Paris, but which the American ladies thought "a little dowdy, and *so* plain." "You are never happy unless you have one or two murders per week on your conscience. If you were to be chased by a bear, now, you would get only what you deserve."

"God bless my soul, Helena!" said the earl. "Are you aware what you are saying? And all these ladies and gentlemen looking on!" he added in a whisper. "I trust you will enjoy your multitudinous escort." And he pointed first to the captain, then to Colonel Hodges, who was resplendent in his best blue cloth coat, and who had assumed the dignified air of a great banker and investor; then, finally, to Mr. Floyd, who came hastening down, rather carelessly dressed, just as the train was beginning to move off. The earl was so stupefied at the manner in which Mr. Floyd sprang on to the steps of the last car as it slipped past him that he did not hear the young man's pleasant salutation. "Great heavens! he might have been killed!" he cried. And he went back up the hill, shaking his head gravely.

When Mr. Floyd reached the car in which Lady Helena was seated he found that Captain Jobson had already introduced her to a family party of his acquaintance from St. Louis. The ladies of this party seemed somewhat startled by such immediate contact with British aristocracy, and for the first five minutes (during which Mr. Dulon got himself presented to the group) they were in doubt as to which direction to take. But presently discovering that Lady Helena was very much like other ladies of culture and high social position — except that as one of the St. Louis party afterward expressed it, she "seemed sort o' to want to talk down to you, instead of keepin' on a level" — the ice of conversation was broken, and the party reached Minneapolis — the pretty little city of mammoth flour mills, lumber yards innumerable, broad streets shaded by handsome trees, and high swelling ambitions — before they realized that they were beyond the confines of Minñetonka.

At Minneapolis there was thunder in the air. It was not without a severe twinge of jealousy that the Minneapolites allowed the excursionists to pass through their city and to be first "received" officially at St. Paul. Minneapolis stood proudly upon its dignity, asserting its autonomy with that fierce earnestness which Americans all display when their rights, however obtained, are called in question. The two cities, situated only ten miles apart, and undoubtedly destined to become one at no very distant day, had railed at each other for weeks before this event. St. Paul, as the capital of the State, and as the official eastern terminus of the new Northern Pacific Railroad, over which the excursion was to go, had claimed and insisted on precedence. But Minneapolis had arisen in her might and had said: "Priority you may have, but we will excel you! Our procession shall be longer, our music shall be louder, our collation sweeter, than yours! Your puerile and pusillanimous festival shall be blotted out of the memories of the distinguished visitors by the greater glories of ours." Thereupon the governor of the State, who was something of a wag, laid a trap for Minneapolis. He had summoned the mayor of that city, who was the colonel of a State militia regiment, to repair with his troops to St. Paul on the celebration-day, and there to do duty in humble tribute to St. Paul's greatness. When the Minneapolites heard this they were all but choked with rage. What! should their civic chief magistrate leave the city which adored him, and crawl in the dust for the delectation of the purse-proud citizens of St. Paul? Perish the thought! Minneapolis shouted defiance to the governor of the State. The noble militia of Minneapolis, with the mayor at their head, would do escort duty at home; not one step would they stir toward St. Paul; and if the tyrannical governor chose to consider their decision as rebellious, and to decimate their ranks, he might try it on, sir, he might try it on!

"Oh, I sincerely hope there will be no fighting!" said Lady Helena, to whom a Minneapolis man in the car had been talking in this vein. The citizen of Minneapolis drew back with a reproachful air.

"Fighting, madam?" he said. "We are not Irish nor I-talians — to disgrace ourselves by fighting."

"Then if the governor should insist upon having your Minneapolis regiment at St. Paul this morning, I am to understand that there would be no resistance?"

"Hum!" said the man. "But you see the governor will *not* insist. He is too wise to do that."

"Then," continued Lady Helena, looking puzzled, "I fear your rivalry is not so fierce as it is painted. I begin to suspect that it is put on — assumed, you know — the better to bring out the advantages of each other."

"Wal!" said the man, laughing. "I reckon, madam, that you're more'n about half right. But you'll judge for yourself, when you come back this afternoon. Why, St. Paul aint a patch on Minneapolis! It's only a kind of a — er-er suburb — a leetle further down stream." And with a wave of his hand he dismissed St. Paul from his consideration, as a burgher of Rimini might have done for Ravenna.

They were whirled away to St. Paul, which certainly was very pretty on its terraces, with its substantial mansions overlooking the majestic sweep of the Father of Waters. Lady Helena and the three gentlemen of her escort were placed together in a handsome carriage drawn by prancing black steeds, and followed the procession to a little park, where the guests were seated to witness the parade of the trades. St. Paul — with its fine railway station, in and out of which dozens of trains were puffing, with its handsome streets lined with stone buildings, with its throngs of well-dressed people standing in long rows to greet the visitors, with its braying bands and marching and countermarching regiments — did not not look exactly like "a suburb a leetle further down stream." As their carriage neared the park the driver turned to his passengers, and in husky voice and with confidential air remarked: —

"When I came hyar, in '53, thar warn't nothin' hyar at all. No town, no nothin'. Them bluffs wasn't cut away. Had ter crawl up 'em. That was thirty year ago. Wasn't ten people hyar then. Now they's nigh on ter a hundred thousand, *ef* not more."

This driver was a shrewd-faced fellow who had evidently risen from the bottom round of the ladder. He informed Lady Helena that he owned the black horses; that he had "done well;" that thirty years ago "Saint Paul warn't on the map. Now they's more'n ten thousand workmen employed in factories hyar."

"Is that more than are employed in Minneapolis?" inquired Lady Helena with a sudden malice which she could not resist.

The driver looked sternly at her. "Minne-*opo*lis?" he said, with infinite scorn. "Wal, I haven't ben up there for ten year or so, but *we used* to consider Minne*opo*lis then as a kind of a leetle town on the outskirts. I reckon 'taint changed much sence that time. Git up!" And the prancing blacks brought them to the entrance of the park. Here Mr. Floyd took charge of Lady

Helena, much to the annoyance of the group from Saint Louis, and he explained to her the seemingly interminable procession of militia regiments, white and black; the Indians, with their wigwams and their weapons of the chase, retreating before civilization, represented by artisans of all classes, working at their trades as they were drawn along on huge wheeled platforms; and, lastly, the great train of wagons decorated with symbols of the agriculture and the forest resources of the State. Then they had luncheon under a huge tent in the park, and Lady Helena was introduced to General Grant, who held her plate for her, and impressed her as "one of the most modest and courteous gentlemen of distinction that she had ever seen."

By and by Saint Paul announced that its celebration in honor of the opening of the Northern Pacific Railroad was over; and that those who had the courage to affront the muddy streets and the meagre cheer of Minneapolis were free to depart thither. So the excursionists rode back to the station under prettily decorated arches, and were pelted by rosy damsels with blossoms, and deafened with music and cheers. They found Minneapolis nearly gone mad with the joy of a suppositious triumph, for Providence had sent them a crowning blessing in the shape of the President of the United States, who, on his way homeward from a far Western excursion, had arrived there just in time to be "taken" for the festivities. "Minneapolis had the Chief Magistrate of the nation at her celebration; he disdained to stop at Saint Paul!" Such would be the proud boast of the local journals. Mr. Floyd and Lady Helena entered into the spirit of this rejoicing, and followed the processions, and studied the flags and trophies, and witnessed the vast parade of the flour and lumber industries, and laughed until they were quite weary. And although they laughed, they were duly impressed with the magnificent energy which, in less than a generation, has built up in these far north-western lands cities and towns and fortunes and a new State, than which none are fairer in America's wide domain.

When they entered the train to return to Minnetonka, they found Captain Jobson and Colonel Hodges seated together, looking a bit dejected, and solemn as wise men are who have had within one glass of too much champagne.

"Do you know, colonel," said Lady Helena, *sotto voce*, "that I am going to ask the earl to-night in what part of Minnesota my investments lie? Suppose I should discover that they are half in Saint

Paul and half in Minneapolis? Would not that be dramatic?"

Mr. Floyd was moody, because, on the way home, he had learned from one of the managers of the excursion that the earl and his two ladies and their servants were assigned to a "private car," but that he was to be billeted with the journalists during the long excursion. Would the two cars be on the same train? Because there were to be four trains, running half an hour apart. The manager could not say. Mr. Floyd was perplexed. Lady Helena's presence near him seemed suddenly to have become necessary to the continuance of his existence.

CHAPTER XI.

TWO OF A TRADE.

Mr. Dulon sat down on the huge valise which he had been carrying for some minutes, and looked around him. It was midnight, and he was on his way to the railway to find his "section" of the excursion. At the foot of the long hill in front of the rambling Minnetonka Hotel four trains were drawn up, each awaiting its contingent of excursionists. The locomotives were crooning harmoniously together in low and melancholy refrain, as if the majestic silence of the night brooding over the great lakes and their wooded shores had subdued them to respect and reverence. The small army of train employés, colored porters, cooks, and body-servants, and the country boys impressed into the service of the travellers to transfer baggage from the hotel porch to the different trains, all moved about silently. The mighty banquet, given by the citizens of the rival cities, in the hotel's capacious dining-room, had long been finished. But two or three strayed revellers were piping staves in a dark corner, obviously under the impression that they had got into the train for Minneapolis and were comfortably speeding to their homes. The rather spasmodic gayety of these indiscreet representatives of Minnesota was the only thing which affronted the dignity of this noble September night, moonless, perfumed, and serene.

The electric lights on the long porch were dying out one by one. Although there were fifteen or eighteen hundred people moving rapidly to and fro, claiming their baggage, inquiring for each other, and nervously shouting the names and numbers of their cars to their guides, they made no more impression than if they had been so many ants on an ant-hill. The night seemed to cast its mantle over them, and to smother their Liliputian bustle.

"Two thousand miles of this new country to traverse before we reach the Pacific!" thought Mr. Dulon. "This is the first time that the distances have seemed impressive to me. There is a forbidding mystery about these new lands which I never appreciated before. If I were alone I should positively be afraid to go on. Nonsense! What a fancy! Stop! I know that voice! Lady Helena, by all that's delightful! And the whole family party behind her! They must be going on our train or they would not have been directed to take this path. *She* must not see me, or she will think I have sought a meeting."

Mr. Dulon said these last words in an undertone, and, arising and catching up his valise, moved quickly out of the path and turned from the friends who were approaching, lest he might be recognized by them. The young painter's pride had been touched during the evening by one or two chance remarks from the earl, which led him to believe that that gentleman was not especially anxious for the close companionship of any of his American friends on the long overland trip. In his heart of hearts Mr. Dulon just then considered the earl an assuming creature, who had altogether too exaggerated a notion of his own importance. "He has doubtless taken pains to secure a private car in the first train, with the directors and magnates," he whispered to himself, "and is only coming down this way by mistake. I shall soon know."

"Third section, this way," said the cheery voice of Captain Jobson, addressing the earl, and Mr. Dulon's heart gave a great jump. It was Fate, then: why had he not recognized and admitted it from the start? "Private car belongs to the Baltimore & Ohio Railroad, and I managed to secure it for you without difficulty. My old friend Barrett — one of the managers — couldn't refuse me anything; brought him home from Singapore in 1856. That was a memorable voyage. My learned pig, Jim, died on that trip. Cute feller, Jim was. Friskiest, knowingest pig that ever went to sea. Could always tell when it was comin' on to blow by Jim's actions; for he would cavort around the deck like mad. Had a regular funeral for him when he died; and swung him off sewed up in a sheet, with a lump of lead fastened into it. Great pig, Jim was. These private cars are very comfortable. Just like being in your own house."

"It was really very considerate of you, captain, to see that we have this — er — this — vehicle all to ourselves. Do you think — er — that we shall be — er — quite secluded and private?"

"Certain sure," said the good captain, looking amused, and nudging Colonel Hodges, who marched beside him.

"Of course," continued the earl, "we wish to do the thing — er — in American fashion, but — er — we cannot be expected at a — er — moment's notice to adopt the — er — promiscuity — er — to which we have not been accustomed, don't you see?"

Lady Helena and the countess and eke Jenks were mute, and as weary as mute. They stole along behind the earl, growing each moment more and more appalled at the immensity of the journey which they were about to undertake. After they had passed, Mr. Dulon "fell in," at a safe distance, and soon had the satisfaction of seeing them halt in front of the third train, which had just drawn up on the rails vacated by the second, now slowly moving away with various admonitory shrieks to those luckless persons who might have forgotten to take their places.

"It *is* Fate," murmured Mr. Dulon, "for the car to which I am assigned is the 'Alsatia,' and here is the 'Alsatia' directly behind the private car in which Captain Jobson is about to bestow the earl's party. This is really charming. I had begun to doubt that there *was* a Providence watching over my affairs; but this looks"—

He sprang up the steps of the "Alsatia," found his way into the huge, palatial "sleeping car," dragging his heavy valise, and was encountered by a colossal porter, who told him to "take a seat and he would be attended to presently." After his long residence in Europe, this refreshing impudence of the American servant jarred a little upon Mr. Dulon's nerves, but he stifled his vexation in a laugh and went out to look after his sketching-gear and his trunks, which he found carefully piled with others, labelled for "train number four." The excitement of hastily rescuing them and having them placed in the baggage-car of the third section thoroughly shook off the drowsiness which had been assailing him, and when the error was rectified he went upon the platform of the "Alsatia" to smoke a cigar.

He found the door of the earl's private car open, and in a blaze of light from a huge lamp, he saw the earl's face, flushed with anger. Captain Jobson stood beside the worthy gentleman, trying to pacify him, but the earl would not be pacified, and the gravity of his annoyance had betrayed him into an excess of gesture and a redundance of speech usually foreign to him.

"It's all very pretty to call it a mistake, Captain Jobson; I call it an outrage. For two days in succession I am assured by the directors of this excursion that I shall have a private car for this tremendous journey of a fortnight. I confide — er — in these promises — er — bring the ladies of my party here — and er — what do I find? I discover that the best places in this famous private car are already taken up by an — er — an English somebody — er — and his two sons, who seem to make themselves pretty much at home, I must say. The American conception of privacy seems slightly at variance with ours, I find. These countrymen of mine are determined to stay where they are, on the plea that they have been 'assigned' — they actually had the impudence to say 'assigned' to this car, and we have before us the prospect of passing the night in intimate communion with a fat father, who calls himself the Hon. Goliath — something, and his two sons — who — d—n it, sir! I shall take my ladies into a public car; I will not be classed with these — these people." And the earl stamped his feet and raised his voice so that there was some danger that he might be overheard by the Hon. Goliath Reachall and his two sons.

Mr. Dulon was amused. The ladies had disappeared, presumably to retire to rest in a section uninvaded by the Hon. Goliath and his intruding sons, and it was evident that the earl would have to suffer the profanation of his "private car" by the fellow-countrymen to whom he so strenuously objected. Besides the train was beginning to move.

Captain Jobson made a final effort to pacify the earl. "I must go and join Colonel Hodges," he said. "I hope you will not allow this small inconvenience to spoil the pleasure of your journey. All the trains are crowded, and the managers of the excursion have, at the last minute, had to make some new assignments. We shall all shake into place in time, as I used to tell my passengers on the 'Invincible.' Good sleep needed, to-night; see big wheat-fields in the morning," and the captain stepped nimbly across to the "Alsatia's" platform, failing, in his haste, to recognize Mr. Dulon, and disappeared within the car. The earl was so angry that he scarcely noticed the good captain's departure, and went on talking to himself. "The Hon. Goliath Reachall! And his two sons! One of them smoking a clay pipe. The Hon. Goliath *is* something huge in the Clerical Establishment of the War Office, is he? God bless my soul! This infernal caravan is actually moving!"

And the earl, finding that the third section of the excursion was rapidly leaving behind the sylvan glades and pellucid waters of Minnetonka, threw himself into a comfortable chair in the small anteroom of the "private car," and glowered desperately at the door behind which the Hon. Goliath Reachall of the Clerical Establishment of the War Office and his two sons were snugly ensconced in their cosey berths, chuckling over the fact that they had been assigned to the same car with the earl and the countess.

When Mr. Dulon's amusement at the earl's vexation had died away he began, still standing on the platform of the "Alsatia," to enjoy the solemn beauty of the night, and felt less than ever inclined to sleep. Light mists had spread themselves in silvery festoons between the pretty trees, whose trunks were fringed with pendent vines. The night air was strong and cool. Mr. Dulon felt that there was inspiration in it for him. Perhaps there was also a kind of intoxication in it, and the young painter was indulging in a strangely variegated dream of vast forests, noble rivers, seemingly illimitable wheat-fields through which squadrons of harvesters were making their devastating way with the precision of well-trained cavalry; rocky summits of mountains with ragged and wind-twisted trees, balancing insecurely among the gigantic stones; Indian encampments, picturesque with gaudy trappings and multi-colored blankets and sensuous dusky faces, and frightful cañons through which impetuous torrents went snarling—when a sudden jar loosened his footing; the train went recklessly around a sharp curve; a keen breeze tugged at his hat, almost taking it from his head, and he concluded that it would be prudent to go in.

. . . .

The sable porter gravely took his name and qualities, and, on learning that he was a painter, led the way through the car to the smoking-room, which had been transformed into a studio, and which, as Mr. Dulon was informed by the dignified darkey, already had one occupant. "He's an Englishman," added the porter, pausing with his hand on the door as if, after the announcement of this important fact, Mr. Dulon might take it into his head to bolt incontinently; "but I don't guess he'll give ye any trouble. Calls himself the 'Hon. Bevis Ringdale;' hyar's his card on de do'," and the darkey pointed to a neat sketch, comically conceived, representing an enraged buffalo charging madly upon a frightened painter, who had been bold enough to sit down in front of the monarch of the plains, with the intention of depicting him.

"Another honorable, and a fellow-artist," said Mr. Dulon; "I am sure that I shall find him agreeable. But — perhaps he is retiring?" for the negro opened the door of the little compartment, without knocking at it.

The Hon. Bevis Ringdale was not retiring. On the contrary he had the appearance of a man who intended to sit up all night, with that profound disdain for repose which one always manifests at the beginning of a long journey. He was a handsome, dark-haired, dark-eyed young Englishman, neatly dressed in a gray travelling-suit, and his Hungarian felt hat, with a feather in it, gave him a jaunty air. He had rigged above the seat, in which he was installed with his sketching-tools around him, a strong reflecting lamp, which threw a bright glow on a sketch that was undergoing his critical inspection. He turned the picture from side to side, daintily caressing it with his delicate white hands, flicking the dust from it and smiling at it as if its contemplation awakened amusing memories. He was quite absorbed in his sketch, and it was not until Mr. Dulon had been able to study him for a full minute that he looked up and said, hastily: —

"I beg pardon. I fancy my things are in your way." And he sprang forward, beginning to bring his belongings, with the adroitness of an old traveller, into the smallest possible compass.

Mr. Dulon explained that he had come to share

the room, and begged the artist not to give himself the smallest trouble.

"Then you are the other artist. Two of a trade. Yet we *shall* agree. This is to be our home for the next fortnight. A sleeping-room by night, a studio by day. If it were not for the dust it would be positively delightful. The gentlemen beyond the partition are somewhat noisy over their cards; but one might find the same inconvenience at a country inn. Here is my sketch of the platform at Minnetonka Hotel, with all the notables at the table of honor. Huge banquet, wasn't it? How do you like the sketch? President Arthur frowning as ex-President Grant comes in late and finds his way to his seat, amid thunders of applause. Wasn't it amusing? Allow me to introduce myself, and so disabuse you of the notion that I am troubled with British shyness. Bevis Ringdale, at your service; nation, English; manufacturer of novels in three volumes, and pictures in colors too lively to please my compatriots. They think my Venetian subjects ought to have woolly skies. On the contrary they find my novels too sad. I suspect that I was born too late in a world too old. And you?"

Dulon Floyd was heartily pleased with this new acquaintance, and he said so, giving the enthusiastic young Englishman a frank account of his own identity, and the circumstances which had prompted him to undertake the mammoth excursion. He now began to remember that he had seen the name of "Bevis Ringdale" in print more than once, in connection with amateur theatricals in high life, the designing of costumes for a grand revival of "Romeo and Juliet," and in critical correspondence, in daily journals, concerning the annual exhibitions of the Royal Academy. He ventured to say so to the Englishman, who colored like a girl, and smiled mischievously as he answered: —

"Yes, the study of costumes for the theatricals was a source of great annoyance to my family — or, I should more correctly say, to some members of my family. When I dabbled in literature they groaned in spirit; my appearance as a painter was considered by some of them as a crowning stroke; but the stage! I went away to South Africa on a sketching-tour to escape from my mother's wrath, forgetting that she could send it after me by letter; and she did send it. In the course of your visits to London perhaps you saw the 'Croydon,' an Arcadian pastoral for which I designed the scenery and costumes. No! It was quite a success. I will show you the sketches of the dresses to-morrow.

By the way, are we rivals? I promised to send notes of the tour to the 'Illustrated' in London."

Mr. Dulon explained that he had but one commission directly connected with the excursion, and hoped that they might both be able to enjoy themselves frankly without too much thought of engrossing duty. He found that the Hon. Bevis Ringdale, who was evidently a younger son of an aristocratic English family, intended to visit San Francisco before his return from the Pacific Coast. "I have a mission there," he said, "a painful one." His bright features clouded, and he glanced hastily at the young American, as if he regretted his frankness. "I am told," he added, "that we can take steamer from Oregon to California, when the excursion is ended. And now I shall clear away my traps, and I am sure you are ready for bed."

Just then the colored porter peeped in, and informed them that the train would stop for half an hour at a junction. "Ef I make up de bed now, yo' kin turn in quiet when the cyars is standin' still," he ventured to remark.

The young men took the hint, and went out to the platform as the long train drew up in the midst of an odorous forest, near a picturesque wooden station. The great boughs of the tall trees waved majestically in the night wind; and in the distance some hounds could be heard musically baying. "These new States have a powerful attraction for my countrymen," said the Hon. Bevis Ringdale. "I fancy there are an hundred English noblemen and — investing men among the members of this excursion party. Have you met any of them?"

"I have had the pleasure of meeting the Earl of Offast. I crossed the ocean on the 'Athabaska' with him."

"The Earl of Offast here?" said the young Englishman. "A walking arsenal, as usual, I suppose. Intent on the destruction of the humbler animals! He is a very distinguished sportsman. He should have taken Lady Offast with him to restrain his instinct for slaughter."

"Oh, Lady Offast and — and her cousin, Lady Helena Roderick, accompany him."

"Lady Helena Roderick!" The Hon. Bevis Ringdale spoke almost sharply, imperiously, and looked up so quickly at Mr. Dulon that the youthful American felt his heart beating faster than usual. He found himself staring at the Englishman, and beginning to regard his newly found acquaintance with a curiosity not unmingled with vague suspicion.

"Yes, Lady Helena," he said, his lips unconsciously caressing the name which was daily becoming dearer to him. "May I ask if you know her?"

"We have met," he answered. He had not quite regained his self-possession, and turned away for a moment as if to hide his face. Mr. Dulon heard him say: —

"Lady Helena? and going in the same direction! How strange! What can it mean?"

Mr. Dulon was mystified; and he now perceived more clearly than at any time since he had left Liverpool, by the unreasoning jealousy which suddenly sprung into his heart and burned there like a consuming flame, that he loved Lady Helena.

Was the bright and frank young English painter a rival? This was a question for the present so environed with mystery that Mr. Dulon found, when at six o'clock in the morning he sprang out of his berth in the improvised studio bedroom, that its consideration had prevented him from sleeping a wink.

CHAPTER XII.

IN DAKOTA.

On the morning after the start most of the excursionists had aching heads. Some of them were frank enough to attribute this to the prolonged festivities of the preceding day; others to the excitements attending the midnight departure; but the truth was that the keen air of the early day in the great uplands across which the four trains were making their way was responsible for the majority of the headaches. Mr. Dulon and his new acquaintance were up betimes, glad to quit their somewhat dusty bedroom studio, and, after a hasty toilet, they went out on the platform of the "Alsatia." Just then the train stopped, and the colored porter came to inform them that they could have an hour's walk if they desired it, "as our train kaint move crost de Red River afore de trains with General Grant an' de rest of de big fellers moves out of Fargo."

The young men, without entering into the details of their geographical situation, swung lightly down from the platform and were starting for a brisk walk on the breezy plain when Captain Jobson's voice was heard hailing "Mr. Dulon." The painter turned, and his heart beat a bit faster than usual as he saw Lady Helena, escorted by the venerable mariner and followed by the earl, Lady Offast, and one or two strange gentlemen, issuing from the private car.

"Wait for us; we will be alongside in a minute," cried the cheery captain.

Now it happened that the Hon. Bevis Ringdale went straight on ahead, as if he had heard nothing, and Mr. Dulon did not ask him to halt. The young Englishman was curiously examining the tall grasses, and gathering small stones and thrusting them into his pockets, as Lady Helena and her escort came up with Mr. Dulon, who bowed, and waited to hear Lady Helena's appreciation of the first night of the excursion.

"Good-morning," she said, merrily, "and it *is* a good morning. This is paradise, after the baking ovens of New York and Chicago, and — yes — I will not except Minnetonka. And fancy you are at present walking on my domain. For here — on the borders of the Red River of the North — is *my* investment. Cousin, please tell Mr. Floyd all about it. These gentlemen," pointing to the strangers, "have been kind enough to come an hundred miles out of their way to show us our purchase. Is it not grand?"

Mr. Floyd was pleased, and said so.

"It extends for twenty miles, does it not, cousin? And it is to be all in wheat, and every autumn we are to come to see the harvest, are we not, cousin? With the harvesters in long lines, like cavalry manœuvring, did you not say so, cousin?"

"Helena," said Lady Offast, faintly, "how can you talk of crossing that odious Atlantic twice every year? It makes me quite giddy to think of the nauseous green water. And, my dear, remember that there are strangers present."

Lady Helena blushed at the reproof. She felt inexplicably gay on this fresh and bright day, and the contemplation of the broad acres, all hers, and capable of such limitless development, had put a fever in her brain. She was just beginning a second enthusiastic series of remarks about Moorhead, the route to Pembina and Winnipeg, the great lakes of Manitoba, and other details which she had heard from the new-comers who had "boarded" the train at a station called Brainerd, expressly to pay their respects to the earl and his pretty cousin, when she noticed the Hon. Bevis Ringdale, who, at the sound of her voice, had turned quickly enough, and now stood gazing at her and irresolute to approach her. Mr. Dulon's heart was not comforted by what he now observed. At sight of the dark-eyed young Englishman, Lady Helena grew deadly pale, and, retreating a few steps, reached out her hand to the countess as if she were about to faint. Lady Offast was also evidently much disturbed, and turned hastily away, as if hoping to escape the Englishman's notice. There was an embarrassing silence, broken suddenly by the round, full tones of the earl, who strode forward, saying: —

"By Jove! there's young Ringdale! Now, who would have thought of seeing him here? How do, Master Amateur? How came you here and what may you be trying your agile hand at just at this particular time? Sketchin', hey? Well, well; I trust you will not make guys of us in the 'Illustrated.' Surely you recognize Lady Offast, and my cousin, Lady Helena?"

The young Englishman, after cordially greeting the earl, advanced to the ladies, and bowed, rather stiffly. His manner was so constrained, and the meeting was so evidently trying to him that the earl looked on in surprise. But in a moment he fancied that it "was all the young fellow's shyness," and he turned away to talk about birds and other game with the new-comers. Mr. Dulon observed that Lady Helena's hand trembled as she gave it to the Hon. Bevis Ringdale, and that she did not give it without a singular hesitation. The subtle instinct of love told him that there was a secret between these two persons, and a dull suspicion sent a pain into his heart. Lady Helena spoke but a minute or two with the youth, and of her low and hurried words Mr. Dulon heard but three. They were, "Westward," and "Lord John."

The Hon. Bevis Ringdale turned from this brief interview with a shadow on his face, and Lady Helena grew paler and paler, as if she had seen a spirit instead of a fine, frank young fellow, clean of feature and symmetrical of limb. Lady Offast beckoned to Jenks, who was hovering sympathetically near at hand, and attempted to commit her cousin to the maid's care. But the young lady suddenly rallied, and resumed her promenade with Captain Jobson, gossiping about the future resources of her domain, and appealing to Mr. Dulon from time to time for support of her enthusiastic prophecies. Meantime Bevis Ringdale calmly took a seat among the grasses, trying to contemplate the far away horizon; but it was not of the horizon that he was thinking.

Presently there was a warning whistle from the locomotive, and people hurried to resume their places in the train. Lady Helena and Captain Jobson, closely followed by Mr. Dulon, ran nimbly back from the knoll whence they had been surveying the future "estate," and were in the "private car" long before it began to move; but the earl tried to be dignified, fancying that the engine driver would not dare to move off until the dignity of England had been safely lodged on the train. The earl found that he had made a mistake, and had to run like a deer (which he could do if he liked), to avoid being left alone on the banks of the Red River. He was much annoyed, and his annoyance was doubled when he discovered that the Hon. Goliath Reachall — who was something important in the Clerical Establishment of the War Office — and the Hon. Goliath Reachall's two sons, were grinning unreservedly at his rather undignified speed.

As for the Hon. Goliath and his two sons they were this morning absolute thorns in the earl's flesh. The Offasts had a horror of anything in the faintest degree like roystering, and when the earl found the Hon. Goliath, clad in a red and black striped coat, a pair of plaid trousers, thick boots and a most absurd straw hat, seated at a small table in the saloon of the car and refreshing himself from a bottle of "prepared cocktail," found in the car pantry, his annoyance was not dissembled. The ladies had also been greeted, on their entrance into the car, by the apparition of one of the sons in a very fragmentary condition of toilet and towelling himself vigorously after an extempore bath at the marble tank in the wash-room.

"D—n it!" said the earl under his breath; "this is horrible! I shall not be able to exist until we can make a change! I—I should like to pitch the Hon. Goliath, with his red and black coat, into the Red River. I—I shall state the case to Mr. Villard; as manager of this excursion I am certain that he will not allow our privacy to be invaded in this extraordinary manner."

As fortune would have it the Hon. Goliath Reachall and his sons were anxious, when the train had reached the little town of Fargo, on the Dakota side of the Red River, to witness the rejoicings of the citizens, and, during their absence, the earl and the ladies managed to breakfast quietly, a colored cook attached to the car serving them many wonderful new dishes evolved from the resources of his rolling larder. But the excellence of the claret and the juiciness of the steak were lost upon the earl, who was in mortal terror lest the invading Reachalls might return and claim seats at the table, and recognition from their aristocratic fellow-travellers.

Fargo was a wooden town with brick variations and "with an electric light system in full operation before there was the slightest need of it," the earl said. But Fargo looked larger to him when he was told that its population of ten thousand people, and its banks, hotels, churches, opera-houses, grain-elevators, newspapers, and high-schools had all been fixed there within a single decade. Lady Helena silently contrasted Fargo with Branley, the sleepy, centuries-old town near the earl's country-seat in ancient England; and she was forced to admit that Branley had not grown much more in ten hundred years than Fargo in ten. Branley was the more solid of the two; but Lady Helena was not sure that solidity was so tremendous an advantage after all. She admired the beautiful altars erected to the goddess Ceres in this enterprising Fargo, and was duly surprised at the mammoth yet coarse-fibred vegetables piled in appetizing heaps in front of these altars.

But her greatest surprise came when, a score of miles beyond Fargo, the train stopped in the midst of a seemingly boundless wheat farm, and in every direction, as far as the eye could reach, she saw the yellow stubble, the odorous heaps of grain, and the steam threshing-machines at work with remorseless accuracy and tireless energy preparing food for the millions. She had heard of the American tendency to exaggeration, and so she listened with an amused smile to the brown-bearded, clear-eyed gentleman-farmer who rode up beside their car on his sinewy little steed, and, touching his hat with the grace of a *preux chevalier*, told her and her companions how this one farm through which their route lay comprised no less than seventy-five thousand acres; how a regiment of men and hundreds of horses and mules were employed thereon; and how no sight, not even that of the summer ocean gently caressed by the breezes, was more fascinating than that of the rippling sea of golden wheat waves, in mid-August, before the reapers begin their devastating labor.

"Do you mean to say," interrupted the earl, who

was standing behind Lady Helena and his wife while this recital was in progress, "that if we had been here two weeks ago we could have seen — er — twenty square miles of waving wheat-fields, and — er — a swath of one hundred and ninety-two feet cut and bound in a — er — in a twinkling, by twenty-four self-binding reapers? — er — that's very extraor" —

"I DID say so, sir," said the brown-bearded horseman emphatically, with that peculiar flash of resentment in his eye which always gives the danger-signal when a Western or a Southern man fancies his veracity impeached.

"Oh, certainly — er — of course," remarked the earl, hastily falling back one or two paces. "I thought — er — I so understood you. God bless my soul! and your reaping-machines on this farm can lay low twenty miles of grain in a swath one-fifth of a mile wide in the course of a single day? Dear me!"

After the brown-bearded man had told them many other astonishing things, and had saluted them and ridden away, glancing backward occasionally, as if he were half-inclined to return and inquire what the earl meant by presuming to question his statements, Lady Helena fell into a revery. She saw, as in a vision, the naked and untilled tract beyond the Red River — *her* investment — transformed into a goodly series of wheat-fields, lustrous underneath the genial August sun. She saw the broad-hatted horsemen swinging along the paths; the "ploughing," the "seeding," the "harrowing," the "harvesting" platoons at work; the mellow stores of grain in fat elevators; and she heard the shrill whistles of the threshing-machines answering each other, as if they were sentient monsters, neighing and champing with unflagging joy. She was so absorbed that she scarcely observed the slow motion of the train as it resumed its journey. But she started when Lady Offast placed one hand gently on her shoulder, and said, in a faint whisper: —

"Helena, were you thinking of Lord John?"

"No, cousin, I was thinking of nothing of the sort," she answered, sharply.

"I am very glad of it," said the countess, taking the girl by the hand and drawing her after her into the car.

. . . .

Next morning the four trains were at Bismarck, a new and pretty town set down upon the bare Dakota hills, not far from the bold banks of the Missouri River. The journey thither from the wheat-farms had been a strange experience to the Eastern folk and to the foreigners, who for the first time were visiting the North-west. Mr. Dulon's impression was that a couple of centuries must elapse before these naked plains, these deep but treeless valleys, these rounded hills, destitute of a single shade tree, could be transformed into cheerful abodes for the children of men. The dusty streets of Bismarck were filled with picturesque processions of school children, rustic beauties, tradesmen, and pioneers; and these enthusiastic residents wound in sinuous line up a long acclivity, on the summit of which the corner-stone of the future capitol of the State was to be laid with appropriate ceremonies, conducted by General Grant, the officials of the newly completed railroad, the Secretary of the Interior and other dignitaries. The earl, who had been instructed as to the excellent shooting to be had in the neighborhood, donned a remarkable hunting-suit, combining all the colors of the rainbow, and accompanied by Captain Jobson and Colonel Hodges, by one or two local sportsmen, and by his valet laden with game-bags, he set forth at sunrise on an expedition, to the consternation of Lady Offast, who had heard that the hostile Sioux had committed depredations in all the country round about only a few years ago, and who fully expected to hear that her lord and master had engaged during the day in a desperate fight with savages. She positively declined to climb the hill and witness the ceremony, and remained closeted in the car with Jenks; the Reachall family fortunately being absent on a tour of observation.

Dulon Floyd, despite his vague suspicions and his heartache, could not refrain from asking Lady Helena to share with him a carryall which an army officer had hospitably offered him, and she accepted readily. Half way to the scene of the ceremonial, they overtook the Hon. Bevis Ringdale, striding along in sturdy British fashion, with a sketching-kit on his back.

"Shall I ask Mr. Ringdale to take a seat with us?" said the young American, reining up the horse.

"By all means," answered Lady Helena, unconcernedly, and the handsome Englishman was hailed. He clambered in, chatting merrily, and appeared to have lost his *malaise* of the preceding day. He had already "got the points of the compass," as he phrased it, and directed their attention to the white walls of Fort Abraham Lincoln five miles away on the western bank of the Missouri — the fort around which the Sioux warriors raged in vain night and day in 1872 and 1873, and where the gallant Custer passed the closing years of the heroic life which he laid down in the disastrous expedition to the valley of the Little Big Horn. He showed them the dark timber line along the stream, and told them of the vast bridge built of iron, steel, and granite so strong as to defy the terrible ice-packs of the capricious Missouri in winter, and its appalling floods in spring. He had already had a conversation with "Sitting Bull," the warrior diplomat of the Sioux nation, who, after having buried the hatchet (in the skulls of many defenceless white settlers), had come boldly into the town which he had so many times tried to destroy, and was posing as a celebrity before the somewhat inimical populace. He told them how the valley of the upper Missouri had, from time immemorial, been known as "The Indian Paradise," because of its mild climate, due to the warm air brought by the westerly winds from off the heated "Japan current" in the Pacific Ocean. In fact, he talked so entertainingly, and with such affluence of facts and figures, that the young American cried out to him in admiration: —

"You talk like a special correspondent. Surely you ought to have been one."

"I *am* one," said this versatile "younger son;" "I am commissioned in that capacity by one of the best of our provincial journals." And he laughed heartily. "I can turn my hand to anything."

They came to the outskirts of the crowd, and the Hon. Bevis called Lady Helena's attention to a bronze-colored elderly man, who looked like a peaceable old woman, and who wore two feathers twisted in his coal-black hair. This was the renowned "Sitting Bull," enthroned in a wagon and busily engaged in selling his autograph, written, not in the picture language of his people, but in painfully elaborated English script, to all who cared to pay the modest sum of one dollar and a half.

While they were contemplating the subjugated chieftain the cracking of pistol-shots was heard, and Lady Helena and her companions looked westward to see half-a-dozen horsemen galloping furiously, attacked and followed by an equal number of Indians. The English lady's heart beat fast. Had the countess' sombre predictions been verified? Had the earl's hunting party already been attacked?

A tall, pale-faced young man, arrayed in gray clothes, a linen duster, and a white felt hat, came briskly forward and addressed himself, with a consequential smirk, to the little group. "There is not the slightest occasion for alarm," he said. "It's only a sham-fight, to show how it was done formerly. Excuse me. Saw you on our train. Colleagues, I believe," bowing to Dulon and the Hon. Bevis. "Saw the lady with the English gentleman, on our train."

Lady Helena turned away, becoming interested in the Indian chief to the utter exclusion of all other terrestrial objects from her vision. But the pale-faced young man was undaunted.

"Whew!" he said. "Isn't it hot! Call this a pleasure-trip. I call it martyrdom, slavery. Look here!" He pulled a voluminous note-book from his breast-pocket. "Twenty-two pages of report on the wheat-crop prospects along the line. Sent it all in by telegraph from here. Nine interviews with German statesmen, chemists, and writers. Sent *them* in by telegraph, too. May I exchange cards? My name is Caswell P. Rusher, of Chicago. Shall I introduce you to 'Sitting Bull'?"

"Oh, thanks!" said the Hon. Bevis Ringdale, with refreshing coolness. "That *would* be a great privilege. Do you happen to be a relative of his?"

Mr. Caswell P. Rusher looked blank for an instant, but his animation was no whit lessened. "Ha, ha! Very good. Not exactly. Thought you might like to interview him. English, I presume?"

"Your presumption," said the Hon. Bevis, showing his white teeth, "is apparently never at fault. Here is my card. And now if you will excuse me for a few minutes, I mean to make a pencil-sketch of 'Sitting Bull.'"

"See you later," said Caswell P. Rusher, and seemed to melt into the crowd as the Hon. Bevis alighted from the carryall.

CHAPTER XIII.

IN THE BAD LANDS.

"THAT was a narrow escape," said Caswell P. Rusher, popping his head into the door of the earl's private car and addressing his remark to Lady Helena, who happened at that moment to be the only occupant of the small "sitting-room."

Lady Helena started, blushed, and then proceeded to look at the intruder with a freezing dignity, which resulted, in a moment or two, in his utter confusion.

"I thought you might like to know," he stammered, as he began to retreat, "that we have just had a most miraculous escape from a grand smash-up. As we were crossing a trestle over the gully, which you can see now if you will take the trouble to look out of the window, a wheel flew off from one of the two locomotives driving this train, and if it had not been for the immense weight of these Pullman cars we should all have gone to 'Kingdom Come.' I thought you and the earl — Good evening!"

Caswell P. Rusher retired precipitately, for Lady Helena had arisen, with anger in her look. There was "a peculiar blaze in her eyes," as he described it afterwards, which made him regret that he had tried to tell her the news. But he found in the Reachalls, father and sons, a most sympathetic audience. They emerged from their lounging-places in the car, lighted their pipes, and set off through the gathering darkness with Caswell P. to investigate the results of the accident which had brought the train to a stand-still and had alarmed two-thirds of the passengers.

"An accident! How romantic!" said Lady Helena, when Caswell P. and his companions had departed. She went out upon the platform and looked down into the grassy, yawning gulf to the bottom of which another turn of the wheels might have sent her. The "sleepers" at the end of the trestle-work were torn and twisted; the locomotives at the head of the train were hissing furiously like monsters angered by delay. One of them was helplessly crippled; the other, ahead of it, had exhausted its strength in useless endeavors to pull its injured companion out of the way. The telegraphers had climbed one of the tall poles by the wayside, and were "tapping the wire," calling for help from the small town five or six miles behind them. Fortunately this town was a "repair-station," where locomotives, workmen, and tools were sure to be plentiful, and the delay would not be very vexatious.

Lady Helena heard the crack of a rifle, and, with Indians in her mind, looked quickly in the direction whence the sound came. She smiled as she saw her energetic cousin tramping across a field a little beyond the sinister gully, and enjoying a season of shooting. Behind him stalked his "man," picking up such small game as the earl had the luck to bring down.

The accident and its consequences delayed "train number three" for many hours, and it was nearly midnight when, on a track built round the disabled engines, the convoy moved away once more. The countess had retired in despair, telling Jenks that she expected to be killed before morning, and that she really must try to get a little nap. But the earl had come back from his shooting expedition with such an interesting account of the Bad Lands, the *Mauvaises Terres* of the old French voyageurs — which mysterious and fantastical region they were to enter upon in an hour or two — that Lady Helena had decided to sit up with him. So she took a seat with the earl upon the broad-railed platform of the private car. The train moved very slowly, and the pair were exceedingly comfortable in their arm-chairs. The earl lighted a cigar, and began to descant upon the various inconveniences of the public dining-car, which an accident to the cook attached to his private conveyance had compelled him to patronize since their departure from Bismarck.

"Just fancy," said the earl, "when I tried to jog the memory of one of the blacks about the brand of champagne at dinner to-day, he said, with the air of a field-marshal, at least, 'You don't need to tell me twice, boss (I believe, upon my soul, he called me 'boss'); it's my trade to remember.' Now, what do you think of that?"

"Fancy!" said Lady Helena. But she was not thinking of that at all. She was thinking of a young painter who, at that very moment, was drawing pencil sketches of her dainty face in his studio bedroom, while the Hon. Bevis Ringdale "washed in" his sketch of the ceremonial of laying the corner-stone at Bismarck.

The darkness was pleasant. The night was warm and odorous. The train rumbled on through the shadows as if it were feeling its way, and were determined to make no mistakes. Now it went cautiously around a curve, and came out upon a vast naked plain, sombre and forbidding as the wide-stretching sea. Now it skirted a belt of timber, or rows of mounds which looked like gigantic tombs of some colossal departed race of kings. Now it stole hesitatingly down a long grade, past broad spaces covered with waving grasses, and in and out of the perfumed juniper thickets. Beside the water-courses were lines of knotted, twisted, and deformed pines, stunted in their capricious growth. Here were no habitations, no camps of cowboys, no signs of the handiwork of man, save this single line of railway track upon its narrow bed. Lady Helena felt as if she were travelling into an enchanted land, full of goblins, fairies, and giants. Presently the train came to a halt in a valley filled with strange formations of earth — some of them like petrified ocean billows, some like pyramids, some lofty as triumphal arches, many shaped like enormous animals, monsters such as might properly be supposed to inhabit so phenomenal a region. Away beyond these strange things there was a red light, as if the earth were aflame. The earl and his cousin gazed with astonishment at this light, which flickered like the fires of a volcano.

"See, cousin! there is a cliff fairly ablaze!" cried Lady Helena. "What a mysterious place! I feel like the huntsman in 'Der Freischutz,' when he is invoking the demon! It would not at all surprise me to see that familiar of devils suddenly peeping up from between these cars and inviting us to a promenade in the bewitched glens hereabouts. What *is* that mass of flame?"

"Will you let me tell you?" said Mr. Dulon's voice.

Lady Helena murmured a greeting, and candor compels the statement that the earl growled his salutation.

Nevertheless Mr. Dulon, who had been delighted to find his love impressed by the freaks of nature in the Bad Lands, seated himself on the railing and told them of the lignite lying close to the surface of the soil, — the lignite which had been smouldering for ages in this strange region where gigantic battle once raged between wave and flame. He told them the secret of the vast buttes, with their horizontal bands of savage color, with their precipitous sides and symmetrical summits, with their dark and brown stripes of impure lignite, or their bases of yellow, their girdles of creamy white, and their cardinal cap of red.

"No sleep to-night for us," he said, gaily, "for Ringdale has sworn to see with me the effects of the first touch of sunlight on this 'Pyramid Park.' 'Dawn in the Bad Lands,' a good title for a picture, is it not? I fancy I can see the hanging committee rejecting it now, on the score of its extravagance and unnaturalness of color!" And he laughed merrily and long.

A moment later he said, "Would it not be charming to wander through this region by night — a night like this — with a brooding sky — an ominous heaven — no moon — and these ghostly fires dancing in the distance?"

Something in his voice appealed strangely to Lady Helena. She felt half inclined to arise, to give him her hand, and to say, "Come! let us wander forth together, despite hobgoblins and magic."

"I don't mind going, just for a lark," suddenly said the earl, "if you let me take a gun and send you one. But suppose the train moves off and leaves us to starve in the Bad Lands."

"Or to be eaten by bears," suggested Lady Helena.

"This train will not stir from this spot for twelve hours; such is the order," said Mr. Dulon. "It was given for our benefit, that we may sketch the dawn and that" —

"Mr. Caswell P. Rusher may sharpen his imagination against the flaming mounds," said Lady Helena in a very low voice.

The painter was dazzled by this prospect of a romantic excursion with Lady Helena in the park at night. He hastened away to invite Ringdale, who had already conceived the same idea of a prowl in the park. When the two painters came back to the private car, they found that the countess and Jenks had been aroused, and, with the air of Christian martyrs about to enter a den of wild beasts, were waiting, wrapped in picturesque cloaks, to undertake what Lady Offast called a "mad promenade." The earl selected a fire-arm from his arsenal for each of the painters, and the little party left the train and stole silently into the shadows. Jenks and the valet, the latter individual provided with a revolver and a lantern, brought up the rear. The countess, at first very timid, and half disposed openly to reproach her husband for his freak, gained courage when she observed that other parties, evidently animated by the same purpose as theirs, had left the train and were "threading the dusky boles" of the dwarf trees, scrambling among the mounds, and waving their torches in front of the broad bands of crimson at the bases of the bluffs.

The earl was perpetually straggling off in pursuit of imaginary game, and, Ringdale gallantly devoting himself to the countess, Mr. Dulon found himself much alone with Lady Helena, who accepted his various offers of assistance with more grace than usual. After two hours of walking and a hundred false alarms from the earl they arrived at the edge of an elevated plateau, where a majestic and singular spectacle awaited them.

In the foreground stood a giant pillar of rock, noble as the figure of Memnon among the Egyptian sands. It was capped with a flat mass, which from a distance looked like a triumphal crown or garland, and Lady Helena said it seemed to her the massive statue of some deity. To the left other pillars, capped in the same fashion, rose to even greater heights than that of their isolated brother. Midway stood a symmetrical rock, which resembled an altar. Through the centre of the plateau flowed a broad and deep stream, which, had the visitors seen it by day, would have appeared to them yellow as the ancient Tiber, and away beyond the sweet calm of this plain and the coursing stream was the broad band of fire, which threw a kind of boding glimmer upon the whole scene.

"Hush!" said Lady Helena, as the countess began to prattle. "Do you not feel like kneeling here, at respectful distance from yonder great altar, and waiting for the procession of priests that is sure to come just at dawn to offer prayers and fruits and flowers to these silent and monstrous gods?"

The countess laughed feebly, and the earl, who came up just then, said that he felt like nothing of the sort, but rather like having a glass of champagne. At this juncture the valet produced from a sack strapped to his back the materials for an excellent punch, including even the coveted champagne. Refreshed, the party resolved to remain in the open air until the dawn came, and the painters were to make their sketches under the critical gaze of their companions.

As faint tints of light began to appear in the eastern sky, dimming the baleful gleam of the far-away lignite fires, and bringing into view one by one the crimsons, the yellows, the whites, the grays, and the browns of the buttes, the countess complained that she was sleepy, and that if there was absolute certainty as to security from bears and other prowling creatures, and most especially from snakes, she desired to be bestowed with Jenks in the comfortable shadow of the great altar rock until the sketching was over and the return journey was announced. The earl and his "man" undertook to keep guard while the painters "laid in wait for the sunrise," as Lady Helena phrased it. Mr. Dulon all at once found that the countess had placed herself under his guardianship, perhaps relying on his superior judgment as to the manor born, and he was busy for some time making her a nest by the rocky edge among the petrified tree stumps and trunks which testified to the former existence of a forest on the plateau.

When he had finished his task, and had promised the countess and Jenks that none of the party should go beyond the sound of his voice, he went back to the vicinity of the isolated pillar god, and was a trifle startled to find himself alone. The others had strayed already; his promise to the countess had been betrayed even while he was making it. He threw down his sketching-kit, which had been strapped to his shoulders, and catching his rifle lightly in one hand, sprang forward over the irregular ground in search of the vanished ones. The silence and the loneliness affected him; they did not cause him alarm, but a vague sense of disquiet.

Now that he was alone he began to notice that everything around him was of colossal proportions, and he seemed the veriest pigmy when he reached the isolated pillar and stood looking up at it. He lost his sense of time in contemplation of this stupendous freak of nature, his artist's eye noting lovingly the contrasted colors which began to define themselves on its huge sides, as the sky became clearer and more clear. Suddenly a breeze of morning touched his brow. He started from his dawn-dream, and resumed his search with vigor.

Making his way with some difficulty around the base of the pillar he came abruptly upon an opening in the rock, through which he might have stepped, had he chosen to do so, down upon a small open space, sheltered, as it were, by the throne upon which the idol might be imagined to sit. He was about to pass through this aperture when he heard Lady Helena's voice, raised as if in indignation, and, looking up, he saw her standing face to face with Ringdale, beneath the so-called throne. The figures of the English painter and the lady stood out in bold relief against the eastern background of fire-illumined sky.

"You have no right to ask me that question," said Lady Helena to Ringdale.

What question could he have asked that might offend her? What secret had these two had in common? These thoughts shot through the young American's mind and left a sting behind them.

Ringdale was very pale. He bowed courteously at Lady Helena's passionate remark, and hesitated a moment before he answered.

"But consider, Lady Helena, that this is no ordinary matter, and that it is something nobler than curiosity that impels me to ask you such a question. It is you alone who can tell me all the truth about Lord John — Do you not think that my motive in asking you to tell me that truth is a worthy one?"

"It is — a noble one, and I respect and honor you for it. But I can tell you nothing."

"Helena, this is absurd; it is wicked. Come; our fathers were friends; we were children together; there is every reason why we should have no issue in such a case as this. Will you not tell me what I want to know?"

"I can tell you nothing."

"Was ever man so bejuggled?" said Ringdale, raising his hands to his head in a most un-English gesture of despair. "It seems like a dream, Lady Helena; if you cannot speak out, I can. It is now four years since I discovered that my elder — my only brother — was on the high road to perdition. How I loved that man! Lord John had been the ideal of my boyhood — and when a sudden revelation showed him to me as I had never dreamed that he could be — the best part of my life seemed taken from me."

"This is not for me to hear," whispered Floyd to himself. "Let me return" —

But as he moved Ringdale ceased speaking, and Lady Helena turned her head quickly towards the aperture in the rock. If he moved again they would hear and discover him. He would wait a moment.

Ringdale began again. "One day I discovered something else. It was that Lord John was madly in love with you, and that he believed his passion was reciprocated."

Lady Helena bowed her head, as if communing with a memory.

"I was thankful for that, as for a great blessing that might redeem my brother's life. At last he told me that he loved you; that he had spoken to you; that he was engaged to you — but that it must be kept a profound secret."

"He dared!" cried Lady Helena.

"And now, Lady Helena, explain to me the rest. Six months ago my brother disappeared from London — from his world. In vain have I sought to find him. I have used every means in my power. I wrote you two letters, which remain to this day unanswered."

"That is true," said Lady Helena. "I should have answered them. But I — I could not. And you must not ask me why."

"In despair," continued Ringdale, "I did something of which you will not approve. I went to your solicitor — my old friend and yours — and I urged him to advise me how to approach you on the subject of my brother's disappearance. Lady Helena, the solicitor gave me but one clue. He told me that the day before Lord John was known to have been seen in London for the last time you came to his office and demanded the sum of twenty thousand pounds in cash for immediate use. He ventured to inquire if you were aware how large was the sum which you took from your principal, and if you meant to make prudent use of it. You were greatly excited, and told him that you were mistress of your own; that there were circumstances in which one did not stop to think of prudence; that you demanded the money, and he could not refuse it. He gave you the money" —

"He has betrayed my confidence!" said Lady Helena, haughtily.

"But only to a friend who adores and reveres you. Tell me truly, Helena, was the solicitor right in his suspicions that that twenty thousand pounds was used to cover some one of the multitude of my brother's sins? And am I right in believing that you know his whereabouts now? Oh, tell me; I can save him!"

She shuddered and turned her face away. "I can tell you nothing," she said.

"The solicitor said to me: 'Look for your brother on the Pacific Coast on his way round the world. Perhaps you will find him.' I start for the Pacific Coast with this slender clue, and on the way I find you, Lady Helena, bound in the same direction. Once more let me ask you, do you know where my poor brother is to be found?"

"You may misunderstand me, condemn me, if you will," she answered, "but I can tell you nothing. And now listen to me for a moment. The secret which your brother confided to you is to remain a secret. No one in this world should know of — of his love for me except we three who know it already, and the solicitor — who guessed it."

"I do not misunderstand you, Helena," said

Ringdale, sorrowfully. "But you are wrong in shielding my brother, whatever he may have done, from one who loves him so truly, so faithfully as I do. I shall trouble you with no more questions."

"It is better so."

They turned, as by common impulse, to retrace their steps to the plateau, Mr. Dulon having emerged from the shadows as if he had been running, and said, "Ah, here you are at last! Lady Offast was beginning to be disturbed about your disappearance."

Just then a flood of rose color appeared on the sky, heralding the dawn, and it was reflected in Lady Helena's cheeks.

Dulon essayed to be cheerful as he strode beside the pair, but one dreadful thought came and laid siege to his soul. She loves another! she loves another! He could hear this phrase in the beating of his own heart.

CHAPTER XIV.

THE FIRELIGHT DANCE.

CASWELL P. RUSHER was seated on the platform of the "newspaper car," busily engaged in writing page after page of description of the characteristic features of the "Bad Lands," when the earl and his party returned from their excursion. As he saw them approaching, weary and dusty, he skipped down from his perch and went airily to accost them. "I am just closing my despatch," he said to Ringdale, who contemplated him with an air of intense astonishment, as if that were the most remarkable piece of news that he had heard for many a day.

"Really," said Ringdale, "you must not allow any solicitude for my welfare, don't you know, to interfere with the instant mailing, or telegraphing of that important document."

"That isn't exactly it," said the unabashed Caswell. "They told me that you had gone on a midnight prowl — ladies and all — and I thought I would just lay for you on your return, and get you to give me an adventure or two, to finish up my column with. See any Indians? Or cowboys?"

"Well, now that you mention it," observed Ringdale, "we heard considerable shooting on our left, while Mr. Floyd and I were engaged in making some studies of sunrise. I think that if you ask Lord Offast, who is fond of sport, he can tell you some blood-curdling things. How many of the poor creatures did you kill, Offast? Chicago pines for information on this particular point."

But Lord Offast suddenly became unapproachable, and, as he went into his "private car," was heard to mutter something which sounded very much like "more of Ringdale's ridiculous d—d nonsense." So Mr. Rusher avoided any further direct inquiry, and allowed the tired excursionists to depart in peace. When they had all disappeared, he bit his pencil savagely, and remarked to himself, "I don't like that Ringdale. He's insufferable. He wouldn't give me an adventure, wouldn't he? That's all right. I'll give *him* one." And he resumed his writing.

This was how the Hon. Bevis Ringdale came to appear in a Chicago journal as having been desperately frightened while sketching in the Bad Lands by the reports of a gun in the hands of one of his fellow-travellers, whom he mistook for a murderous Indian. Furthermore, Caswell P. set forth that on his return to the train, Ringdale was "held up" by a humorous cowboy, who compelled the British painter to lay aside his sketching-kit and hand over his watch and money before he informed him that it was all in fun. When Ringdale read this paragraph, which was handed to him by one of his friends in a London club some months thereafter, he was very angry for a few minutes — angry enough to have satisfied even the exacting malice of the vindictive Caswell P.

But ignorance is certainly comparative bliss, and meantime Ringdale, of course, suspected the enterprising reporter of no attack upon his reputation for courage or good sense. He went to his "studio," anxious to get two or three hours of sleep before the train started again. "How pale you are, Floyd!" he said to his companion. "One might fancy you had seen a ghost. Or is it the fatigue? There, we will not compare sketches now, old man. You are worn out; so turn in. Thank Heaven, it is cool in this box! And no dust for once in a way."

Floyd murmured some excuse for his dulness, and hid his anxiety and sorrow behind the curtains of his berth. But he could not sleep, and presently he arose, noiselessly, made a fresh toilet, and sat down on his camp-stool to work on his sketch. Just as he was beginning, a hand touched him lightly on his shoulder. He looked up; Ringdale was lying in his bed, which was above Floyd's, and had his shapely head propped thoughtfully on one hand.

"Excuse me," he said, "I wouldn't work now. You are too nervous. Will you — will you allow me to ask you a great favor?"

"Why, certainly" —

Ringdale laughed. "Like the man in the comedy of 'The Colonel.' Ever see it? Very good. The fact is, Mr. Floyd, that I want a little help in a delicate matter, and something in your face and manner tells me that I can count on you for that help. Did I not hear you say that you intend to leave the excursion at Portland, and to return to the East *via* San Francisco?"

"That is my intention," said Floyd. "Unless — unless I found the sketching on the North Pacific Coast tempting, I think I said."

"When we first met I hinted to you that I had a painful mission in San Francisco." Floyd laid aside his work, and looked up at the bright, handsome face of the Englishman, with an eagerness which he could not conceal. "You remember that? Well — I have discovered — it is not necessary to say exactly where or how — that my mission is to be more difficult even than I expected. And I all at once made up my mind — in a flash — don't you know? — American fashion — as Offast says — to solicit your aid."

Floyd knew exactly what was coming. He was to be enlisted in the search for the mysterious "Lord John;" for the elder brother in whom Lady Helena was so strangely interested; for the man who had won Lady Helena's heart; the man whom she was apparently at this moment shielding from the consequences of his own misdeeds.

"I shall be happy to help — as best I can," he said.

"I knew you would," said the Englishman; and he *looked* his gratitude. There was no need of hand-shake, or effusive language; Ringdale had the true English eloquence of quiet and intense earnestness.

"It isn't much to tell," he went on. "My elder and only brother, God bless him! has gone to the devil. In addition to that, he has gone round the world. I will spare you the details of the circumstances — most of them, at least. It will be enough for you to know that this brother of mine disappeared from London six months ago, after having committed almost every conceivable folly. He was the head of a family that is — ancient, and that had always been rich. He had encumbered his estates with debts — until he began to be seriously embarrassed. One day he — went mad — I suppose" — Ringdale paused a moment — and caught his breath — "for he committed a crime. I would have sworn that such a thing were not possible; but he did it; he — obtained money by forging the signature of a well-known nobleman who had always been his friend. Before settling-time came he got this deadly paper — which was in the hands of a Jew who had charged him sixty per cent. for discounting it, in irregular fashion — back again, and destroyed it. Indiscreet friends, who loved him, lent him the money to do this, gave it him blindly when he said he must have it or be ruined. The same friends packed him off out of London — away from England, fearful lest he might get into fresh follies — if not crimes."

Ringdale had now lowered his voice almost to a whisper. A faint flush suffused his cheeks. Floyd at once pitied and admired him.

"Loving indiscretion did just what it might have been expected to do; it attracted undue attention to my brother. Poor Lord John! gossip burst forth, and he and his were plentifully scandalized, I assure you. His sudden disappearance got into the papers; there was some sinister talk about the vacant seat in Parliament; and the more charitable suspected foul play. I learned that my brother was making a long tour in China and Japan, possibly in Australia, and that he was likely to come back to England *via* America; but I could learn nothing more. The friends who had saved him seem to have had some strange reason for concealing his whereabouts; they would — they will tell me nothing."

Floyd could not take his eyes from Ringdale's face. He was anxious for the *dénouément*. Although he felt convinced that the young Englishman would not mention Lady Helena, he was certain that he would find some absolute clue to her action.

"Less than a month ago," continued Ringdale, "a dirty-looking fellow, half Greek, half devil, overtook me on the embankment as I was hastening home from a London theatre at midnight. At first I thought he was a footpad, but he soon undeceived me on that point. 'Are you the Hon. Bevis Ringdale?' said he. 'I am.' 'Younger brother of' —'What's that to you, fellow?' I said. 'Stand aside, or'— But something in the blackguard's eye made me listen to him. 'You will be heir to a fine estate,' he said, 'if your brother, who has disappeared so oddly, dies on his travels and is known to have left no issue. But I will do you the honor to suppose that you would rather see your elder brother back in his place, restored to honor and respect, than possess the estate.' I wanted to kick the fellow, but I didn't. The story he told me was this: The old Jew, who had discounted the forged note for my brother, had died suddenly. This creature, the only relative and clerk, succeeded to the ancient thief's business. Among the Jew's papers was found a second bill for a large sum, signed by the same person whose name my poor brother had forged. Something about the circumstances connected with the taking up of the other bill had aroused this blackguard's suspicions, and he concluded that this one was a forgery. So now he came to me to know what he should do. And he actually had the audacity to smile, and to assume a friendly demeanor as we stood facing each other in the dull gas-light down by the Thames."

"How did you learn that the first bill really was a forgery?" inquired Floyd.

"From the solicitor of the friend who had been most directly instrumental in saving him."

Ah! Ringdale had not said this to Lady Helena during the interview of the morning. Perhaps she was still unaware that her lover had committed a forgery. He hardly knew why this thought drifted through his mind.

Ringdale resumed his story: "My first impression was that this midnight prowler was a liar and a blackmailer; that no second note, forged or genuine, had been given by my brother; and that this fellow had been shrewd enough to suspect the first forgery, and had thought he could fleece us all by means of stories about another one. I ventured to suggest this; and the man smiled and answered, 'I see you are suspicious. Very well. I will take the note to-morrow morning to the nobleman who is supposed to have signed it, and we can find out the truth.' —'That,' I said, 'would be conduct entirely unworthy a financier of your distinguished reputation.' —'Quite so,' he said; 'then the only alternative would be for you to give me a couple of hundred guineas, now and then, to help me bear the suspense until we know whether your brother is ever coming back.'—'You are ambitious in your ideas of compensation,' I ventured to remark. 'Not a bit of it,' he retorted, 'and now listen to me. Your brother will arrive in San Francisco in a few weeks, from Australia. I've kept track of him fairly well. Now, you may manage to communicate with him there, and tell him this note must be taken up as soon as he can telegraph the money to England, or get his friends here to furnish it. You tell him so from the old Jew's successor; and you tell him, further, that unless he does it the old Jew's successor will at once test the authenticity of the note. He'll pay up fast enough. There are friends who can do it for him.' You should have heard the cad mouthing his big words. He turned and left me, without another word. Next day a boy brought me a neat letter with a request from this fellow for a loan of two hundred guineas—'a loan for a few weeks.' I sent the money, threw the letter in the messenger's face, and left town for San Francisco next day. Luckily this excursion afforded a cover to my movements, which I attributed to literary engagements. And now you can readily understand what I have to do in San Francisco; can you not?"

Floyd had already leaped ahead of the Englishman's narrative. He saw a vision of the arrival of the erring brother — the sinful lord — in San Francisco; of Lady Helena's joyful meeting with him; of her second interference to save him if there had been a second forgery, and if she were told that ruin was once more threatening him.

"It is romantic, and touching," he said, respectfully. The English painter's complete frankness had affected him deeply. "Yes, I know what you have to do in California. You have to institute a discreet search for your brother; and you have to expect that the money-lender will have an agent on the watch. You must find out to-morrow, if possible, when Australian steamers are expected in San Francisco; and must shape your journey accordingly. And if, as I believe, the Jew's successor is a liar, and the second forgery is a shrewd blackmailing scheme, then you must punish him if you can. In any case, and for anything, count on me."

"Thanks," said Ringdale, simply.

Floyd felt as if he were relinquishing his new-born hopes of Lady Helena's love.

"I trust the imaginative Mr. Rusher has not overheard us," said Ringdale, as he got down from his berth. "And of course — but I need not ask you to keep this secret; I know that you will do so."

There was much whistling of locomotives, and

presently "section three" of the excursion was once more under way. When Lady Helena met the two painters in the "dining-room car" for the one o'clock dinner, she noticed that they were both very pale, and attributed it to the fatigues incidental to "sketching sunrises."

For the next thirty-six hours the trains loitered along the Yellowstone Valley, giving the travellers ample chance to observe the wonders of the new Territory of Montana. The earl was in high spirits here. Everything interested him, and especially the corded buffalo-hides piled like wood at the little stations; the picturesque herdsmen, in their jack-boots and sombreros; the winding river full of flats and shallows in certain sections, and of boiling and tumultuous rapids in others. Captain Jobson and Colonel Hodges brought to him from time to time grim-looking, but polite and serviceable, gentlemen who told him thrilling stories of the campaigns of United States troops against the wily redskins; of the massacre of gallant Custer's command in the valley of the Little Big Horn; and legends of the heroic journey of Lewis and Clark through the Yellowstone Valley, and on to the then mysterious and unexplored Columbia River, at the beginning of the century. Late on the evening of the next day after their visit to the "Bad Lands" the trains were stopped at a huge encampment of friendly Indians, on the Crow Reservation, and the tourists were invited to descend from their rolling-palaces and to witness a war-dance given in their honor.

The first intimation that Lady Helena received of her proximity to the Indians was from Jenks, who came rushing into the private car in a condition bordering on frenzy. "The savages are here, my lady," she cried to Lady Offast, who arose from her comfortable chair with consternation depicted on her usually placid features.

"The savages!" she gasped. "Surely there are men enough at hand to protect us. Where are the guns?" and she looked wildly around for the earl.

"It's only a dawnce," said the Hon. Goliath Reachall, popping into the room with a water-proof coat on. "These are friendly Indians; there are two or three thousand of 'em, and I think there's somethin' interestin' to be seen."

"Thanks," said Lady Offast, with the first graciousness which the Hon. Goliath had ever elicited from her. The relief was intense. Ten minutes later both mistress and maid were ready bravely to join the party which Captain Jobson, with his usual dexterity, had organized. They all clambered down from the cars into the great shadows enveloping the plains, and approached the camp-fires.

The spectacle was odd and wild. In the background was a large village of wigwams, from the streets of which arose an indescribable tumult of Indian jargon, of the beating of rude drums, and the barking of half-wild dogs. Great fires flamed and sent up columns of resinous smoke, and were constantly fed by sensuous-faced boys who brought the wood and threw it down with haughty scorn, as if they indicated thus their contempt for menial employment, and that they did this work merely as part of a state ceremonial. Squatted in a semicircle at some distance from the fires, and so that an intense light fell upon them, were the medicine-men and warriors who were participating in the dance. These men, some of whom were gigantic in stature, others small and wizened, sat crooning and cawing in rude harmony, to the accompaniment of the drums, for some moments, after which they rose and rushed tumultuously forward, flourishing their weapons, leaping, capering and shrieking, as Captain Jobson expressed it, "as if each of them were possessed of seven devils." Their faces were painted with ochre and vermilion; around their necks hung amulets; on their feet were gaudily embroidered moccasins; and many of them wore rich hunting-shirts and leggings. When they had shrieked and gesticulated until they were exhausted, they went back and sat down in semicircle, to begin over again as soon as it was possible. Now and then a sorcerer came, stealing forward, with distended claws and sinister grin, and seemed to invoke malediction on all the world at large except the faithful warriors.

"And they say these are friendly Indians!" exclaimed the earl. "I shouldn't mind seein' a few inimical ones from a safe distance, don't you know? —just to see if they could outdo the violence of these chatterin' apes."

"Their songs sound like the prating of a colony of noisy rooks," grumbled the Hon. Goliath Reachall. "Seen much better things than that in Egypt."

"I wish he were there now," whispered the earl to Lady Offast.

Outside the magic circle of the dance strange figures enveloped in gray blankets stole noiselessly to and fro. Lady Helena, finding herself rudely jostled by one of these, turned instinctively to Ringdale, who was near her, for protection.

She was startled to see Floyd step forward to the offender, seize the black hair which fell over the blankets, and twisting it around his fingers give the wild-looking head a severe shake. The creature glided away out of sight.

"Oh, Mr. Floyd! I am amazed. To chastise a woman!" Lady Helena said this with some indignation.

"That is no woman," he said, smiling, "but a great hulking boy of seventeen."

"Impossible! Are these, then, all men around us?"

"All. Their faces look like those of Italian or Spanish women of the lower class — rude, robust women of the people; but they are men. There is a kind of sensual beauty in their features which, in the civilized races, is bestowed only upon the coarser, feminine types."

"There are but eight or nine hundred of us, all told, in this excursion," said Colonel Hodges, "and at least three thousand of these beggars. They could massacre us all if it pleased them to do so."

"No danger," said a frontiersman, who had been listening with the unrestrained curiosity of the backwoodsman. "The Crows have always been friendly. But if they was inclined to be ugly they'd think about that wire out thar," pointing to the telegraph line, "and they wouldn't strike a blow. They know what the railroad an' the tally-graft means, you bet!"

Finally a capricious night-wind blew the smoke from the fires in the spectators' eyes, and all went back to the trains, whither the clangorous bells of the locomotives were calling them. Then there was much buying of amulets, moccasins, and bead bracelets from whining and begging Crows; then a grand charge by the colored servants to "clear dem gangways;" and the cars moved on across the plains toward the snow-capped mountains. Lady Helena felt as if the visit to the encampment, the semicircle of bedizened warriors, and the infinite jargon, had all been seen and heard in a dream.

CHAPTER XV.

LADY HELENA IS INTERVIEWED.

AND now they were at Livingston, a town which, so far as the travellers could observe, was exactly like all other new towns in this newest of countries; with this remarkable exception, however, that the air was purer and keener, and the sky brighter than anywhere else since they had left New York. They had passed through great valleys, which looked arid and desolate, but which were rendered magnificently fertile by irrigation, and the Hon. Goliath Reachall, after seeing the canal or ditch thirty-nine miles long, destined to irrigate one hundred thousand acres of fertile land, announced his intention of founding "The General Irrigation Company (limited)." He was imprudent enough to ask the earl if he would be a subscriber to the capital; whereupon he received such a snubbing that he still bears the marks of it.

The Hon. Goliath's mention of his project of a company for the creation of irrigating canals reminded Colonel Hodges that the Ocala scheme was getting sadly moss-grown. He sickened at the thought of returning to London and beginning the battle over again. And then and there he made up his mind that he would once more attack the earl on the subject, and would persuade him to give his coöperation before the close of the excursion. Colonel Hodges was a determined man, and the earl, had he known what pressure was to be brought to bear upon him, would have needed all the firmness which, in an unsuspecting attitude, he entirely forgot to summon. When Colonel Hodges came to him at Livingston, engaged him in conversation about the beauties of the Yellowstone Park, and, finally won from him a promise that he would halt there, with the colonel and Captain Jobson, on the company's return from the Pacific Coast, and undertake a week's hunting, the earl was pleased. "Good sort the old colonel; he doesn't feel cut up because I wouldn't go into his canal," thought the earl. "I was near doing it, but I wanted to save my spare tin for investment in these regions. Good sort is the colonel."

How white, glistening, exquisitely ethereal, were the mountains seen from Livingston! Lady Helena, gazing at them, said to her companions that "they looked like the spirits of mountains," as indeed they did. From time to time they seemed hovering in air, and approaching as if to descend and place themselves on earth. "This is inspiring!" cried the girl, gazing out with widely opened eyes and dilated nostrils, a genuine excitement transfiguring her haughty features. "And how romantic that road, winding among the recesses of the hills! I should like to live here." Her enthusiasm increased when the trains had climbed out of the Yellowstone Valley to the approaches to the Bozeman Tunnel. In every direction there were glorious views; tracts of ragged, wind-swept, sinister timber, with here and there little clearings in which families were living in tents; vast hill-sides, ribbed with tremendous ledges; expanses of perfect blue sky, with white peaks standing out in striking relief against them; massive defiles of rock, moss-grown and many colored.

The tunnel was not completed, and the trains, divided into convenient sections, were dragged over a mountain a mile high on a temporary track. During the exciting ascent of this height, it chanced that Lady Helena found herself alone. Her companions had stepped into another car, just before the upward climb began, and the result was that Lady Helena was the private car's only occupant. When she discovered this she was not alarmed. "It is better," she thought, "than being condemned to hear the comments of those odious Reachalls. They criticise scenery as if it ought to have been made exactly to suit them."

Presently the engine drawing the section screamed and stopped. Lady Helena looked out and was surprised and a little amused to see Caswell P. Rusher — immaculate as usual in drab felt hat, alpaca duster of gray buttoned up to his chin, and gray linen gloves — limping forward beside the track. He caught sight of her and lifted his hat with as nonchalant air as if he had known her for a dozen years. Lady Helena drew back, biting her lips with vexation.

In the midst of this magnificent and colossal scenery Caswell P. Rusher looked as a sparrow might look sitting in the lap of Memnon; or like a fly upon the face of the Sphinx. He seemed out of place in the landscape. He required a background of rectangular street, ornamented with telegraph-poles and swinging-sign. He affronted the picturesque. The commonplace average was embodied in him, and in his composition there was no room for anything else. Lady Helena felt this instinctively, and she burned to lean over the platform railing and to say: "O ridiculously *new* man! O consummated mediocrity! what evil fate forced you into this incongruous setting, where all your *défaillances* are an hundred times magnified?"

"I jumped down from a car in the other section up yonder," said Caswell P., addressing himself to Lady Helena with what he conceived to be easy grace, "and I turned my ankle. They pulled out before I could get aboard. So I signalled to this section to stop, and I guess I'll get right in here."

"Pulled out?" said Lady Helena, smitten with pity. "Do you mean to say that your ankles are pulled out? And why did you want to get a board? What kind of boards could you find on these mountains?"

"Ah, ha! Very good. Your ladyship is humorous. Isn't this scenery big?" And, as he spoke, he swung himself up on to the steps of the private car with much agility for one who had a turned ankle. "You will not object to my riding to the summit with you? I can't walk. Oh! you are quite alone?"

"My friends are just behind us," said Lady Helena, stiffly. She was angry with Caswell P. for his intrusion; yet there was something in his cool audacity which amused her. Besides, was he not suffering?

Candor compels the statement that the ingenious Caswell P. had greatly exaggerated the extent of the injury to his foot. But now, seeing Lady Helena alone, a project which he had long desired to put into execution came whizzing through his brain anew, and, as the section started again, he made wry faces, and clutched at the railing for support.

"This pain is dreadful," he said. "I — I think I will have to sit down."

"Do so, by all means," said Lady Helena. "Can I — shall I bring you — a restorative?"

"I thank you, no," answered Caswell P., very coolly. "I — I couldn't permit it; I shall be better now;" and, limping into the car, he sat down in the earl's favorite chair. The curves in the extemporized track were short and the jolting was considerable, so Lady Helena perforce sat down also.

Caswell P. lost no time in putting his project into execution. He took his note-book from his pocket, and his most impudent smile came to his bloodless lips as he tapped the little volume smartly with his forefinger, and said: —

"Three columns of interviews put into this book this morning. All there in short-hand, waiting to be written out. Do you know, my lady, — excuse me if I don't get your ladyship's title right, for you know I have never been to Europe, — that you can do me a very great favor?"

Lady Helena's amusement at Caswell P.'s manner was so great that she could not refrain from laughing. "I am at a loss," she said, "to understand how I can be of service to you." She had never seen any one like this before. The unconscious nature of his impudence was interesting because of its novelty. The man seemed to environ her with his audacity. She would not have been surprised had he asked her to lend him an hundred pounds.

"Over there in Great Britain," said Caswell P., airily, loosening the elastic band on his note-book, "interviewing, I believe, is considered odd. I can't see why. Now, if you would allow me the privilege of an interview I should feel very much obliged."

A flush stole into Lady Helena's cheeks. She had not heard so much about interviewing as the earl, and did not exactly understand Caswell P.'s meaning. She arose. "I fear that you are making a mistake — which you might regret," she stammered. She felt hurt and humiliated.

"There, now, I knew you'd get it wrong, and — and mistake me the first thing," cried Caswell P., reaching out his hand with his pencil in it. "I mean by an interview that I should ask you about your impressions of things — and — and people, and that I should take down your answers — and print them in my paper. Don't you see? Now just let me tell you before you object. It will be a splendid thing for me. See, here's an interview with a German chemist; says our chemists don't know anything, and all that. Quite stunning, you know. Here's another. Hon. Golight — Goliath — something — says our soldiers look slovenly, and all that. Splendid. Another — a London capitalist — says our Western lands will all be owned by England in course of time, and that our climate's hideous. Isn't it interesting? Now, if I could prevail upon you to favor me with some of your ideas about our American things — I should — I should" —

He stopped short, and looked uneasily at Lady Helena, who was eying him so quizzically that he was a little alarmed. At last she said: —

"I quite understand you now. And it is even

more dreadful than I supposed it was. And you," she said, with quite a winning smile, "and you — Mr. — Rusher — it does not affect you at all oddly, then? To ask people — I mean — to insist upon knowing what they think —just for the purpose of selling their thoughts afterward — as if they were your own".— She laughed heartily. "And what a host of mischief you must make!"

Caswell P. smiled, but his smile was a little foggy. "Why, no," he said. "I don't think I make mischief. Most people are glad to be interviewed. I have names in this book — now — names that are known through the length and breadth of the land. Yes, and in Europe, too. Congressmen," he added, reflectively, — "Congressmen, now, are the worst. I know 'em. I've had 'em send around a note to our paper asking to have me come and interview them, which I would do. And then — when I had polished up their ideas, and corrected their grammar, and published their — their lucubrations — they would turn around and abuse 'the scoundrelly reporter before whom they could not speak without finding themselves in print!'"

"Ah! that is certainly ungrateful. But most persons, I should think, would shrink from having their opinions made public. And it seems as if it were offensive to thrust them upon public notice."

"Well, I don't know," said Caswell P.; "people all over the world say pretty rough things about each other, and don't seem anxious to keep their remarks private. But, I assure you,"—and so great was his earnestness that he arose quickly, forgetful that he was supposed to have a sprained ankle, — "I assure you that it would be a great favor if you would allow me to jot down your remarks on our society, and the country in general. It would be the crowning interview of the trip."

"Very well," said Lady Helena, taking a sudden resolve; "I object to it with all my might, and I think it is monstrous. But I will agree to be interviewed, provided you allow me to terminate the interview when I think your questions are becoming indiscreet."

The reporter laid his hand upon his heart. "I hope I shall not ask any question which you cannot answer," he said. "But I suppose you would have no objection, for instance, to saying what you think of our society, — from the point of view of a member of the English aristocracy, if you please."

Caswell P. said these last words in the same tone employed by photographers when they say, "Now head a little more to the right, if you please;" "Hands in your lap, please," etc.

Lady Helena looked aghast. "Your society? You mean American society, I suppose. I haven't seen it."

The interviewer nibbled his pencil, and thought for a minute. Then he said, "You must find everything crude and hard over here, after the mellowness and mustiness of England. The manners rather free" —

"Yes," said the lady, "the manners — or perhaps I should say some of the customs — are rather eccentric; but, stop a minute, how are you putting that down? You must read it out to me from your notes, or I shall not go on."

Caswell P. enjoyed this. It was even better fun than he had anticipated. "I will read it with pleasure," he said; "it runs this way: 'Lady Helena remarked that the crude harshness of the climate was only surpassed by the harsh crudeness of the national manners. As for the eccentricity of the customs, she need scarcely add her expressions of wonder to those of so many aristocratic travellers who had preceded her.'"

"Fancy!" — Lady Helena's face grew dark, — "and I said nothing of the sort. Nothing of the sort! Fancy my classing myself as an aristocratic traveller! This is not interviewing — Mr. — er — Mr. Rusher; it's rank misrepresentation!"

The reporter smiled. "I'm sorry to displease you," he said. "It's a habit we get, putting in the frills. The night editor might not print this if it wasn't just a little spicy."

"No, no, Mr. Rusher, you must report me textually or not at all. You cannot refuse a lady, you know."

"Well, no, that's so," (rather doggedly).

"And now that point is settled you can go on to the next question."

"Ahem!" Caswell P. was growing wary now, but he was determined to ask leading questions, as was his wont. "You find our ladies, American ladies, you know, thin and sallow and with high-pitched voices; do you not?" This was said so insinuatingly that Lady Helena did not gather its enormity at once, but in half a minute she answered stoutly: —

"Not a bit of it! The American ladies that I have seen in Europe and America are extremely pretty and well-bred. Some of the women are perhaps vulgar, but that would also be the case in Europe."

"Ah! then you make a distinction between ladies and women?"

"Naturally, that is — no — but no! no! You must not put that down."

Caswell P. pretended to erase it. "May I ask if you find that democracy makes America an unpleasant country to live in? You think, I presume, that we must go, and are glad to go, to Europe for our culture, and to spend our money intelligently?"

"Really, I have never thought of any of these things at all," said Lady Helena, looking quite distressed. "How should such matters concern me? I — I cannot answer such questions."

"Do you think that our people would be better off if there was an aristocratic class to direct politics and to set the fashions?"

"That is for your people to decide."

"I suppose you find our national cookery quite detestable?"

"Indeed, I do not. I think it is delicious, and I wish England might adopt many items in it. If my cousin were here I am not certain that he would not criticise you for lack of patriotism. He thinks American cookery is quite perfect, I assure you.

But you must not put that down! He would never forgive me."

"Do you think the American accent is disagreeable?"

"Not always," answered Lady Helena, softly. At that particular moment she was thinking of the voice of Mr. Dulon Floyd.

"How did you find the hotels in New York and Chicago? I suppose you thought them very public and glaring, and so on?"

"The heat was the only thing which we found to complain of; and, really, the landlords were not responsible for that."

"Do you think women have too much power in America?"

"Now, Mr. Rusher," said Lady Helena, "I must decline to go on. If I were to answer these questions in the spirit in which they are asked, and you were to print the dialogue, I should appear in print as the most ill-natured woman in the world. So I must ask you to be kind enough to tear those notes out of your book, and to forego the pleasure of printing your 'Interview with an English lady.' Tear them out, please, Mr. Rusher, and present them to me. They will be a souvenir of — of — our ride together."

Caswell P. Rusher looked sharply at Lady Helena to see if any satire were lurking beneath the gentle, almost caressing, tones in which she addressed him. But he could detect none. He looked ruefully at the notes.

"This hasn't turned out as I expected," he said. "I felt certain that we could make a stunning interview out of what you would say. But if you are going to object to letting me color it up, why, I suppose there is no good in taking notes. I'm sure I'm much obliged to you. But I thought you were good for a column and a half."

"The notes, please, Mr. Rusher."

He tore the leaves from the note-book and handed them to her.

"And you will not print my name, nor anything I have said in your paper, Mr. Rusher, because you know that it would be very distasteful to me to have you do so. Ah! here we are at the top. How lovely this breeze is! I hope your ankle does not pain you very much."

Caswell P. Rusher murmured some words the exact sense of which Lady Helena did not gather, and as soon as the section came to a stop he climbed down the car steps, and withdrew in such an abashed and confused manner that the girl was sorry she had been so determined with him. "I might have let him go on a little longer, and then have turned the tables on him by asking him leading questions and drawing him out. What fun it would have been!"

By and by the accidentally separated friends were united on the western slope of the great Belt range, after the heavy cars had been taken, one by one, down the improvised track, through the wild defile of Rock Cañon. Then the trains went on through mysterious gorges and through valleys rich with emerald greens, — valleys so wide and long that thousands of farms might nestle in their broad bosoms; and at night they came, under a blood-red, windy sky, to the little town of Helena, in Montana, prettily ensconced at the base of mountains whose recesses are filled with precious metals.

CHAPTER XVI.

AN UNEXPECTED CLUE.

"THERE is a picture for you," said the earl to Mr. Dulon, "and one which would test pretty fairly the incredulity of our untravelled Academicians." He pointed to the gray and rugged mountains, which formed a background for the town of Helena, and to the sky above them. The blood-red color was slowly fading away now, yielding its place to great, irregular stains of copper and greenish purple.

"The imagination of a scene-painter at Drury Lane might evolve such colors as this for the fairy-land of his pantomime," said Lady Helena; "but I should never have believed, without seeing them, that they could exist in nature."

"There they are, though," said the young painter, stoutly; "and I am glad to know that I shall have reliable witnesses to prove that I am not crazy, when I open my exhibition in Brook street."

They were jolting forward from the railway station to Helena in a shaky omnibus, under the patronage of a saucy negro "conductor," as they talked. Captain Jobson had promised them a supper at the principal hotel, and a view of the picturesque crowd of miners in the street, and they had gladly accompanied him. Young Ringdale was jubilant; he said that the evening breeze, the mountain atmosphere, and the liberation from the slavery of the excursion had given him a wonderful new fund of gayety. Floyd was by no means happy, but he felt excited and eager. A new purpose had come into his life, jostling aside the art ambitions. He was no longer anxious to reach the far shores of Washington Territory, that he might leave his companions and take ship for the outer confines of the Arctic circle, where he expected to find strange subjects for his brush; but he was in a fever of haste to be in San Francisco, and to aid Ringdale — yes, to help Lady Helena, if she required his help — to find the missing "Lord John."

"This Helena is a town of millionnaires," said Captain Jobson, who appeared to know everything about all places, — "millionnaires who are sorry that the railroad has come along here, as they are afraid that it will take away some of their privileges. 'Cute fellers, aint they? See how the old town snuggles up against the foot-hills, and looks sort of scornfully at the railroad depot."

The earl said he thought Captain Jobson was rather poetical in calling Helena an "old" town.

"Well, no," rejoined the captain, reflectively. "Government established a post-office here in 1864. The miners were getting thick then, and some of 'em wanted to hear from home. A good many of 'em didn't, so they moved on into the woods. Crab Town was the first name of this place. 'Taint poetical; so the citizens held a meeting, and decided to name the new city after Helen of Troy; name of Helen always associated with beauty," said the good captain, in a lowered voice, to Lady Helena, who sat beside him.

"A truce to sailors' compliments, now you are on land," said the lady, with heightened color.

"I beg your pardon," said the captain. "Yes — 1864 was the year — and now — here you have a city. Electric light, you observe," pointing to the fixtures for producing this latest phenomenon of civilization, as they entered the streets of the metropolis of Montana. "They even have an opera-house here. Pleasant little occurrence in it last evening. Gives an idea of the Arcadian manners of some of the people in these regions. Man seated in a front seat near the stage interrupts the performance by loud remarks. Man behind him, somewhat elevated by devotion to ardent spirits, remonstrates. Man in front intimates his indifference to sentiments of man in rear. So man in rear pulls out knife and cuts throat of man in front."

"God bless my soul!" said the earl.

"Yes — fact. Man in front is carried to the hospital; man in rear is taken before a justice, in morning, and is put under five-hundred-dollar bonds to appear for trial; after which, — according to my informant, — respectable colored citizen down at railroad depot, — he skips for Idaho."

"He — does what?" inquired Ringdale.

"Skips his bail, — leaves his bondsmen mourning for his sudden departure out of the Montana jurisdiction."

"And is the — the man in front dead?" asked Lady Helena.

"We shall learn that this evening. He might as well die as to live around with a throat so — so badly deteriorated."

"What a dreadful doctrine, captain!" said Lady Offast, who had been quaking with apprehension as she listened to this thrilling tale. "I am sure I hope we shall, none of us, lose our lives in this — this wilderness."

The captain turned around and gazed at Lady Offast in genuine amazement. "We are — guests, madam, and — and you are ladies. We are as safe — as — as if we were in the Bank of England," he concluded, not readily finding a comparison.

Lady Offast — to her credit be it stated — never allowed her apprehensions to endure long, or in any wise to interfere with her appetite; and she was quite radiant after a capital supper at the "inn," as she called it. The snug waiters, in their alpaca coats, who went and came as if moved by invisible wires, and who seemed to fancy that they were conferring a favor on the party by waiting upon them, jarred a little on the good countess's nerves; but the fare was excellent: juicy Montana mutton; immense Montana potatoes, pink to their core, as if blushing violently when offered up; home-made preserves, fragrant tea, and, just as they were about to ask for game, a brace of plump quails. The long, low-studded dining-room was filled with bucolic folk from the fertile "Prickly Pear Valley," which stretches away from the foot of the slope on which Helena stands. The men were strong, lean, rudely handsome, independent of demeanor; the women were sickly and had a complaining air.

"What class, now, do these persons belong to?" asked the earl, in a whisper, of Captain Jobson.

"There are no classes in this country, you must remember," was the answer.

"Ah! well; to what particular branch of activity, then, do they devote their republican energies?" said the earl, a trifle sulkily.

"Farming, sir, farming. Some of them are old miners, tired of digging in the mountains for gold and silver, and liking better to dig potatoes and to grow wheat. They seem to prosper at it," he added, as if courting the earl's opinion.

"They have rather an aggressive air," said the earl, faintly, "as if they wanted to attack something forthwith."

There was a twinkle in Captain Jobson's eye. "The men do look full of fight," he said. "Fact is, that's an expression of physiognomy peculiar to the Western country. It gets to be inherited. It's — a — kind — of — mark of the race. These men belong to a series of generations which have always been tackling something. First, it was the Indians and the wilderness. But the wilderness was the worst of the two. When I was in Oregon, in '69"—

"Astonishing captain — where have you not been?" said Lady Helena.

"Never here before; but I think this is the only place. I've got up the whole history, though, by talks with Montana people on the cars. Curious, aint it? When I was in Oregon, in '69, an old pioneer told me that it wasn't Indians that people feared in crossing the plains; it was the dreadful solitude. Said from the time that he left Peoria, in Illinois, in 1852, — Peoria was frontier then, — until he saw Mount Hood, on the Pacific coast, he and his little party did not encounter a human being; and they were six months on the way. Dreadful, wasn't it? After solitude and the Indians these people have had to fight with the mountains, grappling with them for their gold and silver. And, then, distance has been one of their terrible enemies. They have always been fighting it, and now they have conquered it;" and the captain pointed out the open window of the dining-room in the direction of the railway.

"Really, captain, you are quite eloquent," said Ringdale.

"Not at all. Facts; all facts. These fellows

look fierce and independent because they have had to be fierce, and because they have never had any class above them to keep them down. It would be too late to begin now, I think," he added, somewhat incoherently. "Suppose we go and see the miners," he said. "They come down in thousands from the quartz mines and placer diggings near by at this season of the year, and the town is full of them every evening. It's all gold and silver mines for twenty miles round about here."

The earl was annoyed that he had to push his way through the crowd in the hotel office; he felt that they should have fallen respectfully back until he had departed. So supreme was his annoyance that he did not observe the deference and respect with which even the roughest men made room for the ladies simply because they were ladies. He began to think he should not like this Western world, where every man was expected to take by force what he wanted, and where no allowances were made for any man because of his name or a social position which he had achieved or inherited elsewhere.

They found the short, hilly streets brilliant under the glare of the electric lights; and they were deeply surprised at the unkempt appearance of the miners, who did not compare favorably with the farmers from the Prickly Pear Valley. The old miners were a pathetic spectacle, as Lady Helena whispered to Mr. Dulon. Their faces, framed in grizzled beards, their venerable heads covered with broad slouch hats, looked wretched and woe-begone. They were men who were tired of themselves, tired of the drudgery in which they spent the greater part of their lives, and desperately tired of the dissipation with which they interspersed the drudgery. That which they most craved was an intense and fiery excitement which should lift them out of the cold monotony of their existences; an excitement which should render them regardless of consequences, like the craze of strong liquors or the absorbing thrill which they found at the gambling-table. The young men were hollow-eyed and rather spiritless.

The strong light on the streets served to exhibit more plainly than was proper or necessary certain repulsive forms of vice, at which the excursionists were much shocked. All the gambling-dens were wide open and could be entered directly from the street. Most of them were unattractive, and the gaming had a dull ferocity in it which was without special interest to an outside observer. Ringdale expressed his wonder that men surrounded by such noble scenery, with such Arcadian and bewitching valleys near them, did not beguile their leisure with games of strength and skill, with bathing in the beautiful streams, with wassail at rustic hostelries, instead of in the bare rooms of the prosaic town.

"That's it," said Captain Jobson; "they don't know how to amuse themselves. But it wouldn't be of any use to suggest to them an amusement which did not have a strong spice of excitement and a certain amount of danger in it."

Here they saw the Chinamen mingling with the mining populations, and occasionally receiving kicks and cuffs as assertions of Caucasian superiority. They saw the stages, or "police jerkies," as they are called in Helena, come dashing in from the cañon, out of which the road leads to Fort Benton; and they decided to close their excursion to Helena with a visit to the office of a local newspaper.

They soon found the location of the principal organ of the interests of Montana, and while the ladies waited in the publishing-office, which smelled of gas and paste, the gentlemen were ushered into the presence of a tall, beetle-browed editor, who sat in a small room in front of an uncomfortable desk, and was vexing his soul with endeavors to sharpen a bad lead-pencil with a dull knife.

Captain Jobson, with his usual airy grace, apologized for intrusion upon the editorial labors, and presented the gentlemen as distinguished strangers, purposely putting the earl last to call attention more directly to him, and emphasizing his title. "The earl is a great friend of American institutions," he said.

The beetle-browed editor smiled cordially. "Sit down, earl," he said, taking a hap-hazard flight at a European title, with which he had no direct intercourse, and fancying that he must have got it pretty nearly right. "Take a chair and sit down. Gentlemen, I reckon all that I can do for you is to ask you to lean against the wall — not having no more seats — as the old settler said at his wife's funeral. Wal, earl, we have a great many of your countrymen in Montana, nowadays."

"Ah!" said the earl. This far-western editor ruffled his nerves, and he did not trust himself to say more than "Ah!" just yet.

"Yes; most of them seem to take to horse-raising. Great country for horses, this is — earl. Let me see; there was one of your countrymen in here to Helena yesterday. Yes. He came down to borrow five thousand dollars at one of the banks, as he'd been unfortunate with his stock. Indians and vagabonds run off part of it. I happen to be one of the directors in the bank, and — wal — I reckon we sh'll let him have the money. Maybe you know him — name Hume — great horse man" —

"Can't say I ever heard of him," said the earl, rather shortly.

"That's strange, now, isn't it?" said the beetle-browed editor, leaning back in his chair and twirling his thumbs, as if suspicions about Mr. Hume had been aroused by the earl's disclaimer of acquaintanceship. "England's a small country, too. But you might not happen to know him. He's got a friend on the way over here to join him for a while in the horse-raising business, so he says, — a young Englishman who's coming round the world to San Francisco, from Australia, I believe, and is due here soon; a young lord who has reasons for keeping very quiet, he says to me. Never mind, sir, I'll pick them up."

This last remark was addressed to Ringdale, who had started forward so suddenly that he had sent a pile of well-worn law books, which had been lying near the edge of a small table, crashing to the floor.

Ringdale apologized, and bent over the books; but his hands trembled so that he could not raise the volumes. Mr. Dulon came to his aid, and while the earl was cutting the communicative editor's babble short, and was taking his leave, the young American whispered to the young Englishman: —

"I understand it as you do. The clue is a precious one; but we must not let it slip by losing time."

The little party walked back to the train, the ladies having declared that they preferred the dust of the highway rather than the jolting of the omnibus. Captain Jobson and Colonel Hodges took the lead, and Ringdale and Floyd brought up the rear. It was pitchy dark and quite late, so they walked rapidly, and in silence. Presently they came to the tracks, where a dozen spick-and-span new locomotives, recently fired up, were fretting and fuming, not inharmoniously, while waiting for their start on the midnight eastward journey over the Bozeman Pass. The friendly lights of the "third section" gleamed a few yards away. The young men lingered, bidding the party good-night.

Ringdale lit a cigar. "It will be stifling in the train," he said. "Let us find a cool nook and talk. I say, old man, what is our duty now? Do you think we should let Lady Helena know about — the — the clue?"

"But it may be a mere coincidence, — this arrival of a young Englishman from 'round the world,'" said Floyd, doubtfully. He was at a loss what advice to offer.

"True, true. Ah! it's very perplexing. Will this excursion never end? How long will it take us to reach San Francisco?"

So they talked and planned until the morning began to peep out of the sky; until many of the roaring locomotives had rushed off into the mysterious Eastern distance; and until the night watchman at the railway station had made up his mind that they must be professional burglars from New York, planning a descent upon the depot safe. The last words said by Ringdale, when the young men parted for the night, were these: —

"If I only knew what Lady Helena is going to do!"

"She is certain to do right," said Floyd, with a ring of resentment in his voice. He could not bear the faint distrust of her that Ringdale sometimes manifested.

"Quite so," said Ringdale. And when he was alone in the darkness of his berth, with Floyd silent in his alcove above him, this thought ran through his mind: "The American loves Lady Helena. Here *is* a complication."

CHAPTER XVII.

THE GOLDEN SPIKE.

THE great ceremony had begun. The East and West had once more hilariously met and enthusiastically fraternized. As Caswell P. Rusher expressed it, in the opening paragraph of the copious report sent to his journal in Chicago, the Atlantic and Pacific coasts had "shaken hands, had embraced, had sworn eternal fealty anew." How the two coasts had performed this triple and delicate operation Caswell P. did not specify. He had no time to consider the aptitude of his similes, or the contour of his sentences. He was, in his own language, "on the war-path" that day. He was determined to beat everything else in the West. With linen duster closely buttoned from feet to chin, and with his busy hands neatly encased in Swedish kid, he strode from point to point of the interesting ceremonial of laying the last rails of the vast northwestern thoroughfare. He spied out the pretty red-cheeked maidens who came down from Deer Lodge, hard by the lovely valley in which "Last Spike" station was established, and he skipped away to greet them and to ask each one for her name, that he might telegraph it to Chicago. Next he was among the miners, a cynical and somewhat inebriated delegation of the seekers of the precious metals being on hand, rather scornfully listening to the buzzing of the military band perched in a white-wood pavilion near the "speakers' stand." From the men of pickaxe and drill he collected quaint anecdotes, highly spiced with profanity, and strung them for the delectation of his Chicagoan readers upon a thread of comment as to the mineral resources of the section. Airily, like a humming-bird or a musical-winged bee, he flitted from the miners to the little group of Crow chieftains squatted opposite the platform on which the Secretary of State was haranguing his cosmopolitan audience. "His discourse," wrote Caswell P., in his neat, chippy stenography, commenting on the Secretary, "resembles the new line of railroad. There are long dusty stretches in it; but, just as one is beginning to grow weary of the monotony, the route enters a green valley, where there is a fine river, and where the sunshine is merry on the pleasant grass." Then he sat down, without saying "By your leave," close beside that redoubtable son of nature, Iron Bull, of the Crows.

Iron Bull was full of bitterness, although he managed, with the habitual stoicism of the Indian, to conceal it; for he had come up to this ceremonial in obedience to a hint which was hardly less than a command from the controller of the "Agency" to make his speech at the appointed time, and to welcome the white man who had run his railway directly across his reservation. So when the cheerful reporter clapped Iron Bull on the back and said, "How, John, speak English, don't you? How about the speech you are to make?" a guttural answer came promptly, and a side glance from the Indian's eyes made the adventurous Caswell P. just the least bit cold at the base of his brain. This was the red man's response: —

"Iron Bull. Great chief. D—n!"

"All right, my copper-colored friend," said Caswell P., rising with alacrity. "If you are so easily offended I shall have to write you a speech. And I might as well do it now, for nobody but yourself will understand what you say."

So he unconcernedly climbed the steps of the speakers' stand, elbowed his way through the dozens of American, English, and German dignitaries who were listening to the speeches, and nodded familiarly to the earl, whom he found seated on a bench, with one hand thrust in the breast of his coat and with an air of intense dignity, as if he felt it on this occasion incumbent on him to represent the whole British aristocracy. At the top of the improvised wooden amphitheatre he coolly dispossessed an old lady of a comfortable corner, from which she had momentarily stirred, and sat down to "write out" Iron Bull's harangue.

At the foot of a pretty slope near by some artillerymen from a neighboring fort awaited the signal to fire the salutes. Eastward and westward groups of stalwart workmen were gathered, with rails poised upon hand-cars, and with all preparations made for laying the last quarter-mile of track at the highest rate of speed attainable. On the numerous side-tracks reposed the long trains of Pullmans and Wagners, their locomotives harmoniously "crooning" together. In the western distance was an opening to the valley, where a stream had pierced the rocky barriers. But in all the rich, primitive country there were no human habitations, there was no structure save this railway station, converted for the day into a place of public meeting.

The tremendous chain of the Rocky Mountains, close behind, sheltered this valley from wind and storm. It was a peaceful nook, where tender plants and long grasses and abundant flowers were to be found, and Lady Helena could not persuade herself that it had not been frequented and cultivated for centuries.

The Earl and Lady Offast evidently thought it their duty to sit out the literary exercises connected with this opening of the new transcontinental route; but Lady Helena was troubled with no such conviction, and she stole away, after she had heard one or two of the speeches, and, bidding her maid accompany her, went out through the grassy glades for a saunter to and fro. The idea that she could be in the slightest danger did not occur to her; but Jenks took good care to remind her, by a loud "Ahem!" whenever she had got out of sight of the trains. She was absorbed in thought, and paced rather nervously up and down, plucking now and then at a waving spear of grass. Jenks knew better than to awaken her from her revery, and she might have remained in it for hours had not a bird flown swiftly down before her, almost brushing her face, and uttering a cry of distress. The birdling was appearently alarmed at the proximity of some person or persons to the nest of her young ones. Just beyond, in the direction of the mountains, Lady Helena saw a clump of shapely trees, and thither the bird flew, and then away again, still in her twittering terror.

"Let me see what causes you such alarm, my little winged friend," said the girl, and in a few moments she was at the trees. But she started back and stood quite still and almost breathless. Ringdale and Dulon Floyd were seated on the turf, with their backs to her, and she had heard the young American excitedly pronouncing her own name.

"But is it not clearly our duty to tell her what we have heard?" said Floyd. "After what you have told me it would seem as if Lady Helena must have a pressing interest to know the whereabouts of Lord John. If she knew what we think we know, — what clue we believe we possess, — her whole plans might be suddenly changed."

Lady Helena's face grew rosy, and she turned so lightly on her nimble feet that she was behind a sheltering tree in a twinkling. The young men had not even had time to observe the momentary shadow of her tall, lithe form on the ground. After what Ringdale had told Mr. Floyd? And about Lord John? Lady Helena's heart beat as fast as when the small girl on the "Athabaska" had remarked its tumultuous throbs.

"Quite so," answered Ringdale. "But I am

not sure that I wish her to change her plan, if, indeed, she has one. In her anxiety to shield my poor brother she may contribute to his danger. At first, after hearing what the editor said in his office at Helena, I thought it incumbent on me to tell her; but now I am in doubt. You see, I don't know to what extent she is conversant with his real situation, with the excess of peril that he is in. No, let us go on to San Francisco, and she will declare her purpose there. Whatever it is, we may be sure that it is good and charitable."

Floyd drew a sigh of relief. It would have been inexpressibly bitter for him to have been compelled by the stern promptings of his conscience to tell her that they had news of "Lord John," and that he was coming to hide his troubles in Montana. Would she have stayed here to await his coming? How would she have received the news? With pallor and tremulous joy, with a sweet and sad restraint, or with undisguised alarm? Did she love this mysterious and aristocratic good-for-nothing?

"After all," said he, musingly, but loud enough so that both Ringdale and Lady Helena heard him, — "after all, perhaps it is not Lord John who was meant. More than one young English gentleman may be about to arrive at San Francisco and to come on to a Montana horse-ranch to recruit from his troubles and travels. By the way, why do you always speak of your brother as 'Lord John'?"

"It was one of your countrymen, to whom he was much attached, who first called him so. Poor Jack! I wonder if he will ever come to his own again?"

"I am sure I hope so," said the young American; and he added, stoutly, and a bit louder, as if he wished his conscience to hear and to be convinced that his self-abnegation was complete, "I hope so, for your sake and for *her* sake."

"Oh!" said the Hon. Bevis Ringdale; that odd little English oh! which may be interpreted in half a hundred ways, according to the variation of the inflection. In this particular case it meant approval.

Lady Helena bit her lips and, once again lightly turning, sped away so deftly that her going, like her coming, remained undiscovered. She was vexed with herself for staying to hear so much, yet she could not repress a faint delight which seemed surging up in her heart within the last minute or two.

The situation had all at once become much clearer for her. The few sentences exchanged within her hearing by the two youths had shown her their characters in their true light. She saw them sincere, earnest, self-sacrificing; the brother sternly carrying out his plan of finding the "Lord John" whose presence could be only a pain to him, and whose death would bring to the clever Ringdale title and estates which he would know how to render productive and to care for; the American painter — who loved her — was it not so? did not her own heart confess it? — doing all that he could to discover the man whose permanent disappearance, had he not been of lofty mind, he might have wished for.

These were good men and true. She whispered this to herself as she returned to the scene of the celebration, not daring to look behind her lest the youths should spy her out and suspect that she had been in their vicinity. Jenks, who had remained at a decent distance, had been so mystified by Lady Helena's demeanor that she followed in a state bordering on stupefaction. The young lady went straight to the private car, opened her writing-desk, and wrote the following message: —

"Agent Australian Steamship Line, San Francisco: When does next steamer arrive from Australia? Immediate answer confer great favor."

The earl's man was lounging outside, lazily cleaning one of the noble sportsman's rifles. Lady Helena called him to her.

"I want you to do me a particular favor," she said, "and if you do it acceptably you shall have two guineas. Take this despatch, sign it with your own name, and send it with instructions to have the answer delivered to you at the first practicable point on the excursion, say some time to-morrow. Give the answer into my hand, and tell no one that I have sent this message. Do you understand?"

"Your ladyship shall have the answer as soon as it is possible," said the man obediently; and he went off at once to seek his chance of sending the despatch from the extemporized bureau at the station. "I'll lay this has something to do with Lord John," he said; "but I'll say nothing to the herl. He might give me the sack; and Lady 'Elena's good pay."

And now the speeches and the music seemed mercifully to come to an end, and the booming of the salute guns assembled the strayed excursionists from all parts of the valley. Captain Jobson and Colonel Hodges came to escort the ladies to seats provided for them, where they might see the driving of the "golden spike," to which were to be attached telegraphic wires, so that the blows of the hammer might be echoed hundreds of miles away. Lady Helena presently found herself seated on a little platform, with Ringdale and Floyd on either side of her, busily sketching. This was the point in the ceremonial which Floyd was to commemorate in his historic painting, and he took most careful notes. "I sketched all the scenery and made copious studies of the workmen this morning," he said. "All I want now is the composition of the crowd at the final moment."

"Then you will not have to remain here and labor for a day or two," she queried, rather shyly.

"While you go on to the Pacific?" he said, bending down to her an instant. "Not for all the pictures in the universe. I must go where you go."

Lady Helena's hand trembled, and the haughty look came on her face; but her eyes glistened. The panting gangs of workmen from the East now met the panting gangs of toilers from the West. Down clanged the rails, and ex-presidents of republics and railways, English noblemen, American professors and literati and clergymen from the Atlantic seaboard vied with each other in swinging sledges to drive spikes, and in blistering their hands and bruising their toes. Then the officials drove the "last spike," every member of their families, even the babes in arms, simulating a stroke on the completing rivet's head, and bright little speeches of congratulation were made.

Among this second crop of speech-makers was the Crow chieftain, Iron Bull, who, to do him justice, accomplished his heavy task with grace. He said twenty or thirty words of welcome, and spread out his hands, as who should say: "You have the country; keep it; I cannot get it away from you." Then he stepped back, his feathers and ermine skins swinging in the breeze.

There was a retreat in the throng when the locomotives from East and West moved up to touch noses on the newly completed track, and Lady Helena, looking down, saw Caswell P. Rusher standing directly below her. With grim adherence to his duty he was "writing out" his last despatch, before leaving the scene of the ceremony. He had opened his reporting case and laid it on the back of a miner who was crowded against him. "Don't notice it," he said; "for the press, you know; can't move; *must* use you for a table, or can't file my despatch; minute, that's all."

He was putting the finishing touch to the imaginary speech which he had written for "Iron Bull." Lady Helena could not help seeing the bold script which was spread out beneath her gaze. Caswell P. wrote as follows: "Iron Bull concluded his eloquent remarks thus: 'Tell the Great Father that he has nothing further to fear from us. We are tired of the *ancien régime*, and are ready to come into the common fold.'"

While Caswell P. was contentedly examining this paragraph a peal of laughter rang out on the air. It was the laughter of Lady Helena, who could not control her merriment at the notion that an untutored savage making an address on the north-western plains should gravely allude, in French, to the *ancien régime*.

CHAPTER XVIII.

ON THE TRESTLE.

THE Hon. Goliath Reachall was in trouble. Shortly after the departure of the train number three from the "Last Spike" station, one of his sons, hot and wearied with the long day's ceremonial, undertook his ablutions in British fashion in the wash-room of the earl's private car. The train was just then "at a stand-still" in the midst of a fine table-land, dotted with clumps of trees in and out of which fire-flies were flashing. The earl and his party were at supper in the dining-room car forward, their own cook having "gone on a spree," and doubtless young Reachall fancied that he would not be disturbed. But, as his ill-luck would have it, an elderly lady, the wife of one of the commissioners appointed by the government to examine the railroad, took it into her feminine fancy also to examine the train while the other occupants were having their tea. So passing from car to car, until she came to the earl's vehicle, she found the door ajar, walked in and came pat upon young

Reachall, stripped to the waist and spluttering, as with great enjoyment he threw water upon himself and then scrubbed his cuticle until he looked like a freshly cooked lobster.

"Here, I say, ma'am, this aint your way, you know. This is a private car," said Reachall, advancing upon the lady, and flourishing his towel as if he meant to drive her out.

The old dame turned away her gaze, but she was bristling with indignation. "Private car, indeed!" she ejaculated. "I should think *you* thought it was a public bath!" And she retired, white at the lips, and meditating vengeance dire. She had observed the Reachall family rather narrowly for some days, and had concluded that she did not like them; and now the hour to deal them a master-stroke had come.

Gossip flies with miraculous quickness through cities and towns, but it spreads itself through the narrow area of an excursion party with the vertiginous rapidity of a flash of lightning. In less than an hour the indecorous conduct of the youthful Reachall was a subject for amused conversation in every corner of train number three. Even the Hon. Goliath heard about it, and received the news with becoming dignity. He could see no crime in cleanliness, he said. It had been a source of wonder to him how so many hundreds of persons existed without daily baths during a long run across the continent. But the earl was much disturbed. "D—n it!" he said, "the fellow has gone too far. He must come out of my car, he and his brood. He'll be wanting the ladies' boudoir for a dressing-room next."

Inquiries as to the source from whence the invitations for the young Reachalls had been issued developed the fact that they had no invitations at all. This caused a complication. The father had been invited, but had himself taken the liberty of having his two sons join the excursion at Chicago, to which city they had recently come after a hunting tour. "God bless my soul!" said the earl, when he heard this. "Then they are only intruders! They must come out of this!"

The result was a visit to the Hon. Goliath Reachall by a train official, who, with some circumlocution of language, said he was credibly informed that there were two young gentlemen in his company who had not been invited to become members of the excursion party, and he must therefore ask him to have them leave the train at the next station, which would be Missoula.

The Hon. Goliath admitted that the youths had not been included in the invitation. "But," said he, "you can't put them off in a howling wilderness like this, you know! It's quite impossible!"

"Oh, yes, we can," responded the train official; "just as easy as not. There's twenty men on the cars, any one of whom could put 'em both off at once."

Goliath did not argue the point, perceiving that the officials did not quite comprehend him; and so the two Reachalls disappeared from the excursion that night, being set down, with their innumerous pieces of luggage, at Missoula, where they were to await the first through train to the East over the new road. Their father had no intention of accompanying them, and he went on towards the Pacific with train number three. But he had in some mysterious manner associated the earl with the dismissal of the sons, and he, therefore, took a terrific dislike to the noble lord, and besought accommodation in another car. This favor being accorded him, he suddenly became less critical and exacting, and contented himself with making up for the slight which he considered to have been put upon him by avenging himself on the cold game and the champagne and apollinaris on all possible occasions in the general dining-car. But he raged inwardly, and already meditated a book, in which he would picture the decline of republican institutions, and the disgusting promiscuity of democracy, with a pen dipped in gall.

. . . .

Lady Helena retired early to rest that night, and lay for hours, wakeful and intensely interested, in the panorama of rock-ribbed mountains fringed with yellow pine, and of great barriers along the stream which flowed impetuously in a cañon near which the railway route ran. A faint moonlight cast a mystical shimmer over the gigantic tamaracks and the mammoth pines, and on the islands covered with cottonwood. From time to time the train halted, as if it had lost its way in the forest, and was hesitatingly peering into the uncertain shadows beyond; but at last it would utter a defiant whistle, and move on smoothly and courageously. Then it would shriek, and halt, and back, and move forward and back again; and in the distance Lady Helena would hear the answering whistle of "train number four," valiantly keeping up the rear. It was wonderful and startling to her that in the dense silence of the autumn night in those primeval woods, amid these rocky and dangerous defiles, and on a newly constructed route, she was borne along as safely and comfortably as if her own room in London could have been transported by magic over land and sea. One little accident on these rails, unseen by the men who urged the locomotives along them, and she and her fellow-travellers might go spinning into a chasm, or be rolled down a mountain side, and dashed to pieces among the boughs of the trees! But the accident never came; the journey was magical, enchanting. The railroad impressed Lady Helena — and justly — as the greatest triumph of modern civilization. And while she was musing upon it, with her white hands extended in front of her upon the soft and harmoniously colored blanket overspreading her bed, and with her face turned to the window, she fell asleep.

When she awoke, after a period of fitful dreaming, she was vaguely oppressed with a sense of coming calamity. The train had stopped; men with lanterns in their hands were passing and repassing her window; and a locomotive was whistling plaintively, as who should say, "What shall I do now?" Impelled by some influence which she could not define, she arose, dressed hastily, threw a cloak about her shoulders, drew a hood over her head, and, glancing at Lady Offast, who was sleeping dreamlessly, and finding that there was no danger of awakening her, she opened the door and slipped out into the anteroom. Then, after hesitating a minute, she unlocked the outer door, opened it, and stepped on to the platform.

The keen night air made her shiver. The train was standing on the side of a hill around which the track had been carved with much toil and at enormous expense. Above the narrow strip of iron rails rose the steep slope, covered with firs, tamaracks, and pines. Below was a tremendous stretch of shelving declivity, tufted with coarse grasses and clumps of bushes, in and out of which the moonbeams were playing hide-and-seek. In the distance a brawling stream was coursing among jagged stones and water-worn boulders. Away on the dimly defined horizon was a black line of "timber." This was the untamed wilderness, — untamed, save by the single, slender, iron way.

"Gruesome, aint it?" said a cheerful voice, emerging from a black mass on the platform of the opposite car. "Doesn't give one any desire to get down and go botanizing, does it?"

"Captain Jobson!" said Lady Helena, somewhat startled, "how long have you been sitting there?"

"Hours. I like it. The cars are too warm for

me. I just brace on here with my feet, and the side-railing protects me so that I am as snug as possible in my chair. Yes. I sat up late talking with that boy Dulon. He's a crazy feller. Nice, though! Reg'lar enthusiast. The moon makes him wild, I reckon. He talked lots o' sentiment this evening."

Lady Helena eyed the black mass rather suspiciously. "Indeed! you would much better all have been fast asleep, I think."

"Well, no," said Captain Jobson. "Boys will be boys, you know — full of sentiment. And, as for me, I like to sit out nights and watch the weather. It's kind of second nature. But this railroad travelling is too commonplace for me. No adventures, you know. Aint you afraid of the night air? No? Scenery's gloomy, though, aint it?"

If Lady Helena had told the exact truth at that particular minute she would have declared that she thought the scenery anything but gloomy, for what he had just said about Dulon Floyd had set the moonbeams dancing in her brain, and she saw everything in a fairy glamour. But she feared lest the captain, whose acuteness she had long ago recognized, might discover her secret, so she said, in a voice full of weariness: —

"Dreary, and somewhat monotonous, this wilderness. I trust we shall soon be out of it."

"Oh, no! Only just on the edge of it now; so they all tell me. Woods and cañons, and roaring rivers and Chinamen, and that's all."

"Dear me, Captain Jobson! As if that were not enough! Well, I suppose we must be resigned, until we reach the Pacific coast."

"Excuse me, Lady Helena," said the captain, rising and approaching with a fatherly air, "but it is very late, and the train is likely to start up any minute. Do you think it quite prudent to remain on the platform?"

"Yes — no — perhaps you are — I mean you are quite right," stammered Lady Helena, suddenly feeling that it was very improper. "But I could not stay in my cabin — my berth, I mean; I felt that I must see what was going on."

Just then the locomotive uttered a doleful and foreboding yell, and the train went slowly on. Captain Jobson was in the act of crossing from one car platform to the other to offer the young lady his chair when the sudden movement of the train threw him backward, and he uttered a little cry of pain. "I wrenched my foot," he said, "and I see that the gate to your platform is locked.

I'll just step in and get one of the train men to open it with his key, and then if you wish to stay out awhile I will offer myself as guard."

"Oh, thank you!" she said, and he disappeared in his own car. Lady Helena moved to the side of the platform, looking out as the cars moved lazily onward. A moment later she uttered a faint cry of terror, and clung desperately to the railing before her. It seemed as if the train had left the solid earth and was flying through the air. But a grinding, crunching noise beneath the wheels so far convinced her that they were crossing one of the great trestles which afford such ample testimony to the audacious ingenuity of the western railway-builders. She looked down, shudderingly, into depths which appeared, under the moon's deceptive glare, six times as deep as they really were.

The train was crossing a tremendous ravine in the Coriacan defile, on a trestle-bridge nearly a thousand feet long, and two hundred and fifty feet above the bottom of the valley. It was like looking down from a balloon to gaze over into the vale, in which Lady Helena could dimly discern the forms of trees, and where she could see a few twinkling lights.

The engineers who were driving the locomotives which drew the train of eight heavy cars were evidently determined to be prudent. They went on to the middle of the trestle with great caution, and there halted. Lady Helena grew dizzy as she stood looking down into the gulf, from which the cars, filled with scores of sleeping people, were protected by no railing, no coping. There they were — in mid-air — two hundred and fifty feet high, on a narrow line of planks, supported by a few crazy scaffoldings. The girl felt the appeal of the abyss. "I shall jump down there and be killed if I look another instant," she thought.

Just then she heard the door of the next car opened, and, looking over at it, saw Dulon Floyd come out. For a second his handsome form and manly face were outlined against the light in the background, then he closed the door. Lady Helena pulled her hood about her brows, and stood firm. It was no time to retreat now. "Heavens! what a strange scene!" She heard him say this, and then she saw him start hastily back, and clutch at the side-railing of the platform for support.

For the train had started anew, with a jerk which had wrenched away the imperfect coupling-pin which held the two cars together, and Lady

Helena found herself rapidly separated from Dulon Floyd by a quickly increasing space of shining rail. The car on which Dulon stood, with the one in the rear of it, was left behind on the trestle. But that was not the worst of it. At the point where the train had started there was quite a steep decline, continued to the end of the trestle; it pitched forward so that the cars left behind, having received a downward impetus before the coupling broke, were now following the main train, and, should it stop again before leaving the trestle, they would come crashing into it, and might be toppled over into the abyss, or might kill the innocent sleepers in the earl's car.

Mr. Dulon had been sitting moodily in a corner of his car, watching a game of cards played by two newspaper men who were indisposed to sleep; and when Captain Jobson came in and told him that Lady Helena was wakeful like himself, and was star-gazing, he went out to speak with her, convinced, however, that she would retreat as soon as he arrived. His consternation when the accident occurred may be imagined. One thought only filled his brain; she was in danger; she might be crushed; she might become frightened and leap down; she — a thousand things might occur! What should he, what could he, do?

Lady Helena did not understand the full extent of the danger, but she knew that her lover was there, — helpless on the lumbering cars, left now to their own devices, and, before she realized what she was doing, she had stepped to the edge of her car platform and stretched out her arms to him.

He saw this, for the engineers were slackening speed again, and his car was *gaining* in speed. "Pull the bell-rope!" he shouted, leaning forward and pointing to the place where that rope should be, but whence it had vanished, broken in twain by the shock when the coupling was sundered. She understood him, but made a frantic gesture to show him that there was no bell-rope to pull. "Then run!" he cried. "Run as far as you can away from this end, for we shall be down upon your car in a moment or two. *Run, love, run for your life!* Wake up the others if you can!"

But love did not run for her life. She was far too anxious about another life, much dearer to her than her own. Providence, or chance, just then put it into the head of one of the engineers to look back, and he saw that there was something wrong. He gave the alarm, and the train's movement was instantly quickened, but not in time wholly to avoid the disaster.

It had all happened in two minutes, and Lady Helena stood as if fascinated, waiting the end. She saw Mr. Dulon throw open the door behind him, and shout out an alarm to those within; she saw him desperately signalling to her to withdraw, and she tried to obey him; but her limbs refused to carry her far. She got within the door and a few steps in the little anteroom, and fell down in a faint, just as the loosened cars rejoined the train, with a terrible shock, which smashed the two platforms, twisted their railings and steps, and broke in the end of the earl's vehicle. That worthy gentleman thought that his final hour had come, as he awakened to the situation. It was wonderful that none of the cars had been toppled over into the gulch. Their own immense weight held them to the track, from which lighter cars would have been hurled.

Dulon Floyd never knew how he managed, with an ugly wound in his right shoulder, to get from his car into the other; but he was there before the earl or any one else had left their beds, and he had raised Lady Helena and placed her arms about his neck, and, tenderly supporting her, had called her a hundred endearing names, as she returned to consciousness.

"You are safe!" she said, leaning heavily on his arms, for her strength was gone. "Safe! Thank God!"

"Love!" he murmured. There was no need to say anything more. And I do not think they knew or cared at that moment whether they had been hurled down from the trestle or not.

And now came immense tooting and bellowing from the engines, and much flashing of lanterns, and removing of passengers from the two damaged cars, and rapid work to get out of the way of "train number four." Fortunately no one was killed; there were only half a dozen wounded, including Dulon, with a rift in his shoulder; and presently the wrecked cars and the whole ones behind them were hauled off the trestle with the talent which these road men of the frontier always display in an emergency.

Lady Helena and Dulon were both secretly glad that the accident had occurred. It had done wonders for them.

CHAPTER XIX.

IN THE FOREST WILDERNESS.

The afternoon of the next day was passed by the excursionists in the mighty glades of an ancient forest, through which the sinewy arms of John Chinaman had hewn a path for the "fire-devil," which he would not permit to roam across the sacred earth of China, but which he thought proper enough for the usage of the Anglo-Saxon barbarian.

Wonderful and mysterious was this north-western forest-world, this unsubjugated wilderness, through which the bear and the wolf still roamed at will, and where the tall pines and firs on the mountain-sides, and the cottonwood beside the brawling and rushing stream, stood in armies of hundreds of thousands.

"Here is a mountain so steep that no trees could stick on its side," said the earl to his companions, as they stood looking down on the Clark's fork of the Columbia river, at a point where the waters, urging their eager way year after year and century after century, had carved for themselves a channel deep down between massive walls of rock. Beyond the stream stood a range of hills, majestic, abrupt, almost appalling in their sombre loneliness. In the glades among these hills the grotesque bear sniffed his clumsy way, and humorously went through the daily process of stealing that which he might boldly have claimed as his own; the cautious deer stamped with his delicate foot, and listened shyly; the elk, the caribou, and the moose fed and fought and stupidly gazed, after the fashion of their kind; the grouse sprang whirring from the thicket, and in the small streams the speckled trout disported.

The earl was nervous and excited. He had donned one of his extraordinary sporting-costumes, and was abroad with the firm resolve to kill something. Behind him marched Colonel Hodges, bearing a handsome rifle; Ringdale and Dulon, with their sketching materials and fowling-pieces at their backs, — to gratify the earl's whim, — came next in order; and Captain Jobson, showing marked agility as he clambered over fallen trunks of trees and pushed aggressive brushwood out of the way, escorted Lady Offast and Lady Helena, who were engaged in a frantic course of botanizing.

"There should be brigands in this wood," said

Lady Helena, who was beginning to have a taste for adventure.

"Plenty of 'em here once," said Captain Jobson, who appeared to absorb the history of every tract of country through which he passed. "It's only a year or two ago since over to Weeksville—the trainmen pointed out the place as we came by it this morning — the robbers got to be unpleasantly numerous. So the Vigilantes went for 'em."

"I beg your pardon," said Lady Offast, in a tone which plainly indicated that she did not quite understand the worthy captain.

"Went for 'em, madam; that is, the citizens took the law into their own hands and hanged the villains. One of the robbers was hobbling about on crutches when he was arrested. He had got hurt with a pistol in trying to convince a railroad paymaster that he ought to give him the money intended for the laborers. Wal, they hanged this crippled feller, and, as they didn't have any tombstones handy, they just stuck his crutches up at the head of his grave. Cute, wasn't it?"

"Quite dreadful," said Lady Offast. "And are we sure that the trains will not move off and leave us to be eaten by bears in this forest?"

"No danger, madam. No forward movement until evening."

So they went on, inspired by the keen, pure air, and the aroma of the trees, and the roar of the distant waters. Lady Helena fancied that the procession of towering hills which she could see on the right through the opening in the wood was slowly moving around to enclose them in a magic circle from which they could never extricate themselves. She tried to imagine the place as it was in winter, when the gleaming snow lay heavily upon all this mass of undergrowth, and when the winds howled through the branches of the firs. She might have given her excited imagination still freer range had not her attention been recalled to the party by the sound of a shot.

"Offast has sighted something at last," said his wife.

And so he had. Out from the thicket into which his lordship had fired now tumbled, rather than ran, a confused mass of blue clothing, so agitated by convulsive jerks of yellowish arms and lean legs that it was difficult for some moments to recognize it as a human being — of the Chinese variety. "Choy," said the whirling and trembling object, "no catchee game camp-side; man catchee bullet, die." And this celestial orator indulged in an expressive pantomime, which indicated that if the earl had happened to hit him it would have been a most unfortunate occurrence.

"God bless my soul!" said the earl, striding forward and gazing curiously at the frightened and somewhat indignant John; "I took it for a grouse, and it's only a Chinaman!"

Captain Jobson came up at this juncture and mollified the yellow toiler with a silver dollar, dexterously placed in the palm of his hand. "Nobody hurt, John," he said. "Show us your camp." Then, turning to the earl, he added: —

"It will be more amusing than shooting."

The earl shook his head, and protested that he had been deceived. He had been tempted to America by promises of unlimited sport, in spacious woods, where no permission was to be asked, and where one could roam as he pleased. "And now here, the first shot that I fire to-day I narrowly miss killing a fellow-creature! It's quite exasperating!"

The Chinaman, encouraged by Captain Jobson's gift, and by the prospect of others, guided the party through a thicket, and presently brought them into one of the laborers' camps, not far from a curve in the railway route. Here were hundreds of Chinese, enjoying a brief season of repose before they broke up their encampment and moved westward, where fresh labors awaited them. The ladies shrank from going among them, but they were soon reassured by cheerful smiles and waggings of pagan heads from all directions. A chorus of monosyllabic cackling arose as the earl advanced with dignified air, feeling a sudden return of that power to patronize which he had been taught to consider as an inherited right, but which he had discovered to be singularly out of place when he was in the midst of native Americans. In these peasants from the strange empire of China he instantly recognized the attitude to which he was accustomed at home when laborers were in his presence. He was pleased, and, finding a mild-eyed boy, with a dusky face, singularly devoid of chin and nose, and with a smile which not only seemed to light up his own features, but to communicate a certain radiance to the immediate neighborhood, he entered into conversation with him, and expressed his desire to bestow gratuities on the whole population of the camp before he took his departure.

Dulon and Ringdale were delighted with the quaint types offered to their pencils, and they were very industrious. The camp was of the rudest construction. There were but one or two houses of boards roughly put together; the other habitations were cellars dug in the side of a shelving hill, and banked up with dirt and roofed with boughs. The earl peered into one of these dens, and was so horrified at seeing a young Chinaman extended on a mat, in the third heaven of an opium trance, that he refused to allow the ladies to inspect the interior. At a long table, rigged to the withered stem of a forest monarch which had been felled to make way for the Northern Pacific's track, twenty Chinamen were gathered, discussing fare which seemed by no means indifferent. Their voices rose and fell in wild refrain. The barber was at work in a clean corner, shaving a Celestial's head and arranging the plaits of his cue. Two bright boys, with moonlike faces, arrived with a basket of newly washed clothing from a tributary to the great stream in the cañon. Not all the faces were good-natured. Lady Helena was so impressed with the preternatural ugliness and apparent viciousness of a dwarf, who was squatted on a tree-trunk, that she trembled as she passed him. This creature had enormous wens on his neck, which made him look as if his mottled and hideous head were growing directly out of one of his shoulders. He was meekly eating a few bits of chopped meat and vegetables, which he picked with his long, claw-like fingers from a paper bag. Not far from this creature was a niche in the bank, in which stood an ugly image of some Chinese saint, — "velly good old man," as the guide expressed it, — and in front of this adored personage little sticks of aromatic punk were smoking. Nearly all the Chinamen wore the black slouch hat of the American — the first sign of their gradual absorption into the great homogeneous mass of the nation, which will be — whatever a few timorous and narrow-minded local politicians may think or profess to think — none the worse for a trifling infusion of Chinaman.

At the end of the camp the laborers had arranged a small arch of triumph, prettily adorned with lanterns of paper, artistically painted and bestowed. The earl and his suite were invited to pass under this arch, which they did, and half-a-dozen Chinamen on a hill-side near by fired off some huge bunches of fire-crackers, and leaped into the air, howling and shrieking to indicate their delight at the arrival of the excursionists. The camp was twenty dollars richer for the earl's visit, and Dulon and Ringdale made so many sketches from life that their hands were weary. The felt-sandalled barbarians assumed a respectful air as the earl bade them farewell, and he came away enchanted with what he had seen, and forgetful that his game-bag was empty.

Dulon and Lady Helena had this day hardly spoken together. The young American painter was puzzled and dazzled. He had had a rapturous and tender confession of love from her lips and eyes, in that moment when they fancied that they were to go crashing down into the gulf below the trestle in the Coriacan defile. This was certain; no chance nor change could deprive him of it. But what, then, was the explanation of Lady Helena's devotion to the missing Lord John? Now that he had won from Lady Helena so much — a sudden avowal, which was so precious to him — the jealousy which he had managed to stifle after he had pledged his aid to Ringdale returned with new and alarming force. Might not the young English lady be capricious? Might she not disavow, when she heard news of Lord John, the casual passion of an excursion? Was she not in a peculiar position, which placed her socially almost beyond his reach? Would she prove as haughty of heart as she was sometimes haughty of mien? No, a thousand times no!

He hated himself for his fleeting suspicions; but they came back again and again, and caused him keener twinges than he felt from the cut in his shoulder, which he had, on the morning after the accident, declared a mere scratch, but which the doctor who had bandaged it looked rather serious over. He was ashamed of his sullen silence, as he tramped home from the Chinese camp beside Lady Helena, and he went away to his little den in the newspaper car, to lie down, to nurse his wounds, and to meditate.

After he had been alone for an hour Ringdale came in quite radiant. "News, old man, news," he said. "We shall be in time. I stayed to sketch that mass of tangled vines not far from "train number two," as you know. After I had finished my work I was just about crawling out of the shade of the brush in which I had been seated, when at the back of the thicket I heard Lady Helena's voice, and then the anxious tones of Lady Offast's man. 'I should have had the despatch hours ago, my lady,' says the valet, 'if these 'orrid Americans 'adn't got my name wrong. It came to a station where we stopped last night, just after we was all so nearly killed on that bridge, and it's been follerin' me from train to train until 'ere it is.'—'And what does it tell us, now that you have got it?' says Lady Helena, with a curious tremor in her voice. 'Read it.' John read it out. 'The next steamer from Australia will arrive here in about twelve days.' — 'Good!' said Lady Helena, earnestly; 'we shall not be too late. And now promise me that you will aid me in every way. Your master must accompany me to San Francisco before that steamer arrives! Do you understand? But you must say nothing to him of *my* great desire to be there when this steamer arrives; remember! On my presence there at that time, *honor*, the peace and happiness of a family, *perhaps life itself*, may depend.' The man stammered his complete obedience, and said he thought he could influence his master to make all speed for San Francisco. Now is it not clear that she is going to the rescue of Lord John?"

"I suppose it is," said Dulon, wearily, feeling his suspicions again. Twelve days to wait! It seemed to him an age. He wished to see the mystery unravelled at once. "Perhaps your brother has already arrived by a previous steamer," he ventured to suggest. He half wished that it might be so.

"Your face looks quite dark," said Ringdale, bending down to look at Dulon. "Does that knock on your shoulder give you fresh trouble?"

"Oh, no!" he answered. "I feel a little pressure at the heart." And indeed he did.

The trains moved on that evening through the forests of northern Idaho, and over many a trestle almost as impressive as the one on which the adventure had happened to "train number three." The air was sweet and soft, and the earl's party, reinforced by Ringdale, Dulon, Captain Jobson, and Colonel Hodges, gathered in the anteroom of the private car and on the outer platform. The train moved slowly, and a white moonlight showed with startling clearness the fluted pillars of rock near Cabinet Landing; the old "portage" of the Hudson Bay Company; the glassy surface of Pack River, across which the trains went smoothly on a trestle one mile and a half long; and the exquisite shores of Lake Pend d'Oreille, where the wanderers saw an encampment of Flathead Indians, the wigwams standing out boldly in the moonlight, and the tatterdemalion bucks and squaws grouping picturesquely about them. Then they turned away from the lake into the forests again, and it was not until midnight that they once more came into open country, — the broad and fertile Spokane valley, through which the pretty Spokane river, which is born in Lake Cœur d'Aléne, flows impetuously, now making great leaps between jagged rocks and basaltic shores, and culminating in a roaring and spray-enshrouded waterfall at the place where the town of Spokane Falls sprung up.

"One might fancy one's self in an English country-side here," said Dulon, approaching Lady Helena, who stood bareheaded at the door of the car, gazing at the moonlit expanse of valley with delighted eyes. "See, there is a hedge, or something which at night looks much like one."

"Oh, no! that's a pile of railroad iron, and a long and big one, too!" said Captain Jobson. "That reminds me that when I was in Java, in 1854, I was on a country road one night, and I thought I saw a tiger waiting to spring on me. My hair arose and remained standing, I assure you. But by and by I saw that the tiger didn't move, and so I concluded that I'd jog along and get back to the harbor. Next morning I went up to the same place, and my tiger of the night before was a big mound of earth, thrown up in front of a ditch."

"Away, destroyer of romance!" said Lady Helena, waving her hand gaily to him. And he disappeared, for he never lost an opportunity to leave Dulon in *tête-à-tête* with her. The others, within the car, were engaged in a discussion as to the relative merits of Swiss and American mountain scenery.

"Captain Jobson has spoiled my bit of poetry," said Dulon, laughing. "My hedge has vanished. You look weary and abstracted. I suppose you will not be sorry when this long journey is finished?"

"No," she said, "I do not feel weary. I could have gone on forever through those grand old forests. That is like what I had fancied America to be. Not like New York and Chicago, you know. But when does our journey end?"

"Mine must terminate for the present, I think, at Vancouver's Island, where we can be in four or five days. I am anxious to see that place, which we looked at with awe on the map when I was a school-boy. We thought it was Ultima Thule. I hope I may find there the subjects that I am in search of." Dulon looked sheepish as he said this, for he felt that Lady Helena was regarding him with a quizzical air, as if she understood his motive in thus threatening a separation from her, when he had not the slightest intention of carrying out his threat. "I suppose," he added, cautiously, "that the earl will be in no haste to return to the Atlantic coast, and that you will wish to see all the wonders of the North-west?"

"I think," said Lady Helena, "that my cousin has changed his plans a bit, and means to get to San Francisco as soon as possible. But perhaps you will meet us there after you have been to Ultima Thule?" He looked up hastily; the quizzical expression was still in her eyes, but her voice had trembled.

"What nonsense it is for us to talk so coldly!" he said, with his old earnestness. "Can you not see that I cannot, must not leave you — unless — unless you send me away?"

"Well, I certainly hope that we may journey together as far as San Francisco," said Lady Helena, calmly, as if she had not heard his last words. "Is it a long voyage from Oregon?"

"Only forty-eight hours."

"Oh! fancy!" The wearied and abstracted expression which he had noticed was gone now. "I had a notion that it was — ever so far. Your American distances are so very magnificent!"

"Did I not say the other day that I go where you go, in spite of all the pictures in the universe? And do you think that — after last night — I — I could change my mind? No, I shall go with you to San Francisco;" he drew nearer, and, impelled by a resistless desire to know the truth, he added, "and if

I can help you there — if there is anything that I can do in case of need — trust me fully."

He paused, utterly abashed. The quizzical look had returned to Lady Helena's face. "Ah — I don't think — I am sure — there could be nothing" — She fixed her gaze upon him fearlessly. "But if there *were* anything — I *should* trust you fully. I think my cousin is coming this way."

"Say, can you tell me in which car I can find Klasson, — Klasson of Illinois?" said a sharp voice; and the pale face of Caswell P. Rusher came out of the darkness. The reporter caught at the railings, and swung himself up on to the steps of the earl's car. "There's about two thousand citizens out here want to see him and have him make them a speech. Seems he used to live here. Lord, you should see the bonfires they've built! What a noise that plaguy old waterfall makes! Haven't seen Klasson?" And he swung back into the darkness.

CHAPTER XX.

"WHERE ROLLS THE OREGON."

OUT of the valley and away all night, through cool glades, wide forests, and across romantic ravines on the slender trestles. When morning came the excursionists found themselves in the main street of a "city" built entirely of boards. This mushroom community could not have been more than two years old, but it had all the self-complacent calm of an old-established metropolis. It had a hotel, somewhat larger than a Saratoga trunk; innumerous "saloons," in front of which, at seven o'clock on this hot September morning, an Irish person, of Herculean build and rubicund countenance, was delivering huge blocks of ice to serve later on in the fabrication of cooling drinks for the hundreds of workmen employed on the construction of the stone piers of the mammoth bridge over the Snake river. A Chinaman was peacefully ironing clean garments at the door of his shanty, which was decorated with this legend: "WAH LEE. Washing Done Her." A lady of a flamboyant style of beauty was seated in an easy-chair on a portico of thin planks, and from the somewhat extravagant tone of her remarks it was to be presumed that in older communities she might have been compelled by the social code to take a more retired position; but here no prejudice existed to annoy her, and she relished her liberty.

Back of the town lay a wavy waste of sand-hills, dotted with a sickly growth of bunch grass, and over these miniature eminences came riding, on a sorrowful-looking pony, an Indian chief, dressed in rags and a much-battered tall hat with a feather in it.

Here, near the confluence of the Snake and the Columbia rivers, the great excursion trains were ferried across the Snake on a steamer constructed expressly for carrying railway cars; two of the Pullmans were taken at each trip, the steamer breasting the rapid current with disdainful strength. Lady Helena and Dulon sat on the upper deck, where the breeze was fresh and cool, and surveyed with interest the strangely colored banks of the Columbia; the awful solitudes which must have seemed enchanted by the adventurous white men who first penetrated them. Here vegetation was sparse, and the mottled rocks towered savagely.

Beyond the sage-brush and the sand Lady Helena fancied that she could see a ruined castle or fortress.

"No," said Dulon; "that is a crag too magnificent to have been fashioned by the strength of man; but one could almost affirm that these admirably contrasted colors at the summit were applied by human hands. No; these are the works of nature, and they will tower up, as noble and rugged as now, centuries after the American nation, with its railroads and its town-meetings and its tremendous impetus, has accomplished its mission, and disappeared."

"What heresy, Mr. Floyd! Are you not a good patriot? Do you not expect your nation to endure — forever, I was about to say — and — now that I reflect — it would have been absurd to say it?"

"Why — no," — answered Mr. Floyd, smiling; "I don't expect it to last — any more than the Aztecs or the Mound-Builders — or — I don't know much about such things; but I feel quite certain that this ravenous old continent of ours has already devoured a dozen civilizations, and will pick the bones of ours as remorselessly as it polished those of our predecessors."

"Dear me!" said Lady Helena, laying her hands in her lap, and speaking musingly; "I expected to find every one in America rejoicing over the conquest of nature and the subjugation of the wilderness, and here I discover a youthful pessimist, who sees in the land on which his countrymen are building their proud nation only the grave which is to emtomb their edifice shortly after they have got it built. Is not this stated correctly?"

"I am a pessimist now, am I?" said Dulon, with by no means a doleful expression of countenance. It was pleasant to him to be rallied by Lady Helena. "Why not call me a Nihilist at once?"

"It would have been more appropriate," she said. "I believe America will grow up strong and grand, and will endure. I — I like to think so. My cousin says it will fall to pieces some day. Of course — of course I mean the nation, not the country. But he keeps on buying land here, in spite of his gloomy forebodings."

"Your cousin is an English nobleman, and has small liking for republics," said Dulon, warmly; and Lady Helena smiled, and felt convinced that had she not deftly changed the subject she would have had the "pessimist" energetically defending the eternity of the American republic, just as he had prophesied its decline and disappearance a few moments before.

"But I don't know," said Dulon, slowly. "I can only feel — I can't reason — on such things as this solemn and majestic wilderness here. I feel as if it would resent civilization's inroads as an affront to its grandeur, I can't tell why. The civilizer has only been here for a generation. No one knows what may happen to him yet."

"No; he may" — said Lady Helena, rising and moving away, as if afraid to let Dulon see her face — "he may be hurled down from a railway trestle and be dashed to pieces — unless Providence interferes. And if Providence does interfere — you know — it looks as if He — or It — meant to protect the civilizer, does not it?"

Dulon made no answer, and Lady Helena was much better pleased than if he *had* tried to respond. Presently the cars were all ferried over; new locomotives came screeching and hooting in barbaric style to draw them down to Portland, the metropolis of Oregon and the end of the excursion across the north-western section of the continent. Hundreds of Chinamen left their work on the bridge and came to salute the departing excursionists with fire-crackers and with Hi Yahs! without number.

Night fell before the travellers had wearied of gazing at the rocky and overhanging cliffs, at the broad current flowing in its deep channel, at the singular contrasts of sandy and verdureless reaches interspersed with Arcadian glades in which ample fruit-orchards displayed their fragrant treasures.

Next morning they were ferried across another river — the quiet and picturesque Willamette — and were safely landed in Portland, where the citizens had arranged a mammoth entertainment for them, and as the earl expressed it to the worthy gentleman who escorted him and his ladies to a hospitable mansion on the heights, "We have not had so much fatigue in the two thousand miles between St. Paul and Portland as we should have encountered in the journey from London to Paris."

The amiable personage above mentioned informed the earl that his wife and daughter were "in the East," and that consequently he was not keeping open kitchen; "but," said he, "the City Committee has provided you with meals at Eppinger's." The earl started and the ladies looked amazed, but that evening, when they walked down through the pretty streets, and entered Eppinger's inviting door, and found within a *cuisine* which would have done Paris honor and wines which were irreproachable, the earl was delighted. "Fancy," he said, "coming into the wilds of Oregon to find as good a restaurant as any in London! And as for your boasted Delmonico, I saw nothing so very elaborate except the prices — don't you know, — in his establishment." Eppinger's was indeed a surprise in the wilderness. Captain Jobson and Colonel Hodges now came out in superb style in frock coats and tall hats, and, during the stay in Portland, daily electrified the earl and Lady Offast with new salad dressings, new and strange receipts for omelets, and new wines, when they were fortunate enough to have seats at the table with the English party. Dulon and Ringdale, who were lodged in a quarter of the town at some distance from the earl's quarters, came regularly to salute the ladies when they sat down to the good Eppinger's feasts; but the earl, now that the excursion was virtually at an end, was distant to Mr. Dulon, and by various vexatious expedients indicated his desire that the acquaintance should not be continued to the extent of intimacy. Lady Helena soon observed that Captain Jobson and Colonel Hodges were both endeavoring to correct the earl's revived prejudice against Dulon, and she silently blessed them for it.

Portland was too much, in its general features,

like an hundred other American towns — so far as the works of man were concerned — to gain much attention from the travelled party; but its location won most generous praise from every one. As the monarch of European mountains, Mont Blanc, is chary about showing himself to the visitors at Geneva, so the gigantic and imposing Mount Hood, away across the Willamette, would only now and then reveal to the eager gazers its snow-white sides. Sometimes, when it flashed out upon the vision through rose-colored or delicate gray clouds, it looked like a mountain hanging in mid-air. From the wooded heights back of Portland, seen through leafy openings between the majestic trees, the glimpse of this mountain was worth the seven thousand miles of travel which the English party had accomplished to get it.

"Mount Hood," said Captain Jobson to the ladies, "is like the old settlers here in Oregon: he's mighty shy. Have you noticed that these good folks here who have been so long shut off from the rest of the country and from Europe, rather scowl at the new-comers? They act as if they were afraid we were going to get their country away from 'em. They thought they had a corner on these mountains and this rampageously big river.

Fact, they did. Cute fellers, weren't they? Now, here we come skipping along, dropping in after our little ten days' loiter across the continent — a journey that it took them six months to do one-half of when they came West — and it sorter makes 'em jealous."

"I say, Captain Jobson," remarked Lady Offast, "do tell us what you mean by these people having a corner on the mountains?"

And it took him more than half an hour to explain, after which Lady Offast told him that "the eccentricity of your phrases quite takes one's breath away, I assure you."

While the festivities attendant upon the completion of the railway went on in Portland, our friends departed for a hurried trip along the Columbia River, up to the head of Puget's Sound, and even to Vancouver's Island. Ringdale had been in constant telegraphic communication with mysterious people in San Francisco since his arrival in Portland, and he informed Dulon that they had a week before them ere they need depart for the Golden Gate. Lady Helena now appeared in no haste to reach California, which much surprised and perplexed the young men, who, of course, did not know what special means of information she might have. And, although an apprehension of some coming event which might bring sadness to them stung the heart of each of the three, they could not refrain from enthusiastic enjoyment of the swift journey up the Willamette to its junction with the stately Columbia; they were delighted at the capricious mountain giants, Mount St. Helen's, Mount Adams, and that old vagabond Mount Hood, who were always playing at hide-and-seek among the clouds. These isolated peaks, according to Lady Offast, were not so impressive as the thick studded and serrated Alpine chains of Switzerland, with their ever-changing colors. But the eail was of contrary opinion. He said that he would give all the Swiss mountains, the Jungfrau and the Matterhorn included, for one good look at Mount Hood, or at the gleaming, marble-like pyramid of St. Helen's, as seen from the banks of the Willamette.

The Columbia, with its basaltic cliffs; its banks covered, in this mellow autumn, with gold-brown tints of the matured grass; its great and little "Dalles," where the foaming water rushes with sibilant defiance or angry gurgle down between the frowning lava walls; the Columbia, with its pictured rocks, its mystic inlets, its cañons in which the waters are fathomless, its broad wood-engirdled stretches in which the dangerous sands are scarcely covered; this river, with its mountainous shores covered with tangled forests of willow, alder, ash, and maple, was, to the little party, vastly impressive. Captain Jobson, who, like all sailors, has a taste for quotation, brought out the venerable Bryant's meditation on the solitudes —

> "Where rolls the Oregon, and hears no sound
> Save his own dashings,"

and told them how the noble river was named after a ship — the "Columbia," from Boston, which entered from a cruise in the Pacific, in 1792.

By and by they landed at Kalama, a railway terminus in the forest, and were whisked away in a comfortable train to New Tacoma on Puget Sound. On their way they passed through many little towns struggling for existence among blackened stumps; man had attacked the woods, and was grappling with untamed nature. New Tacoma, on a handsome eminence overlooking the placid waters of the huge estuary, was "ruther stumpy," as Captain Jobson expressed it, but it was soon to be a metropolis, with fleets of steamers from Europe and Asia lying at its wharves, and every inhabitant knew this, and said so at least once a day. New Tacoma had one thing that no other town in all this strange region of water-ways and fertile coasts could boast, and that was an absolutely perfect view of the monarch of the Pacific Coast — Mount Tacoma, the peerless. At sight of this unexpected Alp, Ringdale and Dulon set up a shout of joy. Forty miles away the inspiring peak towered up, more than fourteen thousand feet high, rejoicing in the sunlight, its stupendous glaciers resplendent in the exquisitely transparent air. The foreground was admirable. First, a long expanse of tidal marshes; then the delicate green range of the cotton-woods, and next the robust monotone of the fir forests. Then — Tacoma! in garments of light, a goddess of the air, a vision to uplift the soul!

"We progress from wonder to wonder!" said Lady Helena, dreamily.

That night they sailed along the peaceful waters of the Sound to Seattle, which enterprising town and bitter rival of New Tacoma was brilliantly illuminated with Chinese lanterns in honor of their arrival and that of other distinguished members of the excursion. Above them the sky was of a soft rose-color, which was reflected in the warm mist arising toward midnight. The earl drew a long breath. "This is like our native air," he said. "None of your thin dry Eastern atmospheres for me! I like to feel as if I were taking something into my lungs."

They stepped on board the tiny steamer which departed from Seattle in the morning, and threading its way in and out among the mountainous and densely-wooded islands, brought them into the harbor of Victoria, in British Columbia, as the sun was setting. A chill fell on the water and on the slopes of the pretty island as the party landed and wandered through the un-American, yet un-English, streets.

"This is neither one thing nor the other," said the earl; "but it is easy to see that it will soon be Americanized. It's an affair of environment."

"Bless you!" said Captain Jobson, who had been here — as he had been everywhere else — before, "these people think they are going to annex the United States! You have no idea of their own opinion of their importance."

Lady Helena had felt a singular presentiment of the approach of some surprise since her arrival at Victoria. A surprise was indeed in store for the gentle lady and her companions on the morrow.

CHAPTER XXI.

LORD JOHN.

Dulon found the atmosphere inspiring next morning when, awaking, as he fancied, before any of his fellow-travellers, he made a hasty toilet and slipped away from the little steamer to the green slopes at the back of Victoria. This remote hybrid settlement, with its motley mingling of English provincialism and American frontier instability, appealed powerfully to his imagination. He got up to the crown of a hill, whence he could see the broad and majestic strait of San Juan de Fuca — the noble highway on which, some day, all the treasures of the world away beyond would be brought to this Ultima Thule. This was not an island peopled by hyperborean savages and monsters of the lower order of creation as he had dreamed in his boyhood; and some day it might be the location of a metropolis, when a new Norway had sprung up in Alaska and in the fertile valleys of British Columbia.

He sketched the harbor and the excursion steamer,

because it would serve some day to remind him of *her*. He sketched the half-breed maidens, who stole timidly up to see what strange operation the new-comer was performing, and when he showed them their own pictures he set flames to dancing in their dusky cheeks. He sketched the mediocre edifice rather ambitiously denominated a cathedral. He sketched the broad headland, with its groups of sombre trees and its glistening marble gravestones, and he was about proceeding to sketch an ancient cow who had begun to graze near by when he heard familiar voices behind him, and looking over his shoulder he saw Lady Helena and Ringdale approaching.

He rose from his camp-stool and courteously offered it to Lady Helena, who did not speak to him, and who at once sat down as if she were quite exhausted. She closed her eyes — her lithe form swayed to and fro, and for a moment she seemed likely to faint. Mr. Floyd was on his knees beside her in an instant, but he arose as hastily as he had knelt, for Ringdale had tapped him on the shoulder and beckoned to him.

The young Englishman's face was more pallid than that of Lady Helena, and his eyes were widely dilated, as if he had just seen a vision.

"I have found him," he said. "Don't notice her; she stood it bravely and she will be all right in a few minutes."

"Found WHO!"

"Lord John. My poor brother, God bless him!" He seized Dulon's hand and pressed it warmly. "It's hard to bear — finding him so" — he said — "in such a condition — but" —

"Finding him how?" queried Dulon, who for the moment had almost forgotten Lady Helena's existence.

"But it's better than not finding him at all. Fancy our being directed here — by the hand of Providence — or fate — or something else — and coming right upon him in the middle of a country road. If we had hastened to San Francisco I might never have seen him again."

Lady Helena had now recovered a little, and sat looking out on the water, with her hands folded in her lap and a curious sadness in her eyes. Dulon noticed this, and his thin lips were tightly pressed together. A wrinkle came into his forehead. It seemed to him as if the love which had been such a delight to him were henceforth to prove his torture. But he would be patient; he would wait — wait, and judge slowly. If his romance were at an end

— it appeared to him as if his life were worthless and useless. It would be, he thought, like a landscape that never saw sunshine.

Ringdale went to Lady Helena and whispered, "We will walk up and down on the brow of the hill and talk this matter over. Mr. Floyd can help us."

"Oh! do you think you would better?" — Lady Helena looked up as if she were half-frightened, and there was a small patch of color in one of her cheeks.

"Meantime," said Ringdale, not seeming to notice her interruption, "do you sit quietly here; and remember — the utmost secrecy, so far as the earl and Lady Offast are concerned, until the proper moment comes."

"Very well," said Lady Helena, wearily; and she began her contemplation of the far-off waters again. Ringdale took Dulon's arm, and the two youths began to walk slowly to and fro on the hill-top.

"For Heaven's sake do not keep me in suspense!" cried Dulon. "Tell me, in the name of all that is wonderful, how you have managed to discover your brother on this island, when you fancied that he was still on the Pacific working his way up to San Francisco from Australia."

"Do you remember," said the young Englishman, solemnly, and with a certain tremor in his speech, "that gruesome tale that Captain Jobson told us one evening as we were forging along across the North-western plains; the tale, don't you know, about meeting one time, in the mighty solitudes of the Southern Pacific Ocean, a derelict craft — a vagrant, broken down, demoralized, almost used-up craft, which seemed helplessly and hopelessly drifting to ruin; and how the spectacle of that melancholy ship fairly frightened him, seemed to make his flesh creep? Do you not remember how he expressed the sorrow and sympathy, strangely mingled with the fright that he felt then? Well, I feel as old Captain Jobson did when he saw that craft."

Dulon began to understand him now, and he pitied him.

"I slept badly in that tiny box of a state-room last night, and I went on deck, roughly dressed, for a walk, just as the dawn was breaking. Much to my surprise, I found Lady Helena sitting on deck, muffled to the chin, and looking very solemn. 'Would you not like a good long walk?' I ventured to say to her. 'I should like it best of all things,' she answered; 'I feel as if I were impelled to march, and being cribbed up on this deck is hateful to me.' So in half an hour we were a mile from Victoria, walking in the still green lanes and beside the hedges, on the way to Esquimault, where there is an English supply-station, and where two or three British government ships are always lying. Esquimault is three miles from Victoria — so a native told us — and we confidently expected to get out there and back again before you and the others had been summoned to breakfast, when — when we saw the derelict. Lady Helena fainted dead away, and, upon my word, I felt uncommonly like it myself."

He paused and drew his breath hard. His pride was hurt, but his frankness would not permit him to palliate a single detail, for he had associated Dulon with himself in the search for the unfortunate Lord John, and considered himself bound to tell his partner all.

"You mean to say that you saw your brother on this country road?" said Dulon in a whisper. He felt the same eerie impression to which Ringdale had alluded in recalling the story of the deserted ship. "Was he — did he — does he know you?"

"There, on a little knoll by the roadside, we saw a man seated, or sunk down, rather, in an attitude of extreme exhaustion. Before I saw the face, a mortal coldness seized me at the heart. I had a presentiment of what was to come. The morning sunshine, which was merry elsewhere, seemed in some unaccountable fashion to have avoided that spot where the man was *assoupi*. A big bird was circling in the air above the man, and now and then making swoops downward, as if to see if it were life or death that crouched there motionless. At first we fancied that we had come upon a dead man. As I approached I noticed a faint, sickly odor, like that one perceives in all the Chinese shops and dwellings. I think if I had been called upon to define it I should have said that it was an *immoral* odor, one that by its strange intoxication could take away all sense of the real world from the human mind, and substitute for it an ideal sphere, full of phantasms and mockeries. It was the smell of opium. I hastened forward, and, bending over the figure, I looked into the face. Floyd, it was the face of my brother; and, with the eyes peacefully closed, he looked, in spite of the storm and stress of his career, almost as fresh and innocent as when I used to climb into his bed mornings, and, holding my breath, admiringly contemplate his youthful beauty until he awoke. Dear old brother Jack! And to think that I should find him thus! I wouldn't have believed that it could have happened. It sounds like a page out of a novel, doesn't it?"

"In this sense — yes," said Floyd, "that most *real* novels merely paraphrase events and incidents of *real* life. And what happened next?" He almost dreaded to ask the question, lest he should learn that Lady Helena, on seeing the unfortunate Lord John in such a predicament, had by unmistakable signs manifested the continuance of an affection for him.

"Next Lady Helena, having heard me cry out that it was Lord John, was lying on the grass, as white as the lace at her throat; and what to do, with these two on my hands, I really didn't quite know, don't you know. But in a minute Helena had revived, and came over to my poor brother and helped me to raise him up. She shuddered as the scent of the opium revealed itself, but she aided me in reviving Lord John, and presently he opened his eyes. That, my dear Floyd, was the bitterest of all. This was indeed the derelict, the helpless ship deserted on the great ocean of life! And to think that all this happened only three-quarters of an hour ago!"

"Where is your brother now?" said Floyd.

"I am coming to that. When Lady Helena looked into the eyes that slowly opened her face was like that of one who suddenly gets a severe wound. She was hurt more than she knew, but for the moment she only felt startled profoundly by the shock. There was no recognition in the gaze that poor Jack turned on us — none. There was a vague questioning — an endeavor to understand his surroundings; but it was vain. It was harder to bear than I thought it would have been. I had been prepared for trouble — but not for anything — quite — like — *this.* I give you my word — much as I longed to bring my brother safely home, whatever trouble might have weighed on his unlucky head — that I would rather have found him dead in that sunless plot by the wayside than to have seen him open his eyes as he opened them on us this morning."

Dulon was deeply touched. "I will not worry you with words," he said. "You must both command me, and I will do exactly as you wish."

Ringdale, whose honest eyes were filled with tears, looked up quickly at the American. "You had steeled yourself to the sacrifice," he said, "and bravely and finely too; but now you will not have to make it." Then he turned away, biting his lips, as if he feared that he had said too much.

For a moment Dulon thought the air was filled with music. Then the thought came again: if she ever loved this man, may she not love him still, even though he has wrecked his life and fortune? What are fortune and reputation and health where love is concerned? They do not weigh a feather's weight in the scale.

"I called my brother by his old pet names of boyhood, and he heard me and smiled; but although he looked steadily at me, he did not know me. As for Lady Helena, she must have appeared to his disordered fancy as monstrous and grotesque alternately, for he would look at her fixedly, and seem spellbound with horror; then would cast laughing glances at her. It was horrible! Now, I know what was meant by trying to cast out an evil spirit. The smell of alcohol and opium, the surprise and anguish of this strange meeting, my anxiety for poor Helena, — all had made me as weak as a cat; and I don't know how I should have arranged matters if I had not just then heard the rattle of wheels. Looking up, I saw a smart carriage rapidly approaching, and on the front seat was the familiar figure of Lord John's old valet and particular servant.

"No sooner had the man caught sight of his master than he made all haste to reach us, jumped down and came to the bank, saying, "How did he get so far? He could not have stirred a step alone when I left him last night." Then he saw me, and his face looked like chalk. The explanation which we had was rather sharp, because I consider that this fellow was in the wrong in concealing his master's whereabouts from us. After the man had recovered his breath he told us these facts: —

"Lord John has not been to Australia at all. He came directly from Yokohama to San Francisco, and thence here to Vancouver, where he knew that one or two of his old friends and acquaintances were stationed at the Esquimault naval station. While he had been in China and Japan he had given way more wildly than ever before to drink, and when in China had suddenly begun to use opium to excess. The long ocean voyage to San Francisco had been passed in a kind of opium dream. 'I thought, sir,' said the servant, 'that if I could get him up here, his friends might persuade him to take a voyage among the icebergs or something like that — anywhere to keep him away from drink and the drug.' They had been in Victoria for three weeks, and no advice had done Lord John any good. He drank until his nerves were enraged, then took opium to quell his sufferings. 'I don't think he rightly knows in what part of the world he is,' said the servant. 'He seems to lose some days entirely. His mind is badly hurt.' And the cruel expression was absolutely just. He had been driven over to Esquimault last evening to dine with his two or three friends belonging to the station. Despite their cautions he had made an orgie of what was intended for a simple repast, and had wandered away in the night, after they had retired to rest. 'It was only when I come 'round to the little inn for him in the morning that he was missed,' says the servant, and there the wretched tale ends. We got my poor brother into the carriage, and the servant took him to his lodgings here in Victoria, where he is to keep strict watch on him until"—

"Until?" queried Dulon—

"Until I am ready to take him back to England. It is very sad—and terrible—is not it? I must think a little now, and then I will come and ask your advice."

Dulon stood looking intently at the young Englishman for a minute. "You have a stout heart," he said, "but it has had a severe trial. I am heartily sorry for you."

"You might tell Lady Helena that I have told you all," said Ringdale. "It will simplify matters."

"Do you think so?" There was not much hope in Dulon's voice, but his eye brightened as he drew near to Helena.

"May I speak to you?" at last he said, impulsively, yet so timidly that he blushed for his own timidity.

"Certainly. Why not?" And she turned her great eyes full upon his face. The expression of the hurt — the violent shock which Ringdale had described — was certainly there. But there was also a proud and grieved look in the eyes which seemed to say to Dulon, "Do you dare to doubt me?"

On the whole he did not, could not, would not, dare to doubt her.

"You were thinking so steadily," he stammered, "that I feared lest I might disturb you."

"Yes, I was abstracted, I dare say. I have seen a ghost — the ghost of an illusion. But let us not talk of that now. Do you not think there is a chill in that breeze coming in from the sea?" She arose and prepared to return to the little steamer.

CHAPTER XXII.

CAPTAIN JOBSON ON DECK.

"Each of my voyages has at least one incident to it," said Captain Jobson, buttoning his ulster tightly about his lean, shapely throat, smoothing back his side-whiskers, and taking a sharp look at Dulon. "And this — why, Lord bless you! — this is nothing at all. I've put that young fellow on to hop tea, and he'll be quite civilized by the time we reach Frisco. But when we smuggled him on to the little steamer at Victoria, do you know, I doubted if he would ever get his mind back? Poor boy! it made my heart jump. Heigh ho! I've seen a many on 'em! This Lord John acts just like a captain from New England that I knew in Manilla. But never mind about that."

They were seated in a comfortable corner on the deck of the steamship "Oceanic," bound from Portland for San Francisco. It was two o'clock in the morning, and they were getting out into the Columbia River, superbly lighted by a magical moon which seemed to have a sensuous Orientalism in its glow. It did not appear to Dulon as if this were the same moon which did duty on the Atlantic coasts. But he had small time to waste in contemplation and admiration of the moon. For the present he preferred to admire Captain Jobson, who had, with wonderful skill and deftness, taken charge of the whole party, including Ringdale's unhappy elder brother, and was transforming what might have been a most embarrassing position for Lady Helena and Ringdale into one of comparative ease. "Mr. Floyd tells me," the good captain had said to Lady Helena, "that for reasons which I don't need to understand you don't wish the earl and Lady Offast to know that this young lord is going to San Francisco on the same conveyances with them. Just put that matter right in my hands, and I'll bring the craft safe into port. I promise you he shall be in a comfortable suite of rooms in the Palace Hotel in Frisco without having come into contact with any one whom he ought not to see. Trust me: I'm on deck now."

And he was as good as his word.

It was Captain Jobson's wise and humane treatment, during the two days that he managed to delay the excursion at Victoria, which was bringing reason slowly back to the abused and wearied brain of Lord John; it was Captain Jobson's cunning which secured the poor fellow complete seclusion on the return journey from Victoria to New Tacoma. The valet had been left behind, with instructions to take the next steamer direct to San Francisco, and Captain Jobson had threatened him with various terrible penalties if he dared to report to any one but himself. When the earl and Lady Offast inquired at New Tacoma what had become of the captain, no one seemed to know, and the earl was inclined to have him looked up, until Ringdale suggested that he would most probably be only a day behind them. "The captain of our steamer says that he may have gone over to Olympia, on the Sound, to see some of his ancient sea-mates who have settled in that particular portion of this young wilderness."

The truth was that the captain had remained behind to bring his charge to Portland without observation, and he had succeeded in doing so. And now the earl was peacefully asleep in a cabin not far from that occupied by his old friend, Lord John, without having for an instant fancied that that wayward youth was on the Western hemisphere. Not once on the journey had the earl spoken to Ringdale of the scandal caused by his brother's mysterious disappearance from London.

Dulon was mystified by the willingness of Ringdale and Lady Helena to have the erring Lord John taken to San Francisco. It seemed to him folly to let the man walk into the very jaws of danger. If Lord John were really guilty of the forgery of the first and second bills — according to the story told him by Ringdale — why take him to San Francisco, where he was eagerly watched for by the agents of the old Jew's successor? — the thirsty leech who threatened to test the authenticity of the second note unless money were telegraphed from California to England to pay it. Were Lady Helena and Ringdale still at odds about Lord John — despite his discovery? Did she still refuse to tell Ringdale why and how she had bestowed £20,000 on Lord John, and whether or not she knew of his supposed second forgery? It was an odd case, he thought; and he wondered how many of the details had been told to Captain Jobson, who appeared to regard the young scion of the British aristocracy simply as a patient to be cured of a passion for unwholesome stimulants and narcotics, and who was putting his whole soul into the task of the cure.

By mutual consent the four conspirators, Ringdale, Lady Helena, Dulon and the captain, were to make few if any mentions of Lord John to each other while the voyage lasted. If Captain Jobson frowned severely now and then, when the conspirators met, it was understood to indicate that the patient was doing finely. Lord John lay quietly in his berth, seemingly lost in revery, and Captain Jobson had him locked in and managed to look at him every hour or two. He seemed utterly tractable, and even took a little food which the captain brought him, eating it with a solemn wistfulness which was pathetic.

So the voyage passed without incident until the second night. The travellers visited Astoria while the great steamship tarried at the wharves to take on tons and tons of canned salmon. They climbed to the top of the hills at the back of the town, and could hardly decide which they found most impressive, the vast extent of charred land, dotted with the blackened stumps of forest monarchs, sacrificed by the Astorians to their desire for more cleared ground on which to extend the streets of their city, or the lustrous and lazy expanse of the Pacific beyond the foamy bar, above which the impatient gulls were hovering and shrieking. They were touched with admiration for the vast and languid swell of the immense ocean, and duly impressed with the multi-colored sunset which filled the west that evening with a thousand fantastic forms that seemed to linger more than sun creations in other skies, and that broke reluctantly into chaos and disappeared as if it cost them a pang to yield up their gorgeous existence.

In the evening Dulon, Ringdale, and Lady Helena quietly stole out of the "social hall," in which the two hundred passengers, including the earl and Lady Offast, were delighted by listening to the melodious singing of a colored lady's maid, who had a veritable talent for song and action, and stealing to the nook where Captain Jobson sat, inquired, forgetful of her agreement: —

"How is he? Better?"

To their surprise and consternation the captain, who was visibly agitated, said: —

"No, worse; much worse. He has got some more opium from somewhere. He must have concealed it in the crown of his hat, for I declare I believe I looked everywhere else. And, if I didn't know that it is quite impossible, I should think that he had had some liquor as well as opium. He is restless, won't eat anything, and mutters to himself."

"Let me go to him," said Ringdale, springing forward.

The captain held him back.

"No, don't," he said. "I will take excellent care of him. It might pain you to see him as he is now. You can bear a hand if wanted. If he should recognize you, it might add to his excitement."

Ringdale turned away to hide his emotion; like a true Briton, he was afraid to show it.

"He acts," said the captain, thoughtfully, "as if he was weighed down by a heavy load and was all the time struggling to throw it off. There is a desperate earnestness in his face;" he drew nearer to the young Englishman, and spoke in a low tone, "which makes me think that he will bear close watching."

"I *must* be with him!" said Ringdale.

"No; I say you *must* not, and now I want you to take that as final. You *must not*. Just let me manage this" —

Ringdale stepped back, and looked rather haughtily for a moment at the good captain, whose voice had unconsciously assumed a ring of command. But the old captain did not flinch.

"What I mean," he said, in such kindly tones that Ringdale's heart went out to him, "is this: I have had a great deal of experience in nursing this kind of malady" — he pointed to the state-room in which Lord John was lying — "and I will bring this out right if I have no disturbing influences. Now, you camp down in your deck chairs, and look at the moonlight, and if there is any need for it, you shall be called."

"I mean to sit here a long time," Lady Helena was at that moment saying to Dulon, as he arranged her comfortable steamer chair for her, and handed her numerous wraps which he had been hugging to his breast for some minutes, almost as fondly as if the owner had been in them. "Let us hope that the earl will go to bed early, and that Lady Offast will follow his example. Colonel Hodges has already attempted to influence them by telling them that they must be up by sunrise if they wish to see the Golden Gate; and he is to spirit them off to the front of the ship to enjoy the moonlight. Isn't it kind of him to do so much for us — in this — this emergency?"

Dulon said that it had been eminently wise to let Colonel Hodges into the secret. "It is a pity," he ventured to remark, "that the earl cannot be told all about — the — circumstances; because I think his advice would be worth having — in —

in the matter which Mr. Ringdale—has told me of."

He meant the matter of paying the second bill, to which, according to the old Jew's successor in London, Lord John had forged a noble signature.

"What matter, and what has Mr. Ringdale told you about it?" said Lady Helena with sudden sharpness. This unwonted vivacity of tone seemed to set a chill on Dulon's heart. He suddenly felt as if with all this mysterious affair he had nothing to do, as if he were an interloper and were lowering his dignity by so racking his brain and soul with what did not concern him. Yet a moment's reflection convinced him that he could not divest himself of the intense, almost maddening, curiosity which possessed him to know what were now Lady Helena's real sentiments for Lord John. While this conviction was, in some unaccountable fashion, making the ice at his heart still colder than at first, Lady Helena added, impetuously:—

"Mr. Floyd, whatever you know, or imagine, about the poor fellow yonder, please do not communicate it in any shape or fashion to my cousin or to Lady Offast, until after we have been for a day or two in San Francisco. We *must* arrange certain matters there before— Promise me that, will you not?"

He was seated on the long bench close beside her, and was looking down into her clear, frank eyes as she thus appealed to him. For a moment he did not answer. He was thinking of that supreme moment after the accident on the great trestle in the Coriacan defile, when he held her in his arms, and when it seemed to him — he could not swear to it now — for something had then strangely confused his senses — as if they had exchanged burning kisses. For that moment, and for all the next day, and the next, he had thought that their mutual confession was clear — that there would never be any occasion to resume their old attitude. Yet at this instant they were talking like mere acquaintances — travelling-companions; and she — she was almost distrusting him in relation to this matter of Lord John's secret arrival in California.

"Do you hesitate, Mr. Floyd?" Lady Helena's voice trembled.

"I — no — not at all. I will do as you wish. It was only a question of the wisdom of having the earl's advice — in case — in case Lord John should — should get into trouble."

"I trust the gentleman referred to will meet with no trouble from which his friends cannot immediately rescue him," said the girl very haughtily. "The fact that they are going toward the trouble indicates that they do not fear it." Dulon had never heard her speak exactly like this before. This was the official tone of a class which she suddenly took on. He felt like resenting it, as it seemed to place a gulf between him and his love. The ice at his heart was more and more painful. Had he been mistaken? He would not believe it.

"I don't think we quite understand each other," he said, gravely, his white face glistening in the white moonlight. "I have no right to offer any suggestions, and perhaps it is better that we should not talk about it any more. I am sure I did not intend to convey in my remarks the smallest reflection upon the gentleman's conduct. After all," he added, the bitterness of suspecting her putting a biting energy into his speech, "I was only judging by what his own brother had told me." Then he was sorry he had said that. His situation seemed momentarily to grow worse.

"But his own brother does not know, does not understand, I am sure he does not," said Lady Helena, looking up with flashing eyes, in which tears glistened. "How can he doubt his own flesh and blood! Oh, can you not see that I am thoroughly wretched?" she said, breaking down, and hiding her face in her hands.

Dulon glanced around in search of the captain and of Ringdale. They were earnestly engaged in conversation at the stern of the ship and with their backs turned to him. He bent down over Lady Helena and said, softly and tenderly: —

"Your will is my will. I shall do as you bid me. Can you not see that I am entirely yours?"

"You must not doubt my friends," she said, again looking up defiantly through her tears.

"I do not," said Dulon, simply.

It seemed to him that he did not. He was subjugated; or was he, rather, reassured by the splendid confidence which she maintained? Yet why was she in tears and wretched? Was she quite certain of being able to conjure the danger which Lord John would probably meet at San Francisco?

On the Pacific steamers a goodly number of state-rooms open directly upon the upper deck; no mean advantage in the mild climate and in seas rarely tempestuous. On the "Oceanic" the sleeping apartments were of very comfortable size, and had doors leading on the inner side directly into the "social hall." Lady Helena presently observed a light in the window of the state-room occupied by the earl and Lady Offast, and called Dulon's attention to it. "They have retired," she said, "and poor Lord John will reach San Francisco without having encountered the earl."

The ship stole with swift rushing sound across the face of the waters. Between the immensity of the sky and the immensity of the sea she seemed like a mere dot, a speck, a mote. Sometimes Dulon fancied that he had lost all consciousness of her identity, and that he was borne along independently of her, by some enchanted and resistless force. Phosphorescent gleams danced and marched and sank and rose and wavered beside the ship as she pressed forward; behind her, on the broad, agitated, beaten water-trail which she left the moon made exquisite *répoussé* work, such as no mortal artificer could hope to imitate in silver.

The sounds of singing, recitations, laughter, and cheers in the social hall had died away. Not a person came to promenade the after-deck. The forward cabin-passengers, the swart Italians, the tall and broad-shouldered farmers from Oregon, the ruddy-cheeked girls from Victoria and Tacoma, the slouching Irishmen from Portland, were gathered around the light which streamed out from the comfortable smoking-cabin amidships, where a mighty poker match had been for some hours in progress. And the philosophical Celestials, clad in blue gowns, were curled up in the imminent neighborhood of the bow, quaintly savoring the rhythmical motion of the "Oceanic," as she rose and fell daintily on the Pacific's languid wave.

By and by Ringdale and Captain Jobson approached Lady Helena and Dulon and sat down rather wearily on the bench. Captain Jobson had just been to look at his patient. "He's flighty — flighty," he said; "but can't get any more stimulant; I'm certain of that. I think we shall get through the night without adventure."

Alas! the good captain really thought nothing of the sort. He saw that a critical moment in the disordered condition of Lord John was at hand when the reason — slowly returning after long wandering upon the shores of chaos — might be wrecked, or might impel the body to strange antics or to terrible deeds. The good old captain's heart beat loudly in his bosom, and he started at every slightest sound.

Presently the light in the earl's state-room went out, and the round voice of Offast was heard exclaiming: —

"The linen's damp. I hope there are no rats on board. Bah! It's like sleeping in a mouldy tomb."

Lady Helena's quick ear caught the faint sounds which embodied the protest against the earl's "gloomy language" sent up by Lady Offast from the lower berth, where the good creature lay cowering in one of her spasms of fright lest the steamer should run into something and suddenly go to the bottom.

The four watchers (for they were really all watching — without being willing to admit it to each other — for some strange thing which might happen to Lord John or because of him) sat still in the moonlight listening to the rush of the waves and the insidious whispers which came up from the phosphorescent billows. Ringdale lighted a cigar and offered one to Captain Jobson, who said: "No, thankee. Can't smoke; it's my watch." As for Dulon, he could have sat forever beside Lady Helena, studying the lines of that face which had such strange fascination for him.

Half an hour passed thus. Ringdale rustled in his place, and was about to speak, when they heard a noise in the vicinity of Lord John's state-room.

"Stand by!" said Captain Jobson in an excited whisper, and they all sprang to their feet.

The sliding window of the state-room, which

Captain Jobson had left slightly ajar in order that the "patient" might have plenty of air, was moved slowly back, and the pallid face of Lord John appeared at the aperture. The face looked spectral as the moonlight fell upon it. The lips moved, and the four listeners drew nearer, impelled toward the face, yet half afraid of it.

CHAPTER XXIII.

LORD JOHN FINDS HIS SOUL AGAIN.

DULON, standing silently beside Lady Helena, began to feel as if in the next few moments his fate would be decided. It was in this manner that the feeling expressed itself in his mind; yet he would have been puzzled to explain what he meant by his "fate." He had, despite the revelations with which he had been blest, during the journey, as to Lady Helena's sentiments, for a day or two past been schooling himself to bear the shock of a possible disappointment. Suppose that the few delicious moments during which she had seemed entirely his were but delusions, and that, now that Lord John were found, she should announce, by act or word, that she loved him and proposed to continue loving him, no matter how wayward and dissolute he might have been?

Here was Lord John found, and although not yet in his right mind, likely enough to be so in process of time. What were those pale lips about to confess? What secret was in those frightened eyes, which seemed desperately striving to see something afar off? In their appealing gaze there was infinite sorrow — not unmixed with apprehension — perhaps tinged with remorse. Dulon's heart was invaded by a profound pity for this lonely face peering out of the darkness, as the face of a lost spirit might be imagined to peep forth from some nook in the Inferno.

The night was phenomenally still now, and the steamer sped along to the harmonious music of her engines, faintly heard below. It was as if she were some monster of the deep, peacefully pursuing her own fantastic course, while around her naiads and sea-fairies kept up a solemn chant. Dulon and Lady Helena, Ringdale and Captain Jobson forgot that they were on a steamship, forgot the majestic and placid ocean, the perfumed autumn night — everything except that pallid face which looked out on them as if it were gazing from another world.

For now the lips moved again, and this time audible sounds issued from them.

"Brother," said Ringdale, in a hoarse whisper, tremulous with grief, — "brother, how is it with you?"

There was no answering look of recognition; no turning of the face toward Ringdale, who recoiled almost as if he had addressed a ghost, and for a moment covered his own face with his hands. It was evident that Lord John knew his younger brother no better than he had known him on the road near Victoria.

"Let me try once more," said the lips, and the voice came fiercely and with an earnestness which was touching. "Oh, let me try once more! If I could only wrench away this cursed curtain! But it is all blank, blank, blank."

"I think I will go to him, and get him back to bed," said Captain Jobson, a little doubtfully, for he saw that the others were intensely interested in what Lord John was about to say.

"No, no! do not disturb him, not for worlds!" whispered Lady Helena, impetuously. Captain Jobson stroked his chin reflectively, and stepped to one side, still keeping a close watch on the movements of the pale face.

"All a blank! Things are not real! They seem to float — to wave — in a mist. But the world seems to be slowly coming back. Oh! if I could but remember what happened at the Jew's. Oh, if I could but remember *that*. Then all the rest would come back. What did I do at the Jew's? The Jew's — the old Jew's?"

Dulon felt a nervous grasp upon his arm, and

found that Lady Helena had seized it. She was dizzy and faint, and had narrowly escaped falling to the deck. "Hold me, please," she whispered to the painter, who was almost as dizzy as herself; "I must hear these next words."

"Lean upon my arm," he said, trying in vain to keep the tenderness out of his voice. "Unless you would prefer to sit down."

Lady Helena appeared to recover her equilibrium suddenly. "Fancy!" she said "to sit down at a moment like this!"

She withdrew her hand, whereupon Dulon took possession of it and drew it through his arm. This time she did not withdraw it. As for Ringdale, he would not have observed the pair if they had jumped overboard. All his soul was with his brother, who was evidently struggling with his disordered consciousness, and who might give them a clue which would prove precious to them in their efforts to save this one "who was lost and now was found." Lord John's soul was struggling terribly with Lord John's body, and out of this struggle might come the solution of the mystery to solve which Ringdale had come across seas and lands.

A loud shout from the other end of the steamer, announcing the delight of the crowd eagerly watching the phases of the great game of poker, broke the silence. Then nothing was heard again but the swish! huish! huish! of the lazy waves, and the roum roum! roum — ur roum! of the engines. Nothing else — until Lord John spoke again. His soul now seemed to be holding colloquy with his body — questioning, blaming, yearning for the harmony which had been wrecked, for the unity of purpose and action which appeared to have been destroyed.

"Let me see," said the lips. "When the money trouble came, I said, 'I must leave London.' I said: 'Here's dishonor ahead — dishonor! Not a pretty word to be used in connection with our name.' Then I went into the country — and then I came back to town. Next, there is a blank — a blank! Drink, drink, and drink! Opium, opium, and opium! A strange blank! I would give anything, everything to know what I did in that blank time! What I did; oh, what I did! The thought of that blank is a nightmare — a horror. It haunts me — haunts me."

Lord John's whispering grew more intense, more sibilant. The painful look on the face deepened. Under the pallor of the moonlight the face would have been appalling to look upon had it not been for a certain sweetness and nobility of expression which seemed gradually returning into it. Lord John's soul was resuming its proper place in its earthly tenement.

Dulon was tremendously interested now. The few disjointed words about the old Jew had shown him that Lord John was perhaps to unravel his own mystery. Unconsciously he tightened his grasp on Lady Helena's hand, and she did not resist. At that moment she would not have known it if live coals had been placed against her cheeks.

"The blank"— murmured the lips. "The dreadful blank — I awake out of it — and in a flash see London, and my coming trouble. Another blank — another flash — and I am in the old Jew's rooms. Now all is clear — for a few moments. The old man is familiar — too familiar; I put him in his proper place — he laughs — a low laugh — that makes my blood run cold. There are two figures in the room besides myself; now they fade. O God! why cannot I distinguish them? Ah, no! Now they are returning. But I can see only the Jew — the Jew — with papers in his hand. Money I must have — money I *must* have — do you hear — Jew — money! What are the papers? To-morrow — not now — not now — not in condition to read and sign them — to-morrow. Again the Jew's laugh: it makes my flesh creep!"

"This is terrible," said Captain Jobson, in a low voice. "These ravings may attract attention. I will go in to him and calm him — he must be put to sleep."

"No, NO," whispered Lady Helena, imperiously; "do not stir; it is of the highest importance that he should not be interrupted."

"But," urged the good captain, who naturally fancied, inasmuch as he had been told nothing about Lord John's money matters, that these were the ravings of a distempered imagination, "but I am afraid that this excitement may mean a crisis — may endanger his life — his life."

"Pooh! What is life where honor is at stake?" said the girl, breathlessly. "*Let him go on.*"

And Captain Jobson, once more stroking his chin, fell back in silence.

Again the spectral lips were opened.

"To-morrow, Jew, to-morrow will do. No? Must I sit down? The mist is falling, falling all around me. 'Write what I say,' says the Jew, and laughs again. I take the pen in my hand. I can see the Jew. I can see the other figure bending above me. I begin to write. Then the mist falls.

All is blank, blank. Next day — is it next day? — I find myself in my rooms in town. I remember my visit to the Jew — all, until the blank comes. In my waistcoat-pocket I find a check — the Jew's check — for twelve thousand pounds. The money — the needed money! I have it; my honor is safe. I wish to pay it. But all day, and every day, I ask myself, What paper did you sign? What paper did you surrender into the Jew's hands in exchange for this money? I cannot remember. It was all a blank — a blank."

Lady Helena trembled; but her hand now lay confidingly in that of Dulon. She gazed, as if spell-bound, on the face — the pleading, stirring face communing with itself. Once more the lips.

"Let me see — let me think! Ah! One day I go to see the Jew. 'Show me the bill I gave you the other night some weeks ago. You will do me a kindness. I was very queer at that time, and my memory' — So I say to the Jew — and his brow clouds — and there is a curious flame in his eyes.

"'The bill is all right,' he says. 'I wish every young gent in trouble would bring such good paper to me. But a safe bill now and then helps to make up for the many bad ones.' Then he laughs again — that mocking laugh. 'Show me the bill!' I cry, for now I am half mad with apprehension. A mysterious something within tells me that I have been betrayed. 'Show me the bill!' The Jew's brow darkens; he goes to his strong box, brings out a bill — my bill — drawn by me — at three months. But what is that written across it? An acceptance — by Lord Chancehill! An acceptance — where — how, when was it got? I have never got an acceptance from Lord Chancehill. He would not accept for a penny for me — and so I tell the Jew. The Jew flies into a passion. 'You brought the bill to me all signed by yourself, and accepted by Lord Chancehill,' he cries, 'and gave it to me as good paper. I should think it is; no better paper in London. And now you come to me and say that Lord Chancehill never accepted for you. Am I to understand that this bill is a — a — a forgery? Well, I must tell you one thing — that on its due date it goes to Lord Chancehill to be honored.' And I, O God! I do not know whether or not it is a forgery! The blank — the blank — the awful blank — what may I not have done on that awful blank? Lord Chancehill would have refused me; it is, it must be — a forgery. I fly away — mad with fires and doubts — I hasten to the only friend — oh, the keen humiliation of it! — on whom

I can rely in this final trouble; from her I implore the money with which to take up this bill — this dubious — this damnable bill. She finds it for me — twenty thousand pounds — ay — twenty thousand pounds that I must pay for the use of twelve thousand — twelve thousand — twelve thousand. I return to the Jew! I clamor for the bill until he gives it up against the money which I have brought him. What can it mean? How should *I* write Lord Chancehill's acceptance — *I* — who scarcely knew until last year what an acceptance was? Yet there it is — I can see it as I take it back from the Jew — as I crush it and tear it into fragments — there it is — in his bold, clerkly hand."

Lord John had leaned his head against the window-sash now, and was talking in a low, but very distinct voice, and far calmer as well as more coherently than at first.

"The Jew laughs as he opens the door for me. That laugh makes my flesh creep now. It sounds as it sounded on that terrible night when I went to him, and the curtain was lowered around me until all was a blank, when there came a sudden flash and I found myself in presence of the Jew and the other figure, and I saw papers presented me to sign, when I heard that voice saying, 'Write what I say.' The blank, the blank again. What did I write, what did I sign?"

Then there was a long pause, during which the breathing of the excited listeners sounded sharply in their own ears. Presently the unhappy man who had been thus communing with himself appeared to awaken to external impressions. "How humid the air is," he murmured, musingly. "Where am I now? Still at sea? No! that cannot be, for the voyage from Yokohama — yet this is the ocean — what strange water — what foreign sky is this? O God! The curtain rises — slowly — slowly, but surely — the curtain rises — rises — rises! Where am I, and what — *oh,* WHAT have I done?"

The face was bowed now, and the listeners heard a sound like the sobbing of a strong man.

"Let no one but myself move," said Ringdale. "I will see if he has returned to reason;" and he stepped cautiously forward to the window of the state-room, and standing full in the moonlight, spoke to the face.

"Brother, look up and tell me that you know me — *me* — your own brother who has come to take you home."

The pallid face flashed into the light again.

There was a great gleam of returned sanity in the eyes. "Is it true?" said the lips — feebly, now. "Is it true? Have you come to save me? I thought I saw you — somewhere — the other day — but then the curtain lowered — the blank came — and your face was gone. I can see you now, but you seem to be in a mist."

"I'll run round and get in the other way, and open this door for you," said Captain Jobson, suddenly appearing at Ringdale's elbow. "But be careful. He's a leetle flighty still, you know."

"I am weary — so weary," said Lord John. "Where are you — brother? — I cannot see you now."

Dulon Floyd had heard enough to convince him that the unfortunate young man had been the victim of designing scoundrels, and he said so, hurriedly, to Lady Helena, intently watching her face as he spoke. "He has proved his own innocence, to my thinking, completely," he said.

Lady Helena looked up at Dulon with a pained wrinkle on her brow. "Oh, thank Heaven for what we have heard!" she said. "Weak he has been — yielding and almost lost — but not criminal — oh, not criminal — is it not so? Yet if those dreadful men had made him commit — I cannot say the word" — she shuddered and looked down again. Meantime Ringdale had been admitted into his brother's state-room, and was doing his best to aid the erring one to get his soul back, and completely to raise the dreadful curtain against which he so bitterly declaimed.

"You are afraid that he was made to commit a forgery — in spite of himself — in his — his condition, when he went to the Jew money-lenders," said Dulon. "I don't believe it. I believe that those fellows forged the acceptances, and intended to persuade him or his friends that he had done it."

"The acceptances?" said Lady Helena, in a curious voice. "Then there *was* more than one acceptance?"

"What have I said?" cried Dulon, thoroughly vexed at his own awkwardness, and the next moment there was a weight upon his arm — Lady Helena had fainted.

Shortly after this occurrence the earl awoke from a troubled nap, and, muttering, with truly British energy, "Confound this infernally damp and musty hole! I feel as if I were buried alive," he clambered out of his berth and began to grope for his garments.

"What's the matter now, love? Where are you going?" timidly inquired Lady Offast, before whom arose a terrifying vision of a wreck on the Pacific.

"On deck, dear, to smoke a pipe." And presently he swung open the door leading to the deck, and, emerging into the moonlight, was not a little surprised to see Dulon kneeling before the chair in which reclined Lady Helena, very white, but seeming very much at rest.

"God bless my soul!" said the earl, stopping short in his tracks, and vigorously cramming the tobacco into the bowl of his pipe.

CHAPTER XXIV.

WHICH EXPLAINS MANY THINGS.

THE earl did not drop his pipe, however. His emotion was not so profound but that he could control it; for he was not at all blind, and had found out the young couple's secret almost before they had begun to suspect it themselves. The fact that the American "painting fellow" was on his knees before Lady Helena was evidently apparent to his vision; but it was not the only disturbing element. The earl had fallen into a fitful doze in his bunk, and had had a dream which startled him. He dreamed that he heard a plaintive voice, — a voice with that little broken chord within the tones which denoted remorse and woe; and the anguish of that voice had stirred the innermost recesses of his heart. He dreamed that one whose unfortunate history he knew, and whom he had fancied thousands of miles away, had come all at once floating down through the air and set his foot upon that very steamship. "Great God! how horrible and — and supernatural!" thought the earl, in his dream, for there is nothing that your vagabond dream so much likes as to seduce the powerless dreamer into comments upon the enchantment of his position. He thought that he saw a face as he had seen it a few months before in London, the face of the eldest son of one of his dear, dead friends, — a face white and woful with struggles to recover its lost nobleness and strength. And at intervals the voice came and went until it made his flesh creep; and when he had awakened and climbed out of the berth there was beaded sweat upon his brow.

Dulon was not slow in resuming an attitude of decorous respect in presence of the earl, feeling that, if it had never been necessary before to win him over, it certainly was now. At the same time it occurred to this transparent youthful lover that he ought to make an effort, on behalf of Lady Helena, to save the situation.

"I cannot see the glove," he stammered. "But I will look a little farther this way."

"Nothing but moonbeams there, Mr. Floyd," said the earl, finding it hard to disguise his delight at the painter's confusion. Dulon's timidity seemed, to the earl's thinking, in some curious manner to reëstablish the proper difference between them — to do away with that aggressive boldness which in

America stirred up feelings dire within the earl's soul. "No glove there. I am certain I should see it if there were. I can see a ship's light farther than any man I know — except — except perhaps Captain Jobson."

"Indeed."

"Yes." The questioning flavor of the "indeed" somewhat displeased the earl. "I never exaggerate." Dulon moved away forward, as if he were anxious to join the loiterers about the open door of the smoking-cabin in which the poker players were still fighting their foolish and useless battle. "Don't go," said the earl, majestically waving his pipe in the moonlight.

"Oh, I hadn't the slightest intention of going," answered Dulon in his most provoking tones. And he sat down beside the rail and listened to the huish-spuish of the rushing water.

The earl was so fearful lest he might give way to a display of temper before Lady Helena that he turned his back upon Dulon for a moment, but presently he drew a deck chair beside the girl, sat down, craned his neck, and looked up to the pure sky. Then he drew from his waistcoat pocket a "Vesuvian" and lighted his pipe.

"Do you know, Helena," he said, "I was nearly

frightened out of my life in that cabin. I dreamed of — of Lord John — and I could almost swear that I heard his voice. Here — I say — are you two young people gone mad?"

For Dulon had sprung out of his seat and was leaning towards the earl and listening breathlessly, and Lady Helena had grasped her cousin's arm so tightly as to cause him a sharp twinge of pain. And both these young people certainly did look a little as if they were taking leave of their senses.

"What is it?" continued the astonished earl. "Can't you speak? Your faces are as white — as white — as" —

"Go on, cousin," said Lady Helena. "Tell me what you saw or heard in the dream."

The earl was now thoroughly mystified. How should Lady Helena speak thus, in the presence of Dulon, of a matter supposed to be sacred from the curiosity of strangers. He looked up helplessly at the young painter, as if demanding an explanation.

"Mr. Floyd has heard something about Lord John's adventures, cousin," said Lady Helena.

"Oh, has he?" and the earl's breeding prevented him from expressing further wonder. "Poor Lord John! How I wish he were here, that I might take him by the hand and tell him that he ran away from phantoms."

"From phantoms, cousin?" Lady Helena had lost her self-control now, and was as wildly curious, as impetuous to know the truth, as a child.

"Ay, from phantoms! But then, I didn't know they were phantoms myself until — until the other day — don't you know. I would tell you the whole tale," he added, glancing keenly at the girl, "if" — then lowering his voice — "for I fancy that it would not give you so much pain now as it might have done a few months ago."

"I am going to walk on the other side," said Dulon, "and to smoke a cigar, I think," now finding that it was high time to withdraw; and he was moving away, when Lady Helena looked at him and said, but speaking *to* her cousin: —

"I would like to have *him* stay and hear all that you have to say about Lord John."

"God bless my soul! In that case, don't you think Mr. Floyd would better sit down?"

Mr. Floyd needed no second invitation, although his cheeks burned, for in that one look which Lady Helena had given him, and which, he doubted not, had been remarked by the earl, there was open confession of her love. She had bravely, and with that consummate English frankness which penetrates the veneer of the most artificial manner of the most privileged of classes, claimed him for her own.

"Well, then, there's little to tell, after all, my eccentric and excitable young friends," said the earl, making clouds of smoke fly from his pipe. "Lord John was in difficulties; not a doubt of it. And there is also no doubt that—he bolted. I blame him for that—don't you know,"—laying his hand kindly on his fair cousin's arm—"because it wasn't proper form for a gentleman in his position. But I don't presume to sit in judgment on him. Two or three days before we left London for this excursion there was a Greek-looking scoundrel called on me and told a terrible tale about some forged acceptances by Lord John—how he had discovered one of them through the sudden transfer, because of his partner's death, of all the papers to himself—and would I keep it terribly secret, and as Lord John was coming to San Francisco, would I have him communicated with, and take this compromising document up before it ran its course, and ran its forger into shame? The fellow showed me the bill. It was a forgery of Lord Chancehill's acceptance to a bill drawn by my poor friend,

Lord John, and for a tidy sum — many thousand pounds. So I insisted upon taking up the bill, and, as the Greek-looking fellow was the least bit impudent, I kicked him downstairs. It was worth the money," added the earl, again veiling himself in smoke.

Dulon sat quite still, admiring the simple generosity of these people. Each had carefully hidden from the other a splendid deed of charity, done with a magnificent disdain for the possibility of being swindled.

"I mentioned the matter," said the earl, "merely because there is a very odd sequel to it. On the voyage out to New York on the 'Athabaska' I was impressed, don't you know, with the idea that I must tell some one this circumstance — of course without mentioning poor Lord John — and so I described our Greek friend of the forged acceptance to Colonel Hodges. I considered the colonel's judgment good, and events prove that I have never appreciated it too highly. I fancy I gave a rather neat description of the Greek. 'Colonel,' said I, 'I am inclined to think the fellow was a swindler, and has done me.' The colonel jumped up in a great rage and said, 'The man you have described as the Greek answers exactly to the description of a noted New

Orleans swindler' — and he gave his name. Colonel Hodges said he would bet a hundred thousand dollars — favorite bet of his — that the Greek and the New Orleans swindler were the same. Let us telegraph to London from New York — have him arrested — and find out — says this clever colonel. Perhaps we can recover those thousands of pounds, says he. So we telegraphed; and then I was glad that I had been careful to leave the purported acceptance of Lord Chancehill, which I had paid to the Greek, in the hands of my solicitor. I suppose the Greek thought I would burn it."

"Go on — go on," said Lady Helena and Dulon in one breath.

"Ah — well — we telegraphed, and they got the fellow, and identified him as the New Orleans swindler, a mulatto with Spanish origins, as the French say. He had been doing some quite immense swindling, principally by convincing the friends of rich young gentlemen that forgeries must be hushed up. So when we reached Chicago the colonel and I had a cablegram from London to say that the swindler, who had enriched himself, had been made to disgorge, and that my thousands of pounds were safe again in bank."

"Oh, cousin!" said Lady Helena, remembering

Colonel Hodges on the morning in Craven street, and the statuesque attitudes and the piles of neatly printed pamphlets and maps, "you ought to invest them in the colonel's canal company."

"Which is exactly what I did, Lady Helena," said the earl, this time smoking furiously, and retreating into the smoke to hide his confusion. "I said to Colonel Hodges in New York: 'If we get that money back it goes into your canal scheme,' and Colonel Hodges said to me: 'If we don't get that money back my name isn't Hodges, and there are no snakes in Florida.'"

From which we may conclude that Colonel Hodges had acted sagely in following his capitalist across the Atlantic and across the continent, rather than to relinquish the idea of inducing him to invest.

"So you see, my friends," concluded the earl, "Lord John ran away from a phantom, for he had done nothing but sign a bill across which the wretched youth — I beg his pardon — the New Orleans mulatto of Spanish origins — had forged an acceptance. Poor boy! Poor wandering madcap!"

And now that he had finished his story, told with modesty and excellent humor, the earl began to eye Dulon suspiciously once more. But he could not eye him away from Lady Helena. He seemed to appreciate this; so, for lack of something better, he said, "Wicked place, 'cruel London,' Mr. Floyd."

"No," answered the young man, quietly; "where there is so much noble and beautiful charity, patience, and self-sacrifice, no place can be called wicked. The just outnumber the unjust in your 'dear old dingy,' as you call London; I am certain of that."

Just then the door of Lord John's cabin was opened, and Ringdale came out, with Captain Jobson hovering behind him. "My brother is sleeping quietly," he said to Lady Helena. "He will recover; the strain upon the brain is over." Then he saw the earl, and placed his hand upon his own lips, as if enjoining himself and all the others to silence.

But the explanations which followed, in the midst of which the amazed and excited earl declared that he had gone mad, and they were all "chaffing" him, sent a thrill of delight through Ringdale's heart. His brother innocent; no need to engage in a campaign with wily blacklegs in San Francisco — to save the brother's honor; Lord John to come home to his own! The unselfish Ringdale stole into a corner to hide his emotion, and then began at once to plan new plays, new poems, new novels, new excursions, with all the ardor and energy of a "younger son" who has a good family name and his own independence to uphold at the same time.

Dulon and Lady Helena had but small chance for converse now, although each yearned to the other as never before. Now that her mission to save Lord John's honor was over the girl found her strength gone, and she was glad to accept Captain Jobson's proffered arm as she sought her state-room. While they were traversing the moonlit deck the captain said: —

"Pretty youth, that Lord John! Gentle as a babe, now that his story is off his mind! Wonderful affair, isn't it? His sleeping face looks like that of a child. Reminds me of a youth that died on my ship" —

"Built of mahogany," interrupted the girl with a gleam of chastened merriment on her face.

"Now — now — you mustn't laugh at the old man. He's had a great deal of trouble to-day. Well, good-night. I'll go and walk a stretch or two with Dulon before I turn in. Lady Helena, you must forgive an old man, but that boy Dulon adores the deck you tread on. I hope before my old ship comes into port I shall hear that you are safely married to him. But there! I've said too much — good-night."

"Captain Jobson," said Lady Helena, looking very haughty, but betraying no haughtiness in her voice; "I may safely promise you one thing — and that is that I will never marry any one else — if I do *not* marry *him!*"

But to have seen the blissful Dulon wandering about the decks all the rest of that night, and until the "Golden Gate" began to appear in the glow of a majestic sunrise, no one would have fancied that *he* had any doubts as to his ultimate union with Lady Helena.

Just before dawn the earl and Ringdale were sitting together in a corner under shelter of a boat. They had been talking unweariedly about the strange adventures of Lord John, after which they had relapsed into a long silence. All at once Ringdale laughed merrily.

"Why this sudden levity?" said the startled earl.

"I was thinking what a 'special despatch' Caswell P. Rusher could have made for his paper, had he been with us for the last eight and forty hours," answered the young Englishman.

www.ingramcontent.com/pod-product-compliance
Lightning Source LLC
Chambersburg PA
CBHW031350290326
41932CB00044B/865

* 9 7 8 3 7 4 3 3 4 9 0 4 9 *

www.ingramcontent.com/pod-product-compliance
Lightning Source LLC
Chambersburg PA
CBHW031348290326
41932CB00044B/458

* 9 7 8 3 3 3 7 2 9 5 6 4 6 *